Charles Edward Drummond Black, Józef Popowski

The Rival Powers in Central Asia

The Struggle Between England And Russia in the East

Charles Edward Drummond Black, Józef Popowski

The Rival Powers in Central Asia
The Struggle Between England And Russia in the East

ISBN/EAN: 9783744744010

Printed in Europe, USA, Canada, Australia, Japan

Cover: Foto ©ninafisch / pixelio.de

More available books at **www.hansebooks.com**

THE RIVAL POWERS

IN

CENTRAL ASIA

THE RIVAL POWERS

IN

CENTRAL ASIA

OR

THE STRUGGLE BETWEEN ENGLAND AND RUSSIA IN THE EAST. TRANSLATED FROM THE GERMAN OF JOSEF POPOWSKI BY ARTHUR BARING BRABANT AND EDITED BY CHARLES E·D BLACK LATE IN CHARGE OF THE GEOGRAPHICAL BUSINESS OF THE INDIA OFFICE

WITH A MAP OF THE NORTH-WESTERN FRONTIER OF INDIA SHOWING THE PAMIR REGION AND PART OF AFGHANISTAN

Westminster
ARCHIBALD CONSTABLE AND COMPANY
PUBLISHERS TO THE INDIA OFFICE
PARLIAMENT STREET S·W
1893

CONTENTS

EDITORIAL INTRODUCTION vi

AUTHOR'S PREFACE 1

ENGLAND AND RUSSIA—

   I. Russia's Advance in Asia 7

   II. Russia aspires to the Possession of India . . 65

   III. Can England arrest Russia's Advance in Asia? . 79

   IV. Strategical Relations of the Two States . . 135

   V. England's Value to the Central European Coalition.—Final Conclusions 204

INDEX 225

EDITORIAL INTRODUCTION

IT is more than seventeen years since the issue of Sir Henry Rawlinson's "England and Russia in the East" awoke British public opinion to a livelier sense of the responsibilities and dangers attaching to our tenure of India. At that time it was a far cry from Westminster to Calcutta or Simla, and India was a comparatively unfamiliar topic; its geography and resources were but little known; the network of surveys, topographical, archæological, statistical, and economic, was incomplete; and the literature, official, journalistic, and miscellaneous, had not attained that distinctive character and individual excellence which have since attracted and interested Englishmen. If it were so in the case of Hindostan, public opinion was still less enlightened with regard to its contiguous regions. The most stupendous mountain range and table-land on the face of the earth were indeed known to abut on the northern frontier, and, as history could prove, to have secured practical immunity from invasion in that direction. But this circumstance seems to have lulled us into a mistaken sense of security in respect of the western and north-western frontiers, which were vaguely imagined to be bounded by equally impassable mountains, impracticable deserts, and unconquerable tribes, which would surely repel the intrusion alike of the invaders or defenders of India. Moreover, this lack of knowledge was generally shared by high and low, and more recently still Englishmen have been authoritatively invited to reassure themselves and dispel their anxiety by mere consideration of the size of the maps of the regions referred to. No doubt the teachings of geography are essential to a comprehension of the Central Asian question, but those of history are scarcely less important, and in both respects Sir Henry Rawlinson's treatise was so exceptionally able, while his conclusions were so striking and convincing, that it is not surprising to find a distinguished Russian professor of international law, F. Martens, calling the famous "Memorandum" a historical document, in regard to the influence it had on the public mind and policy.

The gravity of the Central Asian question has in no sense abated since 1875; nay, it has rather increased, but at the same time it may be said to have entered upon new phases. The conquest of the Turcomans and the construction of the Trans-Caspian railway, while they brought Russia into immediate contact with Afghanistan, roused our country to the necessity of strictly defining the respective national limits from the Heri Rud to the Oxus. Again the recent *imbroglios* on the Pamir have brought to light doubts and differences which similarly can only be settled by mutual agreement and local demarcation. Concurrently with these events there has been a vast development of geographical knowledge during the past decade and a half which has forcibly impressed upon the British mind that India's position is continental rather than peninsular, and that, as such, it is amenable to those exigencies to which continental powers find they are subject.

While, therefore, Herr Popowski's work as a recent expert analysis of the Central Asian question will attract deserved attention, it is probably from the standpoint of a Continental observer that his conclusions will be most attentively scrutinized. In the accompanying translation these views have called for editorial comment in but few instances. At the same time readers will do well to remember that during the two years that have elapsed since the publication of "Antagonismus"[1] much that is noteworthy has happened, and it will be impossible to judge of the soundness and present applicability of the author's contentions without a brief retrospect of the more important events that have passed in the interim.

One of the chief factors in the development of the political situation has been the internal condition of Afghanistan, which, during the past two years, has been undoubtedly very troublous, especially in the little known country inhabited by the Hazaras. The Hazarajat proper covers an area of 18,000 square miles in the heart of Afghanistan, and the Hazaras number about half a million souls, divided into eight clans, seven of which pay tribute amounting to between five and six lakhs of rupees annually to the Amir's treasury. The eighth and remaining section, dwelling west of the road from Khelat-i-Ghilzai to Ghazni, is said by Leech to number some 20,000 men, but as the country has not been explored, very little is known as to its present resources. Uruzghan is said to form an extensive plain in this region, and to have been celebrated from the days of Rustam up to the present

---

[1] The German title of this book is *Antagonismus der Englischen und Russischen interessen in Asien. Eine Militär-politische studie.* Vienna. *Wilhelm Frick.* 1890.

day as a breeding-ground for horses. Valuable lead mines exist in the country, which enable the inhabitants to manufacture and export bullets, though their principal occupation is cattle-grazing. The Hazaras are exceedingly hospitable and friendly to strangers, especially to priests and doctors, and they enjoy a great reputation for powers of divination.

In the summer of 1890 the Amir despatched troops into that portion of the Hazarajat which lies in the Upper Helmand Valley, to enforce his revenue dues; and in the discharge of this mission, which appears to have dragged on through two dreary years, the Afghan soldiery were guilty of excesses and cruelty against the inhabitants, their women and children. This treatment drove the Uruzghan section of the Hazaras into revolt, and the rising subsequently spread through the wild and bleak uplands which form the home of their fellow-tribesmen. It is impossible to arrive at an exact idea of the course of the rebellion from the vague and often biassed rumours which have reached us *viâ* Cabul or Candahar, but it is clear that the Hazaras offered a desperate resistance, that their cause elicited wide and active sympathy among their brethren; that success was in no way confined to one side or the other; and that the anxieties of the Amir's situation were so serious that, in consequence, he declared himself unable (probably in all good faith) to receive a mission from the Viceroy to discuss the various important questions pending between the two countries. The advent of the winter of 1892–3 appears to have caused a temporary suspension of hostilities, and recently intelligence has been received of the entire pacification of the country, a welcome piece of news that will not improbably conduce to closer relations between Afghanistan and India.

Although we are without precise data as to these events in the more remote parts of Afghanistan, we do not lack information respecting the capital and its ruler. Of late, in particular, Abdurrahman has shown a growing appreciation of some of the benefits of Western civilization, and has appointed a Calcutta firm, Messrs. Walsh, Lovett, and Co., as his agents. Two members of the firm (Messrs. C. W. Walsh and F. A. Martin) have visited Cabul at Abdurrahman's invitation, and found him very friendly. The Amir expressed himself well satisfied with the machinery supplied for his workshops, and with the admirable manner in which the European employés had set it up. Minting, cartridge-making, cannon-founding, and barrel-rifling machinery are in full swing, and there are also machines for making swords, boots, weaving, saw-mills, and flour-mills, affording altogether employment for about 2,500 Afghan workmen and fifty natives of India. Messrs. Walsh and Martin say that nothing could have been more warmly loyal than the Amir's public expressions of his friendly feelings towards the British Government. He also professed his extreme desire to increase trade with India. It would be easy to reply that these amiable expressions have not always borne fruit, as, for example, in the petition of the tea-planters in the North-West for a reduction of tea duties in Afghanistan, and in similar appeals in respect of the trade which enters Candahar by way of the Sind-Pishin railway. We must, however, beware of judging the despotic ruler of a half-savage Eastern race by too exacting a standard, and allowance must be made for the lack of roads and bridges, and the want of organization among the officials. In the meantime it is interesting to learn that the British Mahommedan agent at Cabul is treated more favourably than his predecessors, and lives in a style not unbefitting our representative. He rides about in Cabul on a richly caparisoned horse, with a dozen orderlies, all conspicuous by the silver-mounted harness of their steeds. He is noted for his generosity, a trait likely to appeal to the full to the impressionable Oriental. An English doctor is in charge of the dispensaries, and, in spite of some recent departures, there are still several English engineers and skilled artisans in Cabul, engaged under the Amir's personal auspices. Mr. Clemens is superintendent of the Amir's stud; mining operations have been instituted under the direction of Mr. A. Collins, mining engineer, and Mr. Pyne, who is the *doyen* of the little English colony in Cabul, and has been there eight years, is in charge of the workshops. Next year it is anticipated that the Amir will start a paper mill, and later on he purposes to engage a professional wine maker from Europe to try his hand at the Cabul grapes. Lastly, but not leastly, it is reported that Abdurrahman contemplates laying down an experimental railway, thirteen miles in length, for the purpose of deporting the refuse of the city of Cabul and bringing back marble for building purposes. Mr. Pyne has given us, in the pages of *The Civil and Military Gazette*, an interesting personal sketch of the Amir. Mr. Pyne has no doubt in his own mind of the Amir's entire fidelity to the British alliance, and that the visit which Abdurrahman contemplated paying to England would have had an immense effect in expanding his Highness's ideas on the subject of railways and the resources of civilization generally. The latter pays keen attention to business details, but nevertheless it is not an unknown circumstance in Cabul (any more than in certain more highly organized States nearer home) for documents to be issued at times, bearing the seal of the ruler, of whose contents or existence the latter is ignorant. Mr. Pyne thinks a meeting, say at Peshawar, between the Viceroy and the Amir, would do much to clear up any possible source of misunderstanding, and cement the friendship between the two nations.

There is no reason, so far as can be judged by an outside observer, to impute undue favouritism or optimism to these reflections. Considering the very imperfect and irregular means of diplomatic communication between the Amir and the Indian Government, and the endless troubles which have arisen and must necessarily arise, at one time with Russia, at another with Kafiristan, Chitral, Bajaur, or other neighbouring states and tribes possessing varying shades of independence, or with our own frontier officials, it is surprising that more ground for estrangement does not crop up between the two nations.

One of these frontier difficulties concerned Umra Khan of Chandawul, in Bajaur, a chief possessing considerable force of character and resolution, and owning supremacy in a fine, extensive, and populous valley of a pastoral character, a little way north of the Khyber Pass. Bajaur is not subject to the Cabul Government, and has only paid tribute when forced to do so, so it is easily conceivable that the relations between the two States were not of the most cordial nature. Hostilities between the Amir and Umra Khan appear to have been on the point of breaking out in 1888, and at the beginning of last year (1892) Umra Khan ousted the young Khan of Asmar, an important village on the banks of the Kunar, a little to the northwest of Bajaur. The sister of the Khan was betrothed to the son of the Amir, who thereupon deputed his general, Gholam Haidar Khan, to lead troops against Asmar, which was captured shortly afterwards. Thereupon the Amir and his general conceived the idea of carrying their conquests further east and annexing Bajaur itself, but this project could in no way be sanctioned by the Government of India, who forthwith conveyed a warning to the Amir, as well as to Gholam Haidar, informing them in unmistakable terms that no interference with Bajaur could be permitted. These movements on the part of the Amir, coupled with the activity of some of his emissaries in Waziristan and near the Gamul Pass, appear to have conveyed the impression that his Highness was bent on a wholesale forward policy, with the object of bringing under control the independent States between Afghanistan and the British frontier. His reply, too, about Bajaur is said to have been touched in a tone the reverse of submissive; but, so far as can be seen, there are no signs of any further aggressive projects, or of any disposition to oppose the wishes of the Indian Government.

Northward of Bajaur the British frontier officials have been confronted with more serious difficulties. Our isolated post at Gilgit has often been menaced by neighbouring mountain tribes, while its proximity to Russian territory invests it with obvious importance. Towards the close of 1891 the British Government determined to improve the road thither as well as the route running northward as far as Chalt on the confines of Hunza-Nagar. This latter proceeding was resented by the Hunza-Nagar tribesmen, who had long maintained a defiant attitude, and hostilities ensued. The brilliant capture of Nilt and Miyan which followed are too recent to need recapitulation; suffice it to say that they fully bore up the reputation of our soldiers for daring and resource, and that in a few weeks the Hunza chief was in full flight, and the secluded refuge of these notorious man-stealers and brigands was at our mercy. The British Government, however, magnanimously abstained from punishing the Hunza-Nagaris who had borne arms against us, and a native ruler, the half-brother of the deposed chief, was formally installed as *Thum*, or Rajah, in the presence of a Chinese envoy from Kashgar, who had been invited to witness the ceremony. This event, from a military and political point of view, was very important, for it established our supremacy in a difficult and quasi-independent region whither the Russian explorer Grombtchevsky had penetrated by the comparatively easy Kilik Pass across the Muztagh range in 1888. Grombtchevsky's reception by the Thum was friendly, a circumstance of some significance when we remember that that of our own envoy, Sir William Lockhart, was of a very different character; in fact, he and his companion, Colonel Woodthorpe, were in some personal danger during their sojourn there. It can hardly be supposed, therefore, that the submission of the country to our arms in 1891-2 was pleasing to the Russians, and our successful *coup* was soon to be answered by a counter-move on the Pamirs.

The territorial rights of England, Afghanistan, Russia and China were a matter of considerable uncertainty in this direction. The Russian view[1] that since the annexation of Khokand in 1878 the Pamir question has remained open, ignores the arrangement of 1873 (which virtually recognized the Upper Oxus as the northern boundary of Afghanistan) and may be consequently dismissed as untenable. At the same time it is rather

[1] Set forth in the *Turkestan Gazette* of the 20th September. See the London *Times* of the 20th October, 1892.

hard to justify the Amir's occupation in 1883 of Shignan and Roshan on the right bank of the Oxus as within the four corners of the Granville-Gortchakov agreement. The frontier between Russian territory and Eastern Turkestan was laid down in 1877, when Yakub Beg was Amir, and, according to the arrangement then arrived at, the lake great Kara-Kul was assigned to Russia, while little Kara-Kul was included in the Amir's share. On the death of Yakub Beg, China re-entered into possession of his dominions, and at the time of Mr. Littledale's journey across the Pamir, her extreme western post was close to Burzila Jai, on the Alichur Pamir. Such, roughly, was the situation in 1890.

In the following year Captain Younghusband was sent by the Indian Foreign Office on special duty into Chinese Turkestan. While at Yarkand in the early summer he was informed of the presence of a body of Russian troops on the Chinese Pamirs. He accordingly despatched Lieutenant Davidson to the Alichur Pamir to make inquiries and himself repaired to Wakhan. At Bosai-i-gumbaz he fell in with a Russian expedition, consisting of about a hundred men under the command of Colonel Yanoff. Here Captain Younghusband was compelled by the Russians to sign a document by which he undertook not to cross certain passes leading into territory now claimed to belong to the Tzar. The most extraordinary thing about this arbitrary proceeding is that it was done at the order of General Vrevsky, the Governor-General of Russian Turkestan, who was north of the Alai range at the time, and was in constant communication with Colonel Yanoff, while Mr. Eliot, attaché to the British embassy at St. Petersburg, who happened to be travelling with the Governor-General, was kept in complete ignorance of Captain Younghusband's arrest. The latter officer ascertained that the Russians had actually crossed the Hindu Kush range by the Khora Bhort Pass into Chitral territory, returning by the Baroghil. On Colonel Yanoff's way back to Marghilan, in Ferghana, his party fell in with Lieutenant Davidson and a Chinese officer on the Alichur Pamir, and having compelled the latter to withdraw, the Russians practically arrested Lieutenant Davidson and made their way on to Marghilan, where, being in some embarrassment as to what to do with the British officer, they finally handed him over to Mr. Eliot. By the advice of the latter, Mr. Davidson returned to Kashgaria and rejoined Captain Younghusband and the Chinese officer in the Taghdumbash Pamir. The two English officers subsequently proceeded to India *viâ* Gilgit and Kashmir.

For this unwarrantable treatment of two British officers, the Russian Government subsequently expressed its regret. But, as M. Popowski very clearly shows with respect to a succession of similar incidents in past years, a disavowal by the central administration at St. Petersburg has no effect whatever, and is probably intended to have no effect, on the action of the frontier officials. Indeed it is even alleged that while the Tzar rebuked Colonel Yanoff and desired him to abstain from crossing the Karakoram and Muztagh ranges in his future reconnaissances, he also promoted him and presented him with a valuable ring set with the Imperial monogram to console him for the reproof which international etiquette had necessitated. It may be recollected that a similar episode marked the Russo-Afghan imbroglio of 1885. Such a state of things is hard to realize in our country, where centralization is far more severe, and where an officer's pettiest actions and movements are rigidly controlled from head-quarters. But the radical difference in the practice of the two countries must be steadfastly borne in mind if we are to form a clear and dispassionate judgment on the probable future of the Central Asian question.

There was but little surprise, therefore, when news arrived in July, 1892, that a Russian detachment of a still stronger character had appeared at Aktash, on the eastern Pamir. This turned out to be a considerable force, composed of infantry, Cossacks, and artillery, and reinforced before starting by numerous volunteers, including scientific men. The expedition left New Marghilan on June 14th, and after overcoming great physical obstacles arrived at Aktash, but on hearing of the presence of a large body of Afghans at Somatash on the Alichur Pamir, Colonel Yanoff and his men proceeded thither. As might be expected, a collision between Russians and Afghans promptly ensued, in which nine Afghans were killed and two wounded. The Russian loss is said to have been one killed and two wounded. The Tzar again expressed his annoyance at Colonel Yanoff's proceedings, but the Indian Government, with a judicious appreciation of the danger of the situation, promptly ordered a substantial reinforcement of the Gilgit garrison. The latter step was, however, of a purely defensive character, and in any case was too late to exercise any influence over the movements of the Russians, who, after "demonstrating" in three separate detachments, viz., in the Alichur Valley, so as to overawe Shignan, at Langar-kisht, by the foot of the Hindu-Kush range, and near Tash-kurghan and the Taghdumbash Pamir in the east, returned to Marghilan on the 3rd October. Detached pickets, amounting in all to about 165 men, were left at various selected points in the Pamirs, and these troops appear to have passed the winter of 1892–3 in this quasi-Arctic region with no serious hurt. Indeed it is obvious from this and from the rapidity of Colonel Yanoff's movements that the difficulties attending the transport, supplies and organization of a force, including Cossacks and artillery, in these elevated regions have been practically and successfully overcome. The strategic importance of this, in connection with the defence of India, can hardly be overrated.

In the meantime an event occurred on the southern side of the Hindu Kush which indirectly will, no doubt, conduce to the increased security of our frontier. In August last Aman-ul-Mulk, the old Mehtar of Chitral, died. Since the British occupation of Gilgit and the activity displayed by recent Russian reconnoitring expeditions in the valley of the Upper Oxus, Chitral has become a post of military importance, commanding as it does a group of passes leading across what has been aptly termed the physical bulwark of India on the northwest. Through Chitral also there runs a road from Jelalabad, which the Amir has been desirous of opening up as a trade route with his province of Badakhshan. This project of the Amir, however, excited great uneasiness in Chitral, and the aid of the paramount Power was invoked to protect the independence of the State. The death of the Mehtar thus found our frontier officials on the alert, but for the nonce the succession was effected tranquilly. Afzul-ul-Mulk, the younger son, took possession of the arsenal and treasury, and was accepted as ruler by the inhabitants, while the elder brother, Nizam-ul-Mulk, Governor of Yassin, fled and took refuge with our officers at Gilgit. Afzul's reign, however, was of short duration. His uncle, Sher Afzul

Khan, a refugee in Badakhshan, collected some hundred Chitrali slaves and a handful of Afghans, crossed the Do Rahah (Dora) Pass, and having captured two small forts, surprised Chitral, and made himself master of the capital, Afzul being shot while attempting to escape. This violent usurpation incensed the Nizam-ul-Mulk at Gilgit, and mustering a strong body of followers, he promptly marched through Yassin and Mastuj, the inhabitants of which rose in his favour, and entered Chitral without opposition, the usurping uncle taking refuge in flight and not daring even to face the vengeance of his victim's brother. Since the Nizam-ul Mulk's accession he bids fair to become a better ruler than was originally anticipated. He has entered into communications with the authorities at Gilgit with the view to the permanent location of a British officer, as representative at his court, in lieu of the native agent hitherto accredited there, and Dr. Robertson is expected to take up the duties as Resident. Dr. Robertson's great experience of frontier politics in Gilgit and Hunza, as well as his recent adventurous journey through Kafiristan, mark him out as possessed of unique qualifications for this important post.

Viewing, therefore, the general course of events during the past three years, we see that while Russia has strengthened her communications from Sarakhs to Zulfikar, and at various other points along the Afghan border, her main activity has been displayed on the Pamirs and on the northern slopes of the Hindu Kush, where the uncertainty attaching to the exact interpretation of the international arrangement of 1872–3 has supplied a more or less ostensible excuse for aggression. A proposal for a mixed commission to demarcate the region in dispute has indeed been mooted, and is understood to be favourably viewed by both the great Powers, but until we are assured of the Amir's agreement, any such delimitation will lack one of the most vital guarantees for its due observance. It is a matter of congratulation that in Hunza-Nagar and Chitral our position is stronger than it was; but after all it is Afghanistan itself that forms the key of the situation, and a frank personal interview between its ruler and that of India becomes more urgent as time goes on, and the unsettled condition of things affords temptation to a fresh Russian expedition to take the field. Such an interview will do more than anything else to enable England and Russia to arrive at some final adjustment of the still outstanding difficulties of the Central Asian question.

A few words are necessary respecting the map which accompanies the present volume. While the western part is based on the last official British map of Afghanistan, in which were incorporated the extensive surveys and reconnaissances executed during the Afghan boundary commission, care has been taken to embody numerous detached and recent surveys of importance, wherever these enter into the area of delimitation. This is particularly the case along the line of the Hindu Kush, where geographical research has been so especially busy during the last few years. The northern part is taken from the last Russian official map of Turkestan, the information in which, so far as it relates to extra-British territory, is, of course, far superior to our own data. Mr. J. Bolton, of Mr. Stanford's geographical establishment, has spared no pains in the collection and harmonization of materials, and on the whole, it is hoped that it will be found to be the best map hitherto published of the region under discussion.

Stated in detail, the principal maps used in its construction are the following :—

On the British side, the sheets of the Indian Atlas, on the scale of 4 miles to 1 inch ; the Trans-frontier maps of the Great Trigonometrical Survey of India, on the scale of 16 miles to 1 inch ; the map of Hundes and Monyul by Messrs. Ryall and Kinney, the Pundits, &c., on the scale of 8 miles to the inch ; the map of Astor and Gilgit, by Lieut.-Colonel Tanner, scale 4 miles to the inch ; map of the Upper Oxus Valley, by Mr. Hennessey, scale 12 miles to 1 inch ; part of Hazara and adjacent independent territory, by Capt. Wahab, R.E., scale 2 miles to 1 inch ; Dr. Leitner's map of Dardistan, 1877, scale 16 miles to the inch ; the above-mentioned map of Afghanistan, in four sheets, by Major Gore, R.E., scale 24 miles to the inch ; and Major Holdich's boundary map of North-Western Afghanistan, scale 4 miles to 1 inch.

On the Russian side, the Russian Staff map of Central Asia, scale 10 versts to 1 inch ; and map of the Amu Daria, by A. Bolchev, scale 30 versts to the inch.

The following are the chief sketches and route surveys from which the intervening territory has been compiled :—

Map of Central Asia in Supplementary Papers of the Royal Geographical Society, 1884, illustrating Mr. Delmar Morgan's paper ; map of Chinese Turkistan, illustrating Mr. Carey's paper in the *Proceedings* of the R.G.S., December 1887, and Supplementary Papers, 1890 ; map illustrating Captain Younghusband's paper in the Proceedings of the R.G.S. for April, 1892 ; map of M. Dauvergne's explorations in the Bulletin of the Paris Geographical Society and Bogdanovitch's map of the Pamirs in the Proceedings of the Russian Imperial Geographical Society, reduced and connected with the results of the work of M. Dauvergne and other explorers by Mr. H. Sharbau, of the Royal Geographical Society.

CHARLES E. D. BLACK.

AUTHOR'S PREFACE

For several centuries past, indeed we may even say from its very foundation, there has been manifest in the Russian Empire a restless, expansive force, highly characteristic of that nation, which has led in the first instance, to the extension of its frontiers in all directions until they have become conterminous with the seaboard on the North and East, and with powerful and united countries on the West. Since then Russia has unremittingly concentrated all her energies on the South, and chiefly in the direction of Constantinople and Central Asia. The European powers, however, and Austria in particular, cannot at any cost permit Russia to take possession of Constantinople. On the other hand, Russia's advance in Central Asia constitutes a menace to British rule in India. Russia can only attain her ultimate object, for which she has so long striven with such incomparable perseverance, by a combat à outrance.

This combat may be regarded as that of two forms of civilisation: the Russian, and that of Western Europe. Russian civilisation is the product of Byzantine and Asiatic ideas implanted in Sclavonian-Finnish-Mongolian soil. Up to the eighteenth century both Grand Dukes and Tzars carefully excluded European influences from their country. Peter the Great was the first who endeavoured to turn Western civilisation—which he admired—to account in Russia ; but the country had gone on too long in her own way to become imbued with the spirit of Western culture.

The old-fashioned beards of his subjects, and the tails of their long caftans succumbed to the strong will of the Tzar-reformer ; the educated classes adopted European manners and other outward forms ; but in their mode of thought, in their treasured associations, as well as in their attitude towards their inferiors, they remained true to traditional habits.

It is, indeed, only recently that they aspired to be regarded as civilised Europeans, and that any distinguishing flattering regard was paid to Europe in the Empire of the Tzar. General Bibikov, Tzar Nicholas's Minister of the Interior, did not fail to recognise this when he exclaimed to the Polish landowners : "The laws are not made for you, but for Europe."

In the sixties Russia quelled the Polish insurrection, and defied France, England and Austria with impunity. As a consequence national self-respect increased enormously ; the Pan-Sclavonic theory of the "*decaying* Western and *quickening* Russian civilisation" soon came to the front, and created a feeling of bitterness mingled with contempt for Europe. This feeling displayed itself first of all towards the Germans, who since the time of Peter the Great had occupied a privileged position in the State, and had held the highest offices and dignities both civil and military. Even the present Tzar Alexander III. when heir-apparent did not scruple to evince his hatred of the Germans on every occasion. They are now being gradually displaced, and the Baltic provinces whose inhabitants justly prided themselves on having always been the Tzar's most loyal subjects, are suffering from the constantly increasing tendency to Russianisation. Russian chauvinism is still on the increase, and the "Moscowskie Viedomosti," organ of the lately deceased Katkov, who for over twenty years had been the leader of public opinion in Russia, correctly indicated the prevalent feeling, when on the occasion of the death of Kaiser Wilhelm I. it stated that "The twentieth century ✓ belongs to us." The Tzar himself is a believer in Katkov's and Pobiedonostsef's ultra-national theory; and it is a favourite remark of his that a sixth part of the globe belongs to him. If such ideas prevail, it cannot be supposed that Russia will voluntarily desist from a policy which she has so tenaciously pursued for centuries past. Since the Berlin Congress the language of the Sovereigns has, indeed, been more peaceable; but the German armaments, the latest additions to the field artillery and the new mortar batteries, in Russia, prove that the situation continues to be grave. For this reason, we regard a war between Russia and Austria with her allies in Europe, and between Russia and England in Asia, as a mere question of time.

Russia's policy both in Europe and Asia is an active one, whilst Austria and England would be only too glad if they succeeded in securing the maintenance of the *status quo*. The English would even submit quietly to Russia's forward-movement, were its pace less rapid, as in that case the fight for India would in all probability be forced on a later generation. From this state of things Russia reaps great benefit. She holds the initiative, and can suit her action to circumstances; and should she now and again, swayed by public opinion or the temperament of her statesmen, be induced to advance somewhat too boldly, she can, as in 1878, purchase peace by surrendering a portion of her acquisitions. Russia will therefore doubtless attain her ultimate object, if the powers concerned be not convinced of the need for energetic resistance.

In the interests of civilisation the final triumph of Russia is by no means to be desired. The lot of those nations which have had the misfortune to fall under Russia's yoke has ever been a hard one. The genial Ruthenian poet Taras Shefchenko describes this in his poem "The Caucasus," and thus apostrophizes the heroic, liberty-loving Circassian : " You will be taught how prisons are built, how knotty knouts are plaited, how chains are forged and—how they are borne!" "The Russians," says the German philosopher Hartmann, "know how to destroy the flower of husbandry in the countries they conquer, but are unable to supply any substitute for that which they destroy. The want of good government embitters the conquered to the utmost, and drives them to desperate attempts to revolt, which cannot be kept in check without the employment of an abnormally large force—diverted from more profitable enterprise." " And though Europe may be said to be in a state of reaction at present, comparisons cannot fairly be drawn between her condition and that of Russia."

As the conflicting interests of Austria and Russia in Europe, and of England and Russia in Asia form the dominant element in the political situation, we make it the subject of our study in the following treatise. We commence our task with the "conflict of English and Russian interests in Asia," as Russia's action in Asia is not so well known, and her need for disguise and restraint is less. Her movements in Asia being less guarded can be observed with greater accuracy, and from them we can learn the meaning of her *modus operandi* in Europe.

Russia menaces by her advance England's possessions in Asia, whilst England's extension in India is a matter of perfect indifference to Russia. Consequently, in the following study we shall devote our attention primarily to Russia. In the first chapter we narrate the history of her advance in Asia since the fifteenth century. In the second chapter we prove that Russia aspires to the possession of India. In the third chapter we examine the political relations of Russia and England in regard to Asia since the commencement of the present century, and arrive at the conclusion that England is powerless to arrest Russia in Asia by means of diplomacy. In the fourth chapter we review the strategical relations of Russia and England. In the fifth and last chapter we discuss England's value to the Central-European alliance; and the reader having now acquired from the foregoing a thorough knowledge of the subject, we conclude by considering what it behoves England to do under the present circumstances.

THE AUTHOR

ENGLAND AND RUSSIA

I

RUSSIA'S ADVANCE IN ASIA

IN the fifteenth century the Muscovite Grand-Duchy shook off the Mongolian yoke, and immediately after commenced its advance on Asia. In the year 1472 the Grand Duke Ivan III. took Perm, and shortly after Viatka. In 1552 Ivan the Terrible occupied Kasan, and in 1556 Astrakhan, in the Delta of the Volga. The Cossacks advanced still further, and in the last quarter of the sixteenth century we find them settled on the rivers Ural and Terek, *i.e.*, both in the East and South, on the confines of Asia.

The Cossacks play a prominent part in Russia's conquests in Asia, and it must be admitted that Russia displayed masterly skill in turning them to the best account. It will therefore be advisable to consider the Cossacks more in detail.

The date of their first appearance has not, indeed, been accurately determined, but as early as the latter half of the fourteenth century they are mentioned both in the Polish and Russian Annals. The Polish Cossacks belong to the Little-Russian, the Russian Cossacks to the Great-Russian stock. We shall turn our attention to the latter.

"Men of energetic temperament and bold, enterprising spirit," observes Colonel Choroshkin of the Russian General Staff in his work on the Cossack military colonies, "who, whether owing to the tyranny of the ruling class, or to their dread of the consequences of some criminal act, or from any other cause, found themselves cramped at home, took refuge in the wilderness which extended for an immeasurable distance between the Southern limits of the Sclavonian and the Northern limits of the Tartar possessions, and was vaguely termed the "plain" (pole).

This desert-life soon compelled the scattered adventurers to band themselves together. The common struggle with wild nature, and with the hard conditions of their life gradually linked them so closely together, that the societies thus formed at length developed into communities ever ready to fight, and mainly dependent for their means of subsistence on robbery and plunder. The more oppressed the inhabitants of the despotically governed States felt themselves, the greater the stream of exiles which poured into the "plain"; and thus the Cossack communities gradually became an army.

They had abundance of room for expansion, inasmuch as the Southern border-districts of the Russia of that day comprised merely the present governments of Kursk, Orel, Riasan, and Nijni-Novgorod, whilst the Tartars occupied only the Crimea and strips of coast on the Black Sea and the Sea of Azov. The intervening space constituted the "plain," which was "no man's land." The Don, Donetz, and other rivers were spoken of as situated beyond the "plain" (zapolnija).

Some of these Cossacks settled on the frontier of the Russia of that day, and were employed as out-posts, and scouts: the rest lived in the "plain," and subsisted mainly on plunder.

After the fall of the Dukedom of Riazan (1523), severer punishment was inflicted on the Border-Cossacks for their predatory incursions on Russian territory, and a number of them were compulsorily transferred to other parts of the Muscovite Empire. To evade this unusual constraint, many of the Border-Cossacks fled into the "plain," and even beyond it, as far as the Don and the Terek, where they formed the nucleus of fresh hordes. "The Cossack colonists, however," says M. Vladykin in his description of the Caucasus, "thrown upon their own resources, were too weak to maintain their independence. To obtain support, they at last submitted to the Muscovite Government, which graciously accepted their allegiance, and thus acquired extensive territories without trouble or cost."

In 1570 the Tzar Ivan the Terrible confirmed the constitution of the Don-Cossacks. Shortly after they figured, too, amongst the Russian troops; but they still considered themselves independent, as is proved by the fact that the Cossacks who were to have taken part in Ivan's expedition against Livonia, returned to the Don without leave or license. The Cossacks still continued to look upon plunder as their chief source of livelihood. With the view of restraining the robbers, the "terrible" Tzar in 1577 sent troops against them under the command of Murashkin. A section of the Don-Cossacks who carried on their system of plunder on the Volga retreated under their leader Jermak in the direction of Perm, and shortly after undertook the conquest of Siberia. Some others escaped, after their defeat by Murashkin, to the Caspian Sea, and settled on the Jaik (Ural).

Another distinct group of Cossacks had settled on the Volga; and on the Terek there were the Grebnian Cossacks. In short, at the close of the sixteenth century, colonies of Cossacks encircled the Tzar's Muscovite Empire on the South and South-East, forming a far-advanced, and continually advancing, chain of defensive outposts.

The seventeenth century was especially favourable to the expansion of Cossack influence. Their adventurous, lively, mounted-freebooter life with its attendant risks was a fascinating attraction to the servile, "earth-bound" serfs. The Cossack was the hero of several of their popular songs, and many a serf took refuge among these free-lances, whose life possessed such attractions, that even merchants who had intercourse with Central Asia, occasionally left their wares in order to join in one of their expeditions. There was a mighty inherent power in "Cossackdom." Up to the end of the seventeenth century the Cossacks fought principally with Orientals, and of their own accord extended the frontiers of the Russian Empire. But Peter the Great almost entirely put an end to their independence. "Thereby," remarks Colonel Choroshkin, "the Cossacks lost indeed much of the fantastic prestige which they possessed in the eyes of the people, but became, instead of a precarious support, a reliable safeguard of the Empire's frontiers." Henceforward they form indeed an essential element of the Russian forces in Central Asia, but are not allowed to undertake independent enterprises, the Russian Government having itself assumed the conduct of Asiatic affairs.

From this period, too, the Government took in hand the organisation of the Cossack hordes and "Lines." Thus, for instance, the Cossacks of the Azov were disbanded in 1865, and the New-Russian Cossacks in 1868; on the other hand, the Amur Cossacks were formed in 1858, and the Semiretchensk Cossacks in 1867. Several lines such as the Ukraine and the Transkama were done away with. At the end of the eighteenth century Potemkin established the Mozdokazov line, and the Lezgin and Laba lines were respectively established in 1830 and 1846. In 1860 the Cossack army occupying the Caucasus was divided into the Kuban and the Terek sections, each being named after the principal river in its district.[1]

The Cossacks form an essential portion of the Russian cavalry, and are employed for the seizure of a territory, or for its protection, in cases where a powerful display of force is necessary. They occupy either a separate district, one, for instance, being named the province of the Don-Cossacks, or else tracts of country comprised in one or more governments. These tracts form, in the case of the Ural and Orenburg Cossacks, a connected whole; in that of the Siberian Cossacks a zone hundreds of miles long; and in that of the Astrakhan, Semiretchensk, and Amur Cossacks, scattered oases.

On the "lines" devolved the task of holding the frontier, and protecting it from attack. The "lines" consisted of forts, or "Stanitzas" (Cossack-villages) placed for the most part at regular intervals. Thus, for instance, the Stanitzas on the Kuban-line were twenty versts[2] apart, and in the intervening space outposts furnished by the Stanitzas were stationed at points commanding an extensive view. In Siberia the lines were formed,—according to the configuration of the

[1] Beside the Cossack hordes a regular Russian army occupies the Caucasus.
[2] About thirteen miles.

country or the character of the neighbouring people,—either of forts or Stanitzas, situated at intervals of over twenty versts.

Lastly, mention must be made of the town Cossacks, who, as their name implies, had settled in the newly built or conquered towns of Siberia. These were the colonists of Siberia, and the pioneers of Russian rule in Asia, "and though," Colonel Choroshkin remarks, "their proceedings doubtless savoured of true Cossack lawlessness, yet we cannot but admire the energy with which they advanced to the easternmost corner of Asia."

When the Government had quite decided on establishing a line, or a more compact nucleus,—a Cossack colony,—it proceeded at once to carry out its intention, regardless of the wishes of the prospective colonists. The Don-Cossacks were the chief source from which the supplies of colonists were drawn. In 1724, 1,000 families were transferred to reinforce the Grebnian and Agrahan Cossacks. In 1732 another 1,000 families formed the nucleus of the Volga horde. Again at the end of the eighteenth century other 3,000 families were to be transferred to Kuban. "This was, however, more than they could bear," says Choroshkin. The old rebellious spirit awoke once more, and manifested itself in a serious insurrection which had to be suppressed by force of arms. Hereupon 1,000 families were removed, and about 2,000 men more or less severely punished. Other divisions of Cossacks were also compelled to transmigrate. In 1792 the Zaporog Cossacks on the Dnieper were transferred with their Hetman to Kuban on the Black Sea. A separate province, called "The province of the Cossacks of the Black Sea," was allotted to them, and they themselves were called Cossacks of the Black Sea.

In 1861 General Evdokimov decided to remove the Circassians living to the south of Kuban to other quarters, and to replace them by Cossacks of the Black Sea. The Cossacks ordered to migrate proved rebellious. "But they soon recovered their senses," observes the admirable Russian writer Vladykin, "and the colonisation was effected without resort to *specially severe measures.*"

When the Governor-General of Eastern Siberia, Count Mouraviev, acquired the Amur territory from China in 1854, he determined to transfer thither 6,000 Cossacks from the Transbaikal Cossack-settlement. To promote the development of the newly-acquired province, he gave orders to select the colonists with the utmost care from among the wealthiest and best families. This was a lucrative business for the officials, who conducted the colonisation, but a severe blow for Transbaikalia, which, both economically and socially, was making rapid progress. The loss of 6,000 souls to so young a colony was of itself grievous enough; but the discontent roused by this compulsory migration from a community as yet unconsolidated led to still more serious consequences. A large number of the colonists, to whom, on the strength of a superficial survey, dwelling-places exposed to frequent inundations had been allotted, perished miserably. This added fresh fuel to the fire of discontent. Transbaikalia has not recovered from this blow to the present day. Had it not been for mistakes of this nature, Russia's possessions in Asia would by this time have reached a very different stage of development.

At present there are ten Cossack hordes: those of the Don, Kuban, the Terek, Astrakhan, the Ural, Orenburg, Siberia, Semiretchensk, Transbaikalia, and

Amur. These occupy a total area of 300,000 square miles, and are recruited from a Cossack population numbering, according to a report issued in 1880, 2,150,837 souls. There are, besides, 775,689 persons living in the Cossack provinces who do not belong to the Cossack class.

In a war the Cossacks furnish collectively 879 sotnias of cavalry, 66 sotnias of infantry, and 248 guns—or, 135,000 horse, 13,500 foot, and 10,500 artillerymen, divided into three levies, according to their ages, and readiness for service.

The question now arises, whence did Russia procure a sufficient number of Cossacks to colonise both the Stanitzas of the "lines," and the Cossack provinces?

A closer consideration of the nature of "Cossackdom" enables us to answer this question. Russian writers would trace a remote resemblance between the Cossacks and the knights of old, with this distinction, that the Cossacks always professed democratic principles, and never formed an exclusive class. They did not inquire after ancestors or antecedents, but hailed every one capable of defending himself as a welcome comrade.

Every able-bodied man was admitted to their fellowship; the fugitive slave who sought freedom in their company, as readily as the Boyar who had come into collision with the Government or the Courts,—in short, all those who would not, or could not, accommodate themselves to the existing *régime.* Hence the Cossacks were recruited partly from Cossack families, and partly from the refugees that joined their ranks. It was not until later, when the Cossacks were thoroughly organised, that their community ceased to be the refuge of outlaws, though even now they do not profess to close their ranks to all outsiders. Especially when fresh colonies were founded, everybody possessed of the necessary qualifications was received with open arms. The Russian writer Vladykin remarks that the Russian is as readily converted into a Cossack on a "line" in the Caucasus, as on any other of Russia's frontier-lines. The Terek, Sunja, and Laba lines were originally manned by married soldiers, serfs, various refugees, and only a small proportion of real Cossacks, and yet this mixed community soon rendered good service.

Their military organisation restricted to a certain degree the free movements of the Cossacks. They could not, as the American colonists, for instance, voluntarily sell their property and migrate elsewhere, inasmuch as their obligation to military service tied them to their division. Besides this it was one of the traditions of "Cossackdom" that its members did not settle singly, but in a body large enough to represent a certain power of resistance. When the Government decided on establishing a new "line," a certain number of Cossack families were ordered to move, and it was generally left to the discretion of the commanding officer whether he would consider in so doing the wishes of the Cossack families selected for the colonisation. In spite of this state of dependence, the Cossacks ranked higher than the mass of the country-people, they being free men, and the others serfs. A serf, even if he betook himself to the boundless ungoverned tracts beyond the frontiers of the Empire, could not be sure of retaining his freedom.

An example of this is furnished by the Government of Stavropol, which was colonised with great success in the latter half of the eighteenth century. The wish of the French King, Henry IV., that every peasant might daily have a fowl in his pot, says our informant Vladykin, was there more than realised, as every peasant saw beef and pork, as well as fowls, on his table. Many peasants possessed hundreds of oxen, thousands of sheep and thousands of roubles, and they were about to add still further to their prosperity, when an unexpected blow fell upon them. The system of conferring rewards in vogue in the Empress Catherine II.'s time—the presentation to court dignitaries of lands with the peasants occupying them—came into operation here as elsewhere, and the colonists became serfs.

Nothing of this sort happened to the Cossacks. They paid for their freedom with the blood-tax,—military service,—and it was for this reason that "Cossackdom" was so popular, and took root so easily in places where the Cossack population formed but a small fraction of the colonists.

In 1861 serfdom was abolished in Russia. No one can, however, become a free man, in the full sense of the word, in a day. The thraldom that had pressed upon the Russian people for centuries had deprived them of the innate, or even acquired, power of initiative, which we admire in the Anglo-Saxons, and to which the latter owe their great success in America and other colonies. If we add, that Anglo-Saxons everywhere remain true to the principles of self-help and self-government, we can easily conceive that they must inevitably obtain results differing totally from those of the Russians, hampered as the latter have ever been by unbending centralisation and administrative caprice, even in the favoured provinces of Northern and Central Asia. At any rate, Russia owes her firm footing in Asia to the

Cossacks, or more correctly to "Cossackdom." The Circassians perceived this, and expressed it in the following simile: A fort is like a stone cast upon the field. Rain and wind may carry it away, or cover it with earth. A Stanitza, on the other hand, resembles a plant, which is firmly rooted in the soil, and gradually spreads over a whole field.

To simplify our survey, we shall first of all review Russia's advance in Northern Asia in an Easterly direction as far as the ocean, then her advance in the south, between the Black and the Caspian Seas; and lastly her advance in Central Asia, *i.e.*, between the Caspian Sea and the Pamir plateau.

* * * * *

In the year 1581 the Cossack hetman Jermak, who had been condemned to death by Ivan the Terrible, conquered Siberia at the head of a handful of outlawed adventurers like himself, and laid his conquest at the feet of the Tzar. This, Russia's first step in Asia, attracted no notice in Europe, inasmuch as the possession of a poor, barren, and sparsely-populated country, the climate of which was, moreover, very harsh, had, in the abstract, no great value. In the seventeenth and eighteenth centuries Russia continued her advance in an Easterly direction, reached the ocean, crossed the Bering Straits, occupied the Alaska Peninsula and a neighbouring portion of North America, and came, in the New World, into immediate contact with the British Empire. This contact, however, created no agitation in the minds of English statesmen. Both the Russian and English possessions in North America were far removed from the administrative centres of those nations, and of little importance. The Russian Government recognised this, and in 1867 ceded Russian

America to the United States for the paltry sum of ten million roubles (7·5 million dollars). At that time the diplomatic relations between England and the United States were, owing to the attitude of the Western powers during the war of secession, anything but friendly, and the Alabama incident, which had reached an acute stage, afforded the Americans the welcome opportunity of making the English feel their resentment. The English and Russian relations were equally strained, owing to the diplomatic intervention of the Western powers during the Polish insurrection, and in consequence of Russia's advance in Central Asia. On the other hand, the diplomatic relations between Russia and the United States were very cordial, and the people as well as the Governments of both nations vied with each other in mutual demonstrations of friendship and sympathy. This being the aspect of political affairs, the cession of Russian America to the United States is easy of explanation. It was an act of courtesy towards the firm believers in the Monroe Doctrine, whereby England's North American possessions were henceforth shut in on two sides—a circumstance which could be by no means agreeable to the English. It testified, moreover, that Russia renounced all claims to America, and restricted herself to Europe and Asia. With the cession of Russian America to the North American States Russia's advance in an Easterly direction came to an end.

* * * * *

The advance of the Russians in the South was not so easy a matter as in the East. Here she encountered on the one hand warlike and rapacious tribes inhabiting extensive, rugged, and inaccessible mountains ; who only nominally recognised the sovereignty of the

Sultan, and were firmly determined to fight to the utmost for their liberty; and, on the other hand, States such as Persia and Turkey, which could only be conquered by Russia's regular troops. Under these circumstances the Cossacks that settled on the Terek at the close of the sixteenth century had to rest satisfied with maintaining their position, abandoning all idea of conquering large tracts of country, as Jermak's followers had succeeded in doing. The Russian Government was, moreover, otherwise engaged, and the seventeenth century closed without any alteration occurring in the *status quo* on the banks of the Terek. It was not until the year 1722 that the Tzar, Peter the Great, on the pretext of avenging robberies committed on certain merchants, led an army against Persia. He took Derbend, but running short of stores and ammunition did not continue his triumphal march further, and returned to his own country. The war was, however, shortly resumed, and in the following year the Russian troops occupied Baku. Hereupon, in 1723, the Persian Government decided to accept terms of peace which gave Russia Derbend and Baku, and the provinces of Daghestan, Shirwan, Ghilan, Mazanderan, and Asterabad. But as soon after as 1736 these conquests were lost, and the Russians retreated again to the left bank of the Terek.

An organised advance in the Caucasus first commenced in the reign of the Empress Catherine II. At about this period numerous colonists settled in the present Government of Stavropol. Prince Potemkin founded the towns of Mosdok, Ekaterinodar, Stavropol, and Vladikavkas, and established the Mosdok-Azov military line. The Empress in 1768 furnished Salomon I., King of Imeretia, with an auxiliary force under the command of General Todtleben, which drove out the Turks. By the treaty of Kuchuk-Kaimardji the Sultan relinquished his sovereignty over Grusia, Imeritia, and Mingrelia, and Russia assumed the protectorate of these countries. In 1795 Heraclius II., King of Grusia, appealed to the Empress Catherine II. for aid against Mahomed Aga Khan, Shah of Persia, who had invaded Grusia, destroyed Tiflis, and carried off 30,000 people into slavery. The Empress sent an army under the command of Count Zubov, which marched along the shores of the Caspian Sea, and took Derbend, Kuba, and Baku. On receiving news of the Empress' death, the Count returned to St. Petersburg.

At this period Grusia was in a state of anarchy. The numerous members of the reigning family, and of the nobility, were in continual conflict with each other, and the St. Petersburg Cabinet, true to its traditions, knew how to aggravate the mischief. King Heraclius, driven to despair, begged the Russian Government to assume the sovereignty over Grusia. His successor, George XIII., also declared his readiness to submit himself and his country to the Russian power, and after his death Grusia was at length incorporated with the Empire of the Tzar. This was proclaimed by Alexander I. in a manifesto, and Knorring and Kovalevski were entrusted with the administration of Grusia. They proved, however, unequal to the task. The agitation amongst the population increased more and more, and the worst was to be feared, when, in 1802, a Grusian, Prince Zizianov, was appointed military governor of Grusia. This extraordinary man commenced his administration by exiling the members of the royal family: he enforced complete obedience to the laws, prepared the way for the annexation of

Imeritia and Mingrelia, and waged a successful war with Persia. In 1806, however, on the occasion of the ceremonial surrender of the keys of Baku, he was treacherously murdered by the Persian General, Hussein Ali Khan.

Russia's settlement in Trans-Caucasia was extremely unpleasant to the Persians. Hence in 1811 they recommenced hostilities. General Kotlarevski, however, at the head of a handful of soldiers defeated the Persian heir-apparent, Abbas Mirza, took Lenkoran on the Caspian Sea, and by the treaty of Gulistan (1813) compelled Persia to surrender Daghestan, Grusia, Imeritia, Mingrelia, and Abkasia. War broke out afresh in 1826 between Persia and Russia. General Paskévitch defeated the Persian forces, and in 1828 concluded a treaty with Persia at Turkmantschaï, whereby the boundary between Russia and Persia, which still exists at the present day, was defined, and Persia paid an indemnity of five million tomans (three and a half million pounds sterling).

Since that date there has been unbroken peace between the two neighbouring countries, and Russia possesses considerable influence at Teheran. By the conquest of Grusia Russia came into direct contact with Turkey in Asia. 'Tis true, however, that the chief towns of both countries are situated in Europe, that their wars were occasioned by European affairs, and were fought out on European battle-fields; nevertheless Russia bore the Caucasus in mind, as far as possible, when negociating the treaties of peace. In 1774, by the peace of Kuchuk-Kaimardji, Turkey relinquished her sovereignty over Grusia, Imeritia, and Mingrelia. In 1829, by the peace of Adrianople, Russia acquired Akhaltsikh, Akhalkalaki, Anapa, Poti, and the coast which lies between the two harbours mentioned. Lastly, in 1878, by the treaty of Berlin, she acquired Kars and Batoum.

With the conquest of Trans-Caucasia, the so-called Caucasian war with the tribes which inhabited the Caucasian mountain-range commenced. These tribes possessed no political organisation, were independent of each other, lived on plunder, and were much attached to their home. They were so convinced of the inaccessibility of their mountains, that they conducted a Russian nobleman from the upper Kuban down to the shores of the Black Sea, in hopes that his description would discourage the Russians from penetrating into their mountains. Up to 1816, *i.e.*, till the appointment of General Jermolov to the command of the Caucasus, the Russians confined themselves to the maintenance of the Kuban and Terek "lines," and of the so-called military road from Vladikavkas to Tiflis.

General Jermolov proceeded, as the Chief of his Staff, General Veliaminov, graphically expresses it, to beleaguer the greatest fortress in the world, which throughout the entire siege was plentifully supplied with provisions, and was defended by a garrison of a million of men. He encompassed the Caucasian mountain-range with a line of circumvallation, and on the arrival of the siege-material the operations were commenced. Parallels extending for hundreds of miles were opened, and were connected by gigantic abattis, and new "lines" which supplied the place of trenches of approach. Forts served as siege-batteries and entrenchments. And when the garrison retired behind the main rampart an assault—lasting six years—took place. The entire siege lasted fully forty-eight years. A kingdom of sixty million inhabitants strained every nerve to take the fortress. Fights occurred daily which might worthily rank with those of the Greeks and Trojans. The Caucasus did not, however, produce its Homer, as the contest was too protracted both as regards time and space.

When the siege of the fortress commenced, to continue General Veliaminov's simile, its garrison was still unorganised. Each tribe fought when, where, and how it pleased, and there was no uniform plan of operation. The Circassians, however, soon perceived the defects in their mode of warfare. They saw that those whom they had hitherto been able to rob with impunity were now getting the upper hand, were destroying their Auls (villages), and taking from them their most productive fields,—and all this, because they acted in unison. These mightier ones were, however, unbelievers. Would not Allah take pity on the weak, and send them his chosen one to protect them from the Giaurs? Moved by such feelings, and by their daily increasing hatred of the Russians, the Circassians were prepared to adapt their social arrangements to the altered circumstances, and the chosen one whom they awaited, and who was to instruct them what to do, appeared in the person of a Murshid (teacher), renowned alike for his ascetic life and his eloquence, the Kadi Mulla Mahomed, the founder of Miuridism. The fundamental principles of the new doctrine were: The complete equality of all believers, the Kazawat (holy war against the unbelievers), the renunciation of individualism, and implicit obedience to the will of the Imam (successor to the Prophet, and mediator between God and the believer). The Miurids formed a sort of society or order. They vowed to obey the Imam implicitly, and to fight to their last breath against the unbelievers. Under their influence the Caucasus underwent a transformation. The Circassians submitted to a dictatorship; an administration was formed which provided provision-stores, powder-factories, fortifications, and artillery. In short, instead of disunited tribes, as hitherto, the Russians were now confronted by an organised association animated by love of freedom and religious fanaticism, and firmly resolved to defend itself to the utmost.

The Murshid Mulla Mahomet soon became convinced that Miuridism was strong enough to take the offensive. He assembled the most prominent amongst his pupils at Jaraglar, and installed his favourite pupil Gazi Mahomet as Imam by laying his hands on his head, and commanding him in the name of the Prophet to open the holy war.

The first Imam formally proclaimed the Kazawat at the close of 1829. In a very short time Daghestan and Avaria acknowledged his authority, and he was in a position to place 15,000 men in the field. He displayed incredible activity, besieged Chansack, Burnuju, Vnezapnuju, Derbend, took Daraul and Kizliar, defeated the Russians on several occasions, and when his troops were exhausted by their superhuman efforts, retreated to Gimry in 1832. There he was attacked by General Rosen, and died a hero's death on the battlefield.

His successor, Hamzat Beg, a moderately gifted, unscrupulous fanatic, murdered those opposed to him, in order to strengthen Miuridism. He fell a victim to revenge in 1834.

The third and last Imam of the Miurids was the celebrated Shamil. He was distinguished by extraordinary strength of mind and character, proved himself an admirable administrator and commander, and conferred an unusual lustre on the Caucasian war. For fully twenty-four years he defied the Russian power, and only succumbed to the enemy's superior strength after years of systematically conducted operations. When at last he was taken prisoner, the news was not credited in Russia.

Shamil had at first great difficulties to contend with. The force at his disposal was inconsiderable, and on several occasions it was only with great trouble that he evaded capture. Not until the year 1840, when the Circassians acknowledged his authority, did he transfer his head-quarters to the Aul Dargo; and two years later his rule extended over Daghestan and the Tschetschna. He now devoted himself without loss of time to the organisation of his territory, and to this period of his life may be traced the most important of his administrative measures. In 1843 he took the Russian fortresses of Unzukul, Zatanich, Moksoch, Gergebil, Chansach and others, with their guns; organised a brigade of artillery, and reached the climax of his power. Just at that time the Russian operations were not conducted, as under Jermolov's *régime*, systematically, or according to a fixed plan. In 1827 Jermolov had been superseded by General Paskévitch. The latter had conducted the Persian and Turkish wars to a brilliant conclusion, and in 1831 was placed in command of the army operating against the Poles, and had thus had no leisure to familiarise himself with mountain warfare. After Paskévitch the post of commander of the Caucasus was left unfilled, and Baron Rosen was merely entrusted with the command of the Caucasian Army Corps. The parallels were divided into four sections: the right flank, left flank, centre, and Black Sea littoral. The commanders of these sections received their instructions direct from St. Petersburg, and were almost entirely independent of the commander of the Caucasian corps. Concerted action was thus sacrificed, until at last the deficiencies in the existing conduct of affairs were recognised in St. Petersburg, and in 1844 Prince Worontzof was appointed commander of the Caucasus.

Prince Worontzof's first expedition on a larger scale came to a miserable end in 1845. He occupied, indeed, the Aul Dargo, where Shamil had established his head-quarters, and destroyed it, but, owing to lack of provisions, was compelled to beat a retreat, in which he sustained severe losses, and only escaped a catastrophe by the unexpected arrival of General Freitag. Thenceforward Prince Worontzof followed the plan recommended by General Veliaminov of proceeding systematically, step by step, as in the siege of a fortress. These tactics rendered success, indeed, certain, but demanded much time and considerable forces. We have already given the dates bearing upon this period, and will now proceed to indicate the constantly increasing strength of the regular army in the Caucasus. In 1804 it numbered 3,000 men, in 1820 28,000, exclusive of Cossacks, and finally, in 1853, 280,000. The defence of the lines demanded, however, such a number of troops, that the Russian army operating against the Turks in Asia consisted in 1853 of only 36,000 men; General Bebutov fought the battle of Bash-Kadiklar with 9,000 men; and in 1854 the Russian army of operation, in spite of every effort to increase it, barely reached a strength of 45,000 men. The magnitude of the Russian army in the Caucasus proves, on the other hand, that the political value of the Caucasus was fully appreciated in Russia, and that no sacrifices were spared to effect its conquest.

From 1845 forward, Prince Worontzof, in accordance with his plan, continued to advance with a success not showy but certain. He fortified advanced posts, connected them with each other by openings through the woods, adapted in width to the range of his artillery, and occupied new lines. In 1855 the Chief of his Staff, Prince Bariatynski, was able to march through the whole of the Chechénia, which since 1840 had been inaccessible to the Russians, with but small loss. Shamil admitted at Kaluga, where he was hemmed in, that, when the Russians began felling the forests, he, at once perceived that they were on the right tack, and that he would be worsted.

In 1856 Prince Bariatynski assumed the conduct of the Caucasian war. The Prince displayed great energy in systematically advancing the siege operations. In the following year he occupied the Chechénian plateau, and in 1858 organised a combined attack on the Black Mountains, where Shamil had his abode in strongly-fortified Vedeno. On the 1st April, 1859, Vedeno was taken, and Shamil escaped to Gounib, where he was again besieged, and on the 25th August, 1859, capitulated.

Prince Bariatynski now directed his forces against the so-called right-flank, *i.e.*, the western portion of the Caucasian mountain-range, which extends to the Black Sea. Here too the Circassians offered a desperate resistance. They succumbed at length to Russia's superior strength, and on 21st May, 1864, the Grand-Duke Michael, who had superseded the invalided Prince Bariatynski in 1863, reported to the Tzar that the Caucasus was conquered.

In the course of this protracted, systematic advance Russian rule in the Caucasus was only once menaced by a serious danger. In 1855 Omer Pasha landed with 20,000 men at Sukhum Kale, and nearly reached Kutais. It is assumed in Russia, that if the Allies, instead of aimlessly lingering in the Crimea, had directed their forces against the Caucasus, the latter would have been possibly lost to Russia. As long as independent tribes, who would have received with open arms any of Russia's enemies, continued to occupy the shores of the Black Sea, the possession of the Caucasus was not assured. And as it was not impossible that a coalition of European powers might again go to war with Russia, the Russian Government resolved, immediately after Shamil's capture, to proceed with all energy against the western portion of the Caucasian mountain-range, and to remove the Circassians settled there to the Valley of the Kuban. Hence the Russian columns were followed by involuntary colonists, destined to occupy the vacated dwellings of the Circassians. The Circassians, however, declined to move at any cost, defended themselves to the utmost, and when they succumbed, decided to emigrate to Turkey. "It was the tomb of an expiring people," says the Russian writer Fadéef. Of the 500,000 Circassians that inhabited the western portion of the Caucasian mountain-range prior to 1859, 250,000 emigrated to Turkey, about 10,000 settled in the valley of the Kuban, and the remainder succumbed to the Russian arms and the hardships of war. The 250,000 Circassian emigrants were soon followed by others, who had already lived awhile under Russian rule. Very many emigrants perished miserably in transit, and in Turkey in Europe, where the Turkish Government allotted them dwelling-places, their number is said to be perceptibly diminishing.

These proceedings cannot of course be approved of from a humanitarian standpoint. But all over Europe humanitarian views are giving place to the idea of'the omnipotence of the State. This idea finds favour in Russia especially, and not only with the Government but with the people too. The writer just quoted, Fadéef, observes: "It cannot be denied that the Circassians have suffered a great deal, but it was unavoidable. . . . We could not give up the conquest of the Caucasus because it was not agreeable to the Circassians. We were compelled to kill half of them, so as to enable the other half to lay down their arms."

Vladykin describes the dangers which might have resulted from the continued residence of the Circassians in their dwellings, and concludes his remarks with the words: "It was a question of Russia's defence in time of peril—even of her existence. It would consequently have been a crime not to have subjugated the Circassians, or to have allowed them to remain where they had hitherto lived."

The Caucasus has, according to the census of 1885, 7,284,547 inhabitants. Of this number 2,591,000 fall to Cis-Caucasia, and 4,693,000 to Trans-Caucasia. In Cis-Caucasia the great majority of the population are Russians, and the 380,000 Circassians still remaining of those who offered so determined a resistance to the Russians have, partly on military grounds, been allotted new quarters. In Trans-Caucasia the Russians form scarcely 3 per cent., the warlike Caucasian mountaineers only about 1 per cent., of the population, which is a very mixed one, and comprises Russians, Greeks, Persians, Armenians, Grusians, Imeritians, Gurians, Mingrelians,

Suanetians, Chichensians, Awars, Darginians, Tartars, and so forth. The proportion of Christians to Mahommedans is as 10 to 7, and the Mahommedan population is by no means as warlike as the Circassian. From this we see that the Russians have nothing to fear from the inhabitants of the Caucasus, and that the conquest of the latter may be regarded as final. This is, however, all the more important, as the possession of the Caucasus opens out extensive prospects of further conquests.

* * * * *

We now proceed to Russia's advance in Central Asia.

When Ivan the Terrible took Kasan, he caused the entire male population, with the exception of the little children, to be put to death. This made a profound impression on all the Khanates into which the ancient empire of Tamerlane was split up. Sultans and Khans sued for the protection of the powerful Tzar, engaged to pay jassak (tribute), and begged to be enrolled as Russian subjects. Shortly after this Russia took Astrakhan, and in the same year (1556) the Bashkirs, who dwelt on both sides of the southern portion of the Ural Mountains, and in the days of the Mongolian rule had formed part of the Golden Horde, proffered their allegiance. The Tzar graciously accepted their submission, presented them with the lands they had hitherto occupied, permitted them to retain their social institutions, ratified the sovereign rights of the old Sultan families that ruled over the Bashkir tribes, and was satisfied with a paltry Jassak of furs. A few years after Russian towns were founded in the Bashkir country: Ufa, on the banks of the Bielaia, Birsk, Menzelinks, Bogulma, Chelyabinsk, etc. The Government allotted each newly-built town a piece of land, and liberal grants were made to high dignitaries and officials. The number of Russian colonies, each with a complete staff of officials, kept on increasing until at last a Governor-General of the Ural province was appointed, with his head-quarters at Ufa.

We defer for the present the description of the further progress made in Russianising the Bashkir-country, and turn to the banks of the Jaik, where Cossacks had settled in 1577, and in 1584 had already built a town near the present Uralsk. As they had no wives, and the women of the nomade Tartars and Calmucks were unwilling to marry unbelievers, the Cossacks kidnapped their wives, like the ancient Romans. Reinforced by new arrivals, they founded the town of Gurjiev, at the debouchure of the Jaik into the Caspian, and ere long became so numerous that they were even able to embark on further expeditions. In 1602 Netchai marched with 500 Cossacks across the desert which divides the Caspian Sea from the Sea of Aral, and took Urgenj, which is barely two days' march from Khiva. He returned with enormous booty, but was overtaken by the Khan of Khiva, and the whole of his force was annihilated with the exception of only three Cossacks, who survived to convey tidings of the disaster on the Jaik. This did not, however, discourage the venturesome Cossacks, and a few years later Shamaj led a second expedition—also disastrous—against Khiva.

Peter the Great concerned himself chiefly with European affairs, but at the same time he did not lose sight of Asia. On the strength of a report from Prince Gagarin, the Governor-General of Siberia, that the rivers of Little Bokhara, in the vicinity of Yarkand, were auriferous, the Tzar in 1714 sent 2,000 men, under the command of Buchholz, with orders to follow the course of the Irtish, to occupy the town of Yarkand, and find out a water-way thence to the Caspian Sea. Buchholz did not indeed reach Yarkand, but he subjugated the country bordering on the middle-course of the Irtish, and founded the town of Omsk.

Shortly after, Prince Bekovitch-Cherkasski, the Envoy at Khiva, produced a Turcoman who asserted that the Amu Daria (Oxus) had at one time flowed into the Caspian Sea, and that the Uzbeks had diverted it by means of dams to the Sea of Aral. The Turcoman declared that the Turcoman population would gladly assist in re-conducting the Amu Daria to the Caspian Sea, and that it would be an easy matter to subjugate the Khanates of Turkestan. This induced Peter the Great to despatch a second expedition—4,000 strong— to Central Asia. The command was given to Prince Bekovitch-Cherkasski, who, starting from Astrakhan, was to sail along the East coast of the Caspian Sea as far as the old mouth of the Amu Daria, and thence to march along the old river-bed to Khiva. He was to induce the Khans of Khiva and Bukhárá to enrol themselves as Russian subjects, and if possible to leave a detachment of Russians with each of them. The expedition embarked at Astrakhan in 1716, built a fort on the Mangishlak Peninsula, a second at Alexander Bay, and a third, named Krasnovodsk, at the old mouth of the Amu Daria. It landed at Krasnovodsk, and proceeded along the old bed of the Amu Daria towards Khiva. As, however, at a distance of nine miles from the mouth of the Amu Daria all traces of the river-bed had disappeared, Prince Bekovitch-Cherkasski returned to Astrakhan, leaving behind him strong garrisons in the newly-erected forts. In the following year he attempted to reach Khiva by the direct overland route. His force comprised 1,500 Ural Cossacks, 500 Grebnian Cossacks, and 500 Nogaian Tartars. In the immediate neighbourhood of Khiva the Khan encountered him at the head of 24,000 men, and after three days' fighting took the Russian army prisoners. Prince Bekovitch was cruelly murdered, a portion of his army were executed, and the rest went into slavery. It was not until several years had elapsed, that any number of them succeeded in returning home with news of the fate of the expedition.

We have dwelt more fully on Peter the Great's expeditions because this Tzar was according to the prevailing opinion in Russia "a colossal figure of such immense power of mind and character that a millennium will scarcely summon another such to the stage of history," and all his plans and aims are regarded as guides for the Russian policy of the future. We now revert to Russia's systematic advance in Central Asia.

By degrees the number of Russian colonists in the Bashkir country increased. The Orenburg line, which consisted of a chain of forts and settlements extending from Ilezk on the Jaik (Ural) past Orsk and Magnitna to the Zvernigolovskaia Stanitza on the Tobol, was completed and connected with the Siberian line which stretched past Omsk to the Chinese frontier. The land covered by a "line" was regarded as an integral portion of the empire and administered as such, and—with a view to a uniform organisation of the Cossacks and other colonists settled in this region—in 1748 the Orenburg Cossack horde was instituted.

The Orenburg line brought Russia into direct contact with the Kirghiz. The Kirghiz led a nomadic life in the extensive tracts of country bounded by the Caspian

Sea, the Ural river, Siberia, Kulja, the Chinese Empire, the Sir Daria, and the Sea of Aral. They are of Mongolian descent and formed part of the Empires of Chingiz Khan and Tamerlane. After the collapse of Tamerlane's empire they waged fierce wars with the Calmucks. In the neighbourhood of Karkaralinsk traces may be found at the present day of a wall 78 miles in length, by which the Calmucks endeavoured to protect themselves from the Kirghiz. In the eighteenth century the Kirghiz were divided into three hordes, the great, the middle, and the small, each of which comprised several tribes ruled by their own almost independent Sultans; so that the authority of the Khans of the three hordes might be regarded rather as a moral one resting on tradition.

The Kirghiz tribes lived, like the rest of the nomads of Central Asia, in continual conflict with one another and with their neighbours, and as early as the close of the seventeenth century many a hard-pressed Kirghiz tribe appealed to the Russian Government for protection. The Russian Government, however, rejected these petitions, until at length in 1730 Abdul-Chair, Khan of the little horde, hard-pressed by the Kokandis, submitted to the Russians. He engaged to maintain order on the Russian frontier, and to provide escorts for the Russian caravans. The Russian Government, on the other hand, recognised the hereditary right of his family to the title of Khan, and promised to erect the fort of Orsk, which formed a connecting link in the shortly after completed Orenburg line. Tevtelev was commanded by the Czarina Anna Joannovna in 1732 to administer the oath of allegiance to Abd-ul-Khair. Besides Abd-ul-Khair, certain Sultans who ruled over insignificant tribes which wandered near the Ural took the oath. Russia had an accurate knowledge of the organisation of the Kirghiz, and of the value to be placed on the allegiance of a few of their Sultans. Nevertheless Russian diplomacy regarded the subject Kirghiz as the entire people, the submission of one Khan and a few Sultans as that of the whole of the Kirghiz tribes, and consequently all the Kirghiz as Russian subjects. For the first few years the subjection of the Kirghiz was purely nominal. It afforded Russia, however, the opportunity of interfering in the internal affairs of the Kirghiz, and of forming a Russian party. With the double view of protecting her new subjects against other Central Asian tribes, and of punishing them in the event of raids on the Russians, flying columns, numbering as many as 2,000 men, were sent into Kirghiz territory.

Westward of the Kirghiz, between the Emba, the Or, the Jaik (Ural) and the Volga dwelt the Calmucks, also of Mongolian extraction. They were governed by their own Khan according to their customs and traditions, acknowledged Russian supremacy, and furnished auxiliary troops, which even took part in the Seven Years' War. No national institutions are, however, tolerated by Russia permanently. In 1761 the Khan died, and his thirteen-year-old son, whom the Russians, contrary to Mahommedan custom, had already recognised as the heir in his father's life-time, was proclaimed Khan. The Russian Government provided him with a council nominated by itself, which usurped all the power. This gave rise to great discontent, which was still further increased by the arbitrariness and the abuses of the Russian officials. At the time, a certain Seryn was conducting fresh bands of Calmucks numbering some 10,000 Kibitkas (tents), from Mongolia to the Volga. Perceiving the risk they ran of losing their national institutions, the new-comers proposed to return to Mongolia. This idea met with general approval, and in 1771 the Calmucks set out on their journey. Their preparations had been conducted with such secrecy that the Russian authorities only heard of their departure when the entire Calmuck population, which numbered about 80,000 Kibitka (*i.e.*, by the way, 320,000 souls), had set itself in motion. As the Russians had no available forces at hand to compel the fugitive Calmucks to remain, they appealed to the Calmucks' hereditary foes, the Kirghiz, and promised, if they would stop the Calmucks, to give them their herds, the chief possession of the nomads.

The Calmucks crossed the Ural safely, but in the desert were surrounded by swarms of rapacious Kirghiz, and when the Cossacks also hurried to the spot a terrible collision took place. In spite of this, a certain number of the Calmucks succeeded in reaching China. Many, however, fell in the fight, and only a few were forced to return, and were quartered among the Cossacks, where they were soon converted into excellent soldiers. This event made a strong impression on the Kirghiz, and Russia's authority in Central Asia increased.

In the year 1797 Sultan Bukéef brought his horde, which numbered 12,000 Kirghiz Kibitkas, into the district where the Calmucks had previously nomadised. His horde was called the Bukeian horde of Kirghiz. At present it numbers 200,000 souls, occupies itself with breeding horses, has long since lost every vestige of independence, and is governed by Russian officials.

The rest of the Kirghiz who remained in their home were placed under the Governors-General of Orenburg and Omsk. The latter soon succeeded in inducing some Sultans of the middle horde to enrol themselves as Russian subjects. Each Governor-General divided the desert placed in his charge into districts, and appointed to each district a reliable Sultan, who was called Ulu-Sultan (great Sultan). In other respects the former division into tribes and families was retained. Sultans ruled them, levied the very moderately assessed taxes, caused the obligatory census to be taken, and decided the disputes of the Kirghiz in accordance with their customs and traditions. The frontier Governments at Orenburg and Omsk constituted the last resort in case of appeal. These authorities comprised Russian and Kirghiz officials, but the latter were in the minority. Each Ulu-Sultan had a division of Cossacks allotted to him as a guard of honour, and their commander had in addition a political mission, namely, that of keeping guard over the Sultan himself.

In Orenburg, too, political business was transacted; Russian trade in Central Asia fostered; the affairs of Turkestan and the Uzbek Khanates attended to; and as accurate information as possible regarding these countries gathered.

Meanwhile Russia was continually advancing in the Kirghiz desert. From her Siberian base she reached in the reign of Alexander I. the sources of the Ishim and the Nur, and established the Cossack settlements of Kokchetav, Karakalinsk, and Bajan-Aul. Under Nicholas I. the Cossack colonies of Akmolinsk, Sergiopol and Kopal were founded. In 1847 the Kirghiz of the Great Horde enrolled themselves as Russian subjects. This event occasioned a further extension of the frontier, and shortly after the Russians established themselves on the river Ili.

Russia's advance from her Orenburg base proceeded more slowly. In 1810 a new "line" was established on the Ilek, and the strip of land between the rivers Ural, Ilek, and Berdianka was incorporated with the territory of the Orenburg Cossacks. This increase of territory necessitated an addition to the forces stationed between the Bashkirs and Kirghiz, and they were accordingly augmented by 13,000 discharged soldiers with their families; the Stavropol Calmuck horde; salt carriers who had been in State employ; crown-peasants living between Isakmara and the Ural; and peasants from the vicinity of Chelyabinsk. By this means 36,700 persons of the most varied types were associated with 42,000 Cossacks, and the amalgamation of these heterogeneous elements was left to time and the force of circumstances.

In the year 1830 a personal friend of the Emperor Nicholas, Count Perovski, was appointed Governor-General of Orenburg. The Count raved about the conquest of India, and desired to associate his name with some important deed, which would bring Russia nearer to India. In 1832 he established a new "line" stretching from the fortress of Orsk to the village of Berezovskoe on the Ui, to which he gave the name of "New frontier-radius." In 1833 he built the fort of Novo-Alexandrovsk on the Caspian Sea. This did not, however, satisfy his ambition; and he looked towards Khiva, which since the time of Peter the Great had been regarded as a stepping-stone on the road to India. Khiva constituted the chief obstacle to the development of trade in Central Asia, as most of the predatory attacks on caravans traversing the Kirghiz Steppe emanated therefrom. Besides this, several Russians, whom the Turcomans and Kirghiz usually captured singly, were pining in slavery at Khiva. On these grounds an expedition was decided on, and equipped with all possible care. The expeditionary corps had a march of 840 miles before it, was 4,000 men strong, and took with it 9,000 camels, and thousands of Bashkir carts.

The chief difficulty which presented itself on the line of march was the crossing of the arid desert, called Ust-Urt, which lies between the Caspian Sea and the Sea of Aral. To provide against a scarcity of water, a winter campaign was decided on, and on the 29th November, 1839, Count Perovski started from Orenburg at the head of the expeditionary corps. Soon, however, unusually cold weather for this region set in, and the desert was thickly covered with snow. Marching became laborious, the temperature was at times as low as $47°$ R., and from the 17th to the 26th December it averaged $30°$ R. The camels—which cannot stand intense cold—died in great numbers. The horses were unable to graze owing to the thick covering of snow, and Count Perovski was compelled to beat a retreat before he had reached the Ust-Urt. In June, 1840, the expeditionary corps returned to Orenburg with heavy losses.

In spite of its miserable ending the expedition made a great impression on the Khivans, and alarmed England, which persuaded the Khan of Khiva to liberate the Russian prisoners, so as to deprive the Russians of any pretext for a second expedition. The Tzar Nicholas, on the other hand, recalled Count Perovski to please the English, and appointed General Obrutchev Governor-General of Orenburg.

General Obrutchev first of all applied himself to the task of conquering the Kirghiz desert from the Ural to the Sea of Aral, going to work slowly but surely, with a small expenditure of money and resources. He first sent surveyors into the desert, who were accompanied by escorts. From their surveys he fixed upon a new line of communication, on which—from 1845–1847—he erected the forts of Kara-Butak on the stream of that name, Uralsk on the banks of the Irghiz, and Orenburg on the Turgai. Finally, at the end of 1847, he reached the Sea of Aral, took possession of the mouth of the Sir Daria (Jaxartes), and built the fort of Raimsk, afterwards named Aralsk. He erected a second fort, named Kos-Aral, on the Sea of Aral. Kos-Aral served as a harbour for the naval captain Butakov, who surveyed the Sea of Aral, gave the islands thereon Russian names, and took possession of them.

Obrutchev now turned his attention to the east coast of the Caspian Sea. There, overlooking Mertvi Bay, the fort Novo-Alexandrovsk, erected by Count Perovski, had already stood since 1833. Its site was, however, so unfavourable as to render it of little efficacy.

General Obrutchev discovered a suitable site on the Mangishlak Peninsula close to the sea, and built a new Fort Alexandrovsk, which developed such a wide sphere of activity that the Government of Orenburg inquired of the Foreign Office which of the nomad Turcomans in the vicinity of the forts were to be regarded as Russian subjects. The reply was, that Russia had no limits in the East.

By degrees order and quiet began to reign in the Kirghiz desert. The Russians punished unmercifully all attempts at plunder and deprived the guilty tribes of their best grazing grounds, which completely impoverished them. Colonel Kuzminski, when he could not get at the robbers, destroyed a few villages belonging to their kinsfolk. This had a great effect on the Kirghiz. The escorts of the surveying parties were gradually reduced, without their ever being attacked. The caravans from Bokhara fearlessly crossed the desert. When, in 1850, a synopsis of the chief events in the reign of Nicholas I. was drawn up, in honour of the twenty-fifth (Jubilee) year of that monarch's accession to the throne, the Governor-General of Orenburg declared with pride that Russia had made such progress in that region that the increase of conquered territory equalled in extent the whole of France and Spain put together.

By the subjugation of the Kirghiz Desert Russia was brought into direct contact with the Khanate of Kokand, which at that time had some small forts on the Sir Daria. I say at that time because firmly-established frontiers or States are non-existent in Central Asia. The various States there are as wanting in consistency as the quicksands of the desert. Almost every more important town of Central Asia has had its independent Khan, and been at one time the capital of an independent Khanate. The Khans are continually at war with each other, and with their rebellious subjects. In consequence of these wars the frontiers are continually shifting, new States arise, and existing ones collapse. Thus, for instance, Andkhui, Balkh, and Khulm and Kunduz in the sixties were at one time independent, at another dependencies of Bokhara or Cabul. Now they form part of Afghanistan.

Kashgar, Yarkand, and Khotan were likewise independent Khanates. They then fell to China; severed themselves again from China during the great Taiping rebellion of 1863, and under the leadership of Yakub

Beg became a powerful State in Eastern Turkestan, which in 1877 was again re-conquered by the Chinese.

The three Uzbek Khanates do not present a more pleasing picture. A few historical details taken from the last few decades will prove this. In 1840 the Amir Nasr-Ullah reigned in Bukhárá. The brother of the Khan of Kokand appealed to the Amir to assist him to the throne of Kokand. The pretext for war was most gladly seized. Amir Nasr-Ullah stormed the town of Uratiube after a three months' siege, killed most of the inhabitants, left a garrison behind, and withdrew. Thereupon the Khan of Kokand arrived, took possession of Uratiube, and massacred the Bokhárian garrison. The second campaign led to a peace, whereby the Khan of Kokand ceded the town of Khojend to the Amir of Bukhárá. Nasr-Ullah appointed the Khan of Kokand's rebellious brother Governor of Khojend. The brothers, however, became reconciled through their mother's mediation, and commenced hostilities with Bokhárá. Nasr-Ullah again besieged the Khan of Kokand, caused him, his brother and the most influential of his adherents to be beheaded in Kokand, confiscated their property, and was apparently master of the entire Khanate. Meanwhile the Kipcháks, who had hitherto remained quiet spectators of the contest, elected a Khan, and assisted him to conquer Kokand. The Amir, too, found a pretender, supplied him with a Bokhárian army, and promised him the Khanate of Kokand, if he succeeded in defeating the Kipcháks. His *protégé*, however, betrayed him, joined the Kipcháks and Kokandis, and helped them to defeat the Bukhárian army. Nasr-Ullah was making preparations for a fresh campaign, to wreak vengeance on the traitor, when his brother-in-law, Governor of the town of Shar, revolted against him. This diverted his attention from Kokand. The town repulsed thirty assaults before it was taken, and when Nasr-Ullah on his death-bed received news of the victory, he caused his rebellious brother-in-law's sister, his own wife, to be beheaded. He died shortly after. His successor, Amir Muzaffer Edin, at once re-opened hostilities with Kokand. He instigated a revolt, and when the Khan was killed, he entered Kokand, and placed Khudayár on the throne. Some months later the Kipcháks rose in arms to secure the throne for Alimkul. A terrible contest ensued. The Amir of Bukhárá was defeated, and appealed to the Turcomans for assistance. The leader of the Kipcháks, Ametkul, fell in battle. His wife assumed command and carried on the war until, at last, in 1863, it ended in a peace whereby the Khanate of Kokand was divided. Kokand remained in the possession of Alimkul, Khojend in that of Khudayár, and the Amir Muzaffar Edin brought great treasure, several guns, and a plentiful supply of arms in triumph to Bokhárá.

Bukhárá was also frequently at war with Khiva. The Khan of Khiva, Medemin-Khan (1842–1855), for his part, was constantly fighting with the Turcomans, and took Merv several times. On one of his expeditions he was surprised by some Turcoman horsemen in his own camp, and slain. His successor Abdulah defeated the Yomúts. The latter sued for peace, but not many months later hostilities were resumed, Abdulah fell, and his younger brother was proclaimed Khan. The Yomúts, for their part, supported another pretender. Before blows were exchanged, however, they sued for peace, and proceeded to the number of 12,000 with their claimant to Khiva to attest their formal recognition of the Khan. The latter came to meet his kinsfolk, but was assassinated. A furious fight ensued in the streets of Khiva, and the Khivans, encouraged by their Ulemas, obtained the victory. The Yomúts were massacred to a man, and a whole week elapsed before all the bodies could be removed. Khiva remained some days without a ruler, until Said-Muhammad was proclaimed Khan. He continued the war with the Yomúts; the Jamshídís surprised and plundered Khiva; several pretenders laid claim to the throne; and in short, under the rule of the weak Said-Muhammad Khiva was brought to the verge of ruin.

It is self-evident that States so feebly constituted were incapable of resisting Russia. When she had established herself on the Sea of Aral, she could proceed against Khiva or Kokand with equal facility. At that time she preferred, however, in deference to English public opinion and in the interests of her own European policy, not to provoke England overmuch, and decided, in consequence, to proceed against Kokand.

A pretext was easily found, as the Kokandis possessed some forts on the Sir Daria, the garrisons of which sallied forth to plunder the Kirghiz, who were regarded as Russian subjects. As early as 1849 General Boghdanovitch took the Kokandi fort Kos-Kurhan by assault, and intimated to the Kirghiz that Russia intended to protect them from the Kokandis. In 1852 General Blaramberg took some small Kokandi forts, and stormed Ak-Mesjed, which was reputed to be impregnable. He was repulsed, and retired. In 1853 Count Perovski, who was again Governor-General of Orenburg, himself attacked Ak-Mesjed, and took it after a three weeks' siege. His army comprised 750 infantry, 400 Ural Cossacks, 200 Bashkirs, with a battery of twenty-three guns. He now at once proceeded to establish the Sir Darian line. Kos-Aral and Aralsk were abandoned, and in their place Fort No. 1 —which served at the same time as a port—was built and garrisoned with 800 men. Fort No. 2 was planned for a garrison of 100 men, and two guns. Lastly, Ak-Mesjed was strengthened with a garrison of 750 infantry, 500 Cossacks, and 125 artillerymen, and was named Fort Perovski.

Between Fort Perovski and the fort on the Ili there was a gap over 600 miles in extent. Now, in order to establish a base for further advance, it was decided at St. Petersburg, after a lengthy conference, in which the Governors-General of Orenburg and Western Siberia took part, to connect the Sir Daria line with the Siberian. To this end operations were to be conducted simultaneously from the Ili and from Fort Perovski. Tzar Nicholas I. ratified these decisions, but, in consequence of the Crimean war, their execution was postponed for some time, and for ten years Russia contented herself with quite insignificant progress in Central Asia. In Siberia, from the Ili base, Fort Vernoe was founded, and soon after Kastek; and in 1860 Colonel Zimmermann advanced into the valley of the Chu, and took two small Kokandi forts, Tokmak and Pishpek, without losing a single man. From the Chu Valley reconnoitring parties were sent out as far as Aulie-Ata. On the Sir Daria line Fort Julek was erected, and Fort Jany-Kurhan on the road from Julek to Turkestan was taken.

At length, in 1864, two expeditions started simultaneously from opposite sides. The one, 2,500 men strong, under the command of General Tcherniaiev, took Aulie-Ata; the other, 1,200 men strong, commanded by Colonel Vierovkin, took Turkestan. The Kokand line was now established. It connected the Valley of the Chu with that of the Sir Daria, and General Tcherniaiev was placed in command of it. In the autumn of the same year he took Chemkent, and made an unsuccessful attack upon Tashkend, but no later than the following year he took Chinaz as well as Tashkend. The last-named town numbered over 70,000 inhabitants, and was taken by a force of 1,950 men with the loss of only 125. From this period Russia's advance in Central Asia has been more rapid. As, however, the events connected therewith belong to modern history, and are generally known, we may confine ourselves to a brief summary of the most important facts.

In 1866 General Romanovski with 3,600 men defeated the Amir of Bukhárá at Irjár, and shortly after captured the Kokandi fortress of Khojend. In the autumn he took possession of the two Bukhárian forts, Uratiube and Jizak, and arranged preliminary terms of peace with the Amir.

In 1867 the military district of Orenburg was abolished, and a new military district of Turkestan instituted with head-quarters at Tashkend. Semiretchensk furnished two regiments of Cossacks, who were named after that province. General Kaufmann on being appointed Governor-General of Turkestan concluded peace with Kokand. An outbreak of Mohammedan fanaticism, however, forced the Amir of Bukhárá into a war in 1868. He was defeated, and Samarkand, Tamerlane's capital, was taken. The Amir sued for peace, and engaged to be in all respects a true ally of Russia. He paid a considerable war indemnity, placed his sons under the Tzar's protection, and even sent them to be educated at St. Petersburg. Besides this, he ceded to Russia, in addition to Samarkand, Djam,

Kerki, and Char-jui on the Amu Daria. Russia in return suppressed the revolt of the Amir's own son, and General Abramov took by storm the two rebellious towns of Shar and Kitab, and compelled them to submit to the Amir. The two foes, formerly so implacable, now cultivated amicable relations, which are still maintained. The Amir, 'tis true, contents himself with a shadow of sovereignty.

In 1871 the Khanate of Kulja, which was said to have supported predatory incursions, was incorporated with Russian territory. After China's conquest of East Turkestan a few years later, Russia surrendered a portion of the territory of Kulja to the Chinese.

Next came Khiva's turn. In 1869 the Russians had already established themselves on the East coast of the Caspian, at Krasnovodsk, and shortly after at Chikishlar; they gradually extended their authority over the Turcomans, and reconnoitred the routes to Khiva. At length, in 1873, a campaign against Khiva was decided on. A pretext was easily found. Three divisions advanced simultaneously from Krasnovodsk, Fort Perovski, and Orenburg. They had a distance to traverse varying from 480 to 840 miles, yet all three reached Khiva safely. Under such circumstances resistance was not to be thought of. Russia occupied the land on the right bank of the Amu Daria, restored the young Khan to the throne of his father, and imposed upon him a war indemnity of 2,200,000 roubles, which cripples not only himself, but his successors, should he have any. Two forts, Nuski and Petro-Alexandrovsk, were erected on the Amu Daria.

In the year 1875 the excessive oppression of the Khan of Kokand, Khodáyár, an adherent of Russia, occasioned a general rising of the people, and their leader, Abdurrahman, preached a holy war against the Russians. General Kaufmann marched against the rebels with sixteen companies, eight sotnias, and twenty field-guns, defeated them, and annexed the province of Namangan. In consequence of fresh insurrections in the following year (1876) the whole Khanate was incorporated with the Russian Empire. After the subjugation of the three Khanates, says General Kuropatkin in his treatise "Russia's Advance in Central Asia," the country of the Turcomans remained the solitary centre of disturbance in the desert. In accordance with her customary procedure Russia had already succeeded, in 1836, in gaining over certain chiefs of the Yomút-Turcomans, and inducing them to prefer a request to be enrolled as Russian subjects. Such requests were, on political grounds, usually refused several times, and it was not until 1869, after Krasnovodsk had been founded, that the country of the Yomúts was annexed by Russia. Certain of the Yomúts, however, would not submit. They were defeated at Kisil-Takir, and the Russians established themselves in Chikishlar. Thereby they came into contact with the Tekkeh-Turcomans, who inhabited the country east of the Yomúts, and were known for their courage, their strength, and their wealth. A succession of fights ensued, which proved that the Tekkehs fully deserved their reputation; for, though quite as badly armed as the other Central Asian races, they far surpassed them in valour and capacity. In 1874 the Trans-Caspian Military Government was instituted, and General Lomakin was placed in command. The Tekkes assured him of their amicable intentions, yet no definitive peace resulted. The wealthier of the Tekkehs wished to submit to the White Tzar; the majority, however, would not relinquish their independence. Nearly every year Russian expeditions were sent out, but were not always crowned with success: and in 1879 especially, General Lomakin suffered a serious defeat. In consequence of this it was decided at St. Petersburg to deal a powerful blow at the Tekkehs, and General Skobelev was entrusted with the command of an expedition which numbered 7,500 foot, 3,000 horse, and about 100 guns. On the completion of the preparations, which were made with care and energy, the operations commenced in June, and on the 24th January, 1881, the fortress of Geok-Tepe, which numbered 30,000 defenders, succumbed to Russian arms. In orthodox Asiatic fashion, all of the garrison that fell into the hands of the conqueror were massacred, and in the pursuit even women and children were fired upon with grape-shot. With the capture of Geok-Tepe the war was practically concluded. One after another the individual tribes voluntarily submitted, and in April, 1881, General Skobelev quitted Trans-Caspian territory. His successor, General Rohrberg, renowned for his administrative talent, was entrusted with the task of persuading the frightened nomads, who now formed the most suitable material for conversion, to return to their homes and become peaceable Russian subjects. From his Askabad base he organised the country, and extended Russian authority. He was soon replaced by General Komarov, who gained over certain chiefs of the Tekkeh-Turcomans dwelling in the oasis of Merv, and they induced the most influential man among them, Makhdúm-Kúlí-Khán, who had conducted the defence of Geok-Tepe and on the capture of the fortress had succeeded in escaping, to attend the Tzar Alexander

III.'s coronation at Moscow. The splendour which he beheld there must have dazzled him, and one can easily imagine how, with the aid of his Oriental imagination, he would excite the astonishment and admiration of his hearers. Meanwhile General Komarov established a Cossack outpost in the oasis of Tejend, and at the beginning of 1884 the Russian Captain Alikhanov, accompanied by a few horsemen and the hero of Geok-Tepe, Makhdúm-Khán, appeared in Merv, and read out at a public assembly a letter of General Komarov calling on the population of Merv to submit to Russian authority. Bearing in mind that the Cossacks in the Tejend oasis might possibly emphasize this summons, the chief Aksakals (grey-beards) set their seals to the fatal document, and on 6th February, 1884, four chieftains and twenty-four of the highest personages took the oath of allegiance to the White Tzar in General Komarov's drawing-room at Askabad.

A few thousand Merv-Tekkes led by Kajar Khan attempted indeed to oppose the Russians, but were immediately dispersed. Kajar Khan took refuge in Afghanistan, and his adherents submitted in silence. With the seizure of Merv the conquest of the Turcoman country was completed, and Russia came into direct contact, in Central Asia, with Persia and Afghanistan.

The Persian Government viewed with uneasiness Russia's progress eastward of the Caspian Sea. The Turcomans were certainly not pleasant neighbours, and were continually plundering the Persian border-provinces; but the vicinity of so powerful an Empire as Russia was still less welcome to the Persian Government. Russia's influence at Teheran was, however, so great that the Government of the Shah issued instructions to the Governors of Mazanderan and

Asterabad to assist the Russians in procuring provisions and confined itself to occasional diplomatic protests regarding supposed infringements of Persia's rights. Secretly, the Persian Government endeavoured to persuade both the Akhal and Merv Tekkehs to acknowledge Persian supremacy. Russian diplomacy, however, easily counteracted these endeavours, and when the Yomút and Tekkeh-Turcomans had become Russian subjects, the Russian Government invited Persia to a settlement of the frontier between the two empires. This was all the more necessary as the Turcomans, being nomadic, often grazed on Persian territory and did not themselves know exactly how far their territory extended. The negotiations were conducted so rapidly that on the 9th December, 1881, the same year in which Geok-Tepe fell into Russian hands, the treaty defining the Russo-Persian frontier was agreed upon, and in the course of the next few years the frontier was accurately determined *in loco*. Finally, in 1884, Russia took possession of Old-Sarakhs, and of a strip of land which lay between Persia and Afghanistan, and was correctly termed by Vambéry "no man's land": Persia had to submit in silence, as was only to be expected.

On the other hand, the settlement of the frontier of Russia and Afghanistan presented several difficulties. The Amir was supported by England. In the early sixties English public opinion had already become alarmed at Russia's progress in Central Asia, and the two Governments had since negotiated frequently on this point. We reserve the consideration of England's and Russia's diplomatic moves for another chapter, and confine ourselves to the observation that as early as 1878 Lord Beaconsfield suggested the establishment of a narrow neutral zone extending from Sarakhs to Khoja-Saleh on the Amu Daria. England demanded a topographical, Russia, on the other hand, an ethnographical, boundary, *i.e.*, that which was Turcoman should belong to the Turcomans, and that which was Afghan to the Afghans. The negotiations lasted some years, and Russia had conquered the whole of Turcomania, before the decision was arrived at to send topographical commissions to the spot with suitable escorts. At last, in 1884, General Lumsden appeared on behalf of the English with an escort of 1,000 men.[1] The Russians declared that they had expected a commission, not a military demonstration, and did not send off their commissioners till later. In March, 1885, a serious collision occurred on the Kushk river in the presence of some of the English officers of the frontier settlement commission between Russians and Afghans, in which the latter sustained heavy losses, and were compelled to evacuate their positions.

In view of the continually increasing tension between Russia and her western neighbours, the Cabinet of St. Petersburg at last decided on solving the question of the delimitation of the frontier of North-West Afghanistan, which was creating much bad blood in England. This took place in July, 1887, after the Afghans had felt Russia's heavy hand, and had arrived at the conclusion that England's intervention had been of scarcely any use to them. The frontier of Russia and Afghanistan is now accurately defined from the Heri-Rud, a little above the Zulfikar Pass, to Khoja-Saléh.

In accordance with the Anglo-Russian agreement of

[1] The military escort, properly so called, was far smaller. The above figure appears to include camp followers.—ED.

1873 the Amu Daria, as far as its junction with the Kokcha, forms the boundary eastwards between Bokhárá—which is entirely dependent upon Russia—and Afghanistan.[1] Lastly Badakshan, and Wakhan, which are also on the left bank of the Upper Oxus (Amu Daria) were conceded to Afghanistan, whilst the two other Khanates on the Pamir plateau, Shignan and Roshan, remained independent. Sir Henry Rawlinson, however, remarks in his celebrated work "England and Russia in the East," that owing to "somewhat hazy notions of the geography" of those remote countries, as well as to a clerical error in the agreement of 1873, it was not accurately defined which feeder of the Oxus from the junction of the Kokcha upwards to its source should form the northern boundary of Wakhan; and, in fact, opinions differ both in England and Russia as to the correct definition of this Oxus feeder. In September, 1887, the *Invalide*, official organ of the Russian War Office, mentioned that the Khanates of Shignan and Wakhan were by the agreement of 1873 to remain independent. Yet in 1883 they were occupied by the Amir, and great discontent is said to prevail there. Thus we see that at present Russia's frontiers in Central Asia from the Caspian Sea to the junction of the Kokcha with the Oxus are accurately defined, whilst eastward of that point to the frontier of the Chinese Empire a similarly

[1] The actual words of the agreement are :—"Badakhshan with its dependent district of Wakhan from Sarikul on the east to the junction of the Kokcha river with the Oxus (or Penjah) *on the west; the stream of the Oxus* thus forming the northern boundary of this Afghan province throughout its entire extent." But, unfortunately, owing to the copyist's error, the words in italics were omitted in the final agreement ("England and Russia in the East," p. 310).—ED.

accurate definition is wanting. But even where accurately defined, it need not on that account remain definitive; for in Europe, also, as we know, the frontiers of States are shifted from time to time.

In conclusion, we will glance at the ethnographical relations and the present condition of the races subjugated by Russia. If we look, remarks Vambéry, at the half million of Kasan Tartars, who in ancient times were renowned for their Moslem culture, we find that, apart from a few very insignificant characteristics, such as, for instance, their familiarity with intoxicants, not a trace of the spirit of our age is observable in their social or political life. The Government has done next to nothing to raise this people's standard of education. It is allowed to continue in its moral apathy, and owes its meagre mental culture solely to the schools founded by itself and supported by its own means. In Kasan there is indeed a Government school, but the spirit and object of the education imparted aim at the conversion of Tartars into Christians and Muscovites.

Russia's rule of three centuries over the Bashkirs exhibits no satisfactory results. As already mentioned, the Bashkirs voluntarily enrolled themselves as Russian subjects in 1556, and in the seventeenth century rendered the Russians good service in their European wars, even against their co-religionists of Turkish nationality. " If the people of Great Russia," remarks Zaleski in his work "Russia's Progress in Central Asia," "aimed at civilising; if they possessed beside their enterprising spirit, their energy and powers of discernment, no savage instincts, no inclination to violence or oppression; if the Russian Government were capable of soaring to Christian ideas and of regarding its mission in the East in that light, it would then be in a position to educate and civilise the nations of Central Asia, to create a considerable power which might benefit the State, and render real service to humanity. This would be all the easier, since Mohammedanism which is elsewhere such an obstacle to the diffusion of Western culture has not struck deep root there. Consequently in Central Asia a people with an ancient Christian civilisation could have accomplished anything. Semi-barbarous Russia was, however, incapable of educating a people."

According as the Russian population in the Bashkir country multiplied, the numbers of officials in the towns and villages increased, and the treatment of the Mohammedans grew worse. This led to frequent local risings, whereby the Bashkirs protested against the injustice done them. These insurrections were, however, soon suppressed, and only rendered their lot harder. At last, in 1676, a general insurrection led by a certain Seit broke out. The then Governor of Ufa ascribed it in a report to the Tzar to the injustice and violence of the officials. The insurrection lasted fully three years, and Strelitz regiments from Moscow and Don-Cossacks had to be requisitioned to suppress it.

The Government, for its part, held the so-called Sultan families, *i.e.*, the aristocracy, or in the Tartar language Ak-sajuk (they of the "white bone"), responsible for the insurrection, and it was decided to treat them with the utmost severity; to exterminate them as far as possible, and to confer the chieftainship of the tribes, which had hitherto devolved upon the Sultans, only on persons who owed everything to the Government. The carrying into effect of these decisions was left to the newly-appointed Governor of Ufa, Sergieev, whose horrible deeds still live in the memory of the Bashkirs, after a lapse of two centuries. In the province of Orenburg it is commonly reported that Sergieev, who built a palace on the river Bielaia in the winter, invited the whole of the Bashkir aristocracy (they of the white bone) to a feast, and after the repast had them all thrown into the river through a hole made in the ice. At all events it is proved on documentary evidence that the Governor used to make his principal Bashkir guests drink themselves to death. Administrative measures were also adopted to effect the Bashkirs' economic ruin. As nomads they lived by rearing cattle, keeping bees, and fishing. In 1707 the rivers were declared fiscal property, and the fisheries an appanage of the crown. This occasioned another insurrection of the Bashkirs. Several Russian colonies were burnt down, the colonists massacred, and the rebels advanced to within a short distance of Kasan, the Governor of which, Kudriavcev, had no more troops available. He cast the families of the noblest Tartars into prison as hostages, and intimated to the Tartars that they must take the field against the Bashkirs, and that in the event of their defeat their families would be put to death. The Tartars thus incited defeated the Bashkirs, and when eight regiments had arrived in haste from Moscow, the insurrection was successfully put down.

A reaction now set in among the Bashkirs. They began to court the favour of powerful Russia, and rendered real service to the Government. Tajmar, a celebrity in his day, beat 10,000 Kirghiz who were about to plunder Russia's border-provinces, and through his mediation certain Sultans were induced to enrol themselves as Russian subjects. Several noble Bashkirs supported him. As a reward the Governor of Ufa in 1732 permitted them to send a deputation to St. Petersburg, which was most graciously received. The delegates complained bitterly of the officials that oppressed their country, and begged that the ancient rights and institutions of the Bashkirs might be restored to them. Redress was promised, and liberal presents were given, but in the end everything remained as before.

Shortly after it was decided to establish a new line, and to transfer the head-quarters of the Governor-General from Ufa to Orenburg. The Bashkirs were ordered to build the forts of the new line rendered necessary by the subjugation of the Kirghiz, gratuitously. This was all the more repugnant to them as they had recognised only too clearly that these forts were directed against themselves. They refused to build the forts, and when an attempt was made to coerce them, they again took up arms. The insurrection lasted this time fully five years, from 1735 to 1740, and the rebels were very severely punished. An eyewitness, Rytchkov, Secretary of the Orenburg frontier government, has bequeathed us an exact specification of all the horrors enacted. About 9,000 women and children of the Bashkirs were presented to Russian Boyars, and transported to Russia; 3,000 men were condemned to hard labour in the Siberian mines; 700 Auls (villages) were burnt down; and some 16,000 men fell in battle, or were hanged in the course of the war. When quiet had been restored in the Bashkir country, the Governor-General of Orenburg, Prince Urussov, held a further strict judicial investigation, in the course of which 600 more culprits were punished. On the 25th August and 17th September, 1740, the sentences were executed on a hill near the town of Buzuluk: 6 were impaled, 11 suspended by iron hooks inserted in their ribs, 135 were hanged in the ordinary way with ropes, 140 beheaded, and the remaining 300 had their noses and ears cut off, and were permitted to return to their homes, that their appearance might inspire whole generations with a dread of Russia's might.

Then followed a further series of administrative measures having for their object the transformation of the Bashkir country. On the western slopes of the Ural the Mestcheraks settled on Bashkir territory, paying an annual rent for the land. When the insurrection of the Bashkirs was nearly overcome, they marched against them, and the Government presented them with the lands they had hitherto tenanted. The salt of the inland seas had hitherto belonged to the Bashkirs; henceforth it was declared fiscal property. The Bashkirs were forbidden to meet together, and at the head of each tribe and every community, Russian officials, complete strangers to them, were placed instead of the hitherto elected authorities. The land of the Bashkirs was regarded, like that of Cossacks, as the common property of the people. Henceforth the Bashkirs were allowed to sell their land, and the Government supported the purchasers. A few examples will show how the Bashkirs were fleeced in these transactions. Three hundred thousand dessiatines, *i.e.*, about 600,000 acres, of forest in which the iron-works of Bieloreck stood, realised a purchase price of 300 paper roubles (about 80 silver roubles[1]). The domain of the factories of Avziano-Petrovsk and Kutaisk, comprising 180,000 dessiatines, were sold for an annual ground-rent of 20 roubles, and these instances might be multiplied. New

---

[1] The silver rouble is worth about 3s. 2d. of our money.

Russian villages and factories sprang up, and the Bashkirs were more and more driven into a corner.

At last it was thought that the resistance of the Bashkirs was finally crushed, and that the Russian Government officials might with impunity take any liberties they chose with the tribes and communities. How hard the yoke was may be seen from the fact that no later than in 1755 a fresh insurrection broke out. On the 18th May of that year nearly all the Russians living in the Bashkir country were murdered. The Mulla, Batyr Shah, who called upon the faithful to rise in the name of Islam, took the lead, and appealed for support to the Kirghiz, Mestcheraks, and other neighbouring Mahommedan tribes. In this grave crisis the Governor-General Nepliuiev, who had only a weak force at his disposal, proved equal to the emergency. First of all he had recourse to the Mestcheraks, told them that if the Bashkirs were victorious they would take their lands from them again, and invited them to march with him against the Bashkirs. Then he drove about 50,000 Bashkir families on to Kirghiz territory and sent a proclamation in the name of the Empress Elizabeth to the Khan and the neighbouring Sultans, in which he offered them the women, children and herds of the Bashkirs, if they would undertake to deliver up the adult males. And in reality the Kirghiz took possession of the families and herds of the Bashkirs, and handed over to the Russians the men that remained alive. The insurrection lasted some time longer, but a reconciliation between the Bashkirs and Kirghiz was not to be thought of. For a time the Russians calmly looked on whilst the Bashkirs and Kirghiz fought with one another, and when it was thought that the mutual hatred had waxed sufficiently strong, further fighting was forbidden. Although this happened more than a century ago, the two neighbouring races have remained implacable foes even to the present day. This insurrection finally exhausted the strength of the Bashkirs, and in the insurrection of the Jaik-Cossacks, led by Purgatchev, only a few weak bands of Bashkirs took part.

To accelerate their assimilation, the Bashkiro-Mestcherak Cossack horde was instituted in 1798. The whole country was portioned out into eighteen districts, and the entire population placed under the military authorities. Every adult Bashkir was regarded and treated as a Cossack, and the military authorities issued orders as to the construction of the houses; the proper way to plant potatoes; what kinds of cereals should be sown; and so forth. At that period the number of the Bashkirs decreased, according to the census returns, to 500,000 souls, of whom 102,000 were found to be capable of bearing arms. The Government did not, however, require such a large force on the Ural, and a few years after a fixed tax was substituted in several districts for military service. The military organisation was maintained notwithstanding. The Bashkirs liable to military service were compelled on emergency to build forts on the lines, and to convey necessaries to the garrisons, in carts provided by themselves, in lieu of cavalry duty. The country became impoverished, every vestige of national character was lost, and the sons of the Bashkir officers and officials were educated as true-born Russians at the college for cadets at Orenburg, and really felt as such.

In 1865, when the assimilation of the Bashkirs was far enough advanced, the Government disbanded the Bashkiro-Mestcherak Cossacks, and the Bashkirs became crown-peasants. For the future there were no more Bashkirs, but simply Russian peasants of the Governments of Perm, Viatka, and Orenburg.

This example clearly demonstrates the view the Russians took of their civilising mission. And let it not be said that the Bashkirs were incapable of being civilised! They are a kindred race to the Magyars, who under the influence of Western civilisation have attained a high degree of development. Hopeless deterioration has been the fate of the races settled on the Volga: *i.e.* the Mordva, Cheremisses and Chuvashes. Their numbers are continually decreasing; they form the lowest class of the population; their everyday life, their mode of thought and their social institutions, as Vambéry says, indicate not the slightest influence of Western civilisation.

The Kirghiz belong in point of numbers to the strongest of the nomadic races of Central Asia. Their population is over 2,000,000, and it is owing to their being split up into an infinitude of petty tribes, clans, and families ever at variance with one another, as Colonel Veniukov remarks in his work "The Russo-Asiatic Borderlands," that they have failed to become a power to be dreaded by neighbouring countries. The great majority of the Kirghiz have been but a short time under Russian rule. The Khan of the Little Horde and a few Sultans submitted indeed to the Russians as far back as 1730, but by far the greater number of them has only acknowledged Russia's supremacy in the course of the present century, and some only within the last few decades. Thus Russia's treatment of the Kirghiz shows us her procedure in the earlier phases of subjugation; in connection with which we may observe that the Kirghiz Steppe possesses few attractions for colonists. The majority of them proceed to the Valley of the Sir

Daria, and many of the complications arising from the support given to unjust claims preferred by the colonists owe their origin to this fact.

At the outset Russia is usually satisfied with a tolerably mild form of allegiance, leaving the power in the hands of the natives, who continue to rule according to their customs. But she busies herself to gain over some of the most influential persons by loading them with honours and presents, to which Orientals are so susceptible. Several Kirghiz Sultans received commissions in the army, and the Bey Mahomed even attained to the rank of general.

On the whole, however, Russia aims at replacing the old families, which, as with the Bashkirs, are called families of the "white bone," by upstarts who owe their all to the Government. In order to maintain respect for the Russian name, examples are made from time to time, when *more Asiatico* the whole tribe is held responsible for the acts of each individual member. If, for instance, a flying column were deputed to punish acts of brigandage, and failed to reach the actual culprits, it destroyed some of the Auls of kindred tribes. And the effect thus produced was so lasting that even the money mail could cross the Kirghiz desert unmolested, without escort.

Brutal manifestations of power exercise a great influence over Asiatics. The slaughter of Geok-Tepe, instead of inciting the Turcomans to further resistance, induced them to submit speedily to Russia. Russian diplomacy, however, by no means rests satisfied with the formation of a Russian party in the countries subjugated. It always anticipates, by endeavouring to gain over a party in adjoining countries as well, so as to have a few influential persons, such as Iskander Khan or the Maharajah Dhuleep Singh, at its disposal for any emergency. It applies with great skill to the heterogeneous population of Central Asia the maxim of "Divide et Impera." The Russian Colonel, Veniukov, whose treatise on "The Russo-Asiatic Borderlands" appeared in the *Voenyjsbornik*, the organ of the Russian General Staff, and who had access to the archives of the Staff, states that the Governors of Orenburg and Siberia received instructions from the Empress Catherine to utilise the antagonism of individual tribes, such as the Bashkirs, Kirghiz, and Calmucks, and to let these restless, disaffected tribes mutually weaken each other. This principle has hitherto been adopted with success. We have seen that the Kirghiz and Mestcheraks co-operated in subjugating the Bashkirs; the Kirghiz compelled some of the Calmucks flying to China to return, the Turcomans fought against the Khivans, and so on. The final aim of the Russian Government is Russianisation. Colonel Veniukov, to whom we alluded above, spares us the trouble of drawing these conclusions from the existing facts; he states that Russia could not grant independent government to the three Khanates, as in that case it would never have effected the Russianisation of the conquered countries. In several Kirghiz Auls in the Orenburg desert Russian is already spoken, and the Russianisation of the Kirghiz is in full progress.

We have dwelt at greater length than we had intended on the description of the Russian system of government in the Bashkir and Kirghiz country, as we wished to place before our readers the method adopted to prepare the way for further advance, and to Russianise the territory conquered. We can now confine ourselves to a very brief notice of the remaining nationalities.

The Calmucks are of Mongolian extraction. The greater part of those who originally wandered towards Russia eventually emigrated to China; but some of them—completely Russianised—are to be found among the Ural Cossacks; and about 50,000 live on the Chinese frontier. The Buruts, who are also called Kara Kirghiz, number about 400,000 souls.

The Uzbeks, of Turco-Mongolian parentage, were a short time since the ruling race in the three Khanates. They number close upon 1,000,000. At the time when they formed independent States they were unable to offer any serious resistance to the Russians. Much less can they do so now that they no longer live apart, but share their country with Tajiks and Serts, races of Iranian origin, who form the agricultural and commercial classes. These latter are, however, by no means anxious for a revival of the Uzbek rule.

The Turcomans are divided, like the Kirghiz, into several tribes, which from the time of Tamerlane have never coalesced, and have frequently had fierce conflicts with each other. Their number probably does not exceed 1,000,000. We shall not name the nationalities that are numerically weak, but merely mention that the Semiretchensk Cossacks are increasing, and that, according to a report of General Kuropatkin in 1885, about 60,000 colonists have settled in the province of Semiretchensk, and about 25,000 in the districts of the Sir Daria, Ferghana, and Zerafshan, within the last thirty years.

From the above survey we see that Russia has obtained a firm footing in Central Asia, and that she has nothing to fear from the conquered races. This fact is of great importance towards the comprehension of our subsequent conclusions.

II

RUSSIA ASPIRES TO THE POSSESSION OF INDIA

FROM the preceding chapter we draw the following conclusions:

1. *Russia has advanced in Asia for centuries past slowly but systematically, without allowing herself to be diverted from her purpose.*

2. *She is not satisfied with the mere conquest, but she exerts herself unremittingly to assimilate and Russianise the countries annexed, and has achieved considerable results in this direction.*

3. *Russia is firmly established in Asia, is not menaced from any quarter, has nothing to fear from the subjugated races, but, on the contrary, already utilises them to a certain extent for military purposes.*

Now the question suggests itself : Does Russia intend to discontinue her advance in Asia in order to further the moral and material progress of her vast possessions, or will she, as hitherto, pursue her triumphal march towards a definite goal?

The principal characteristics which distinguish the people of Great Russia from the Ruthenians and other Sclavonic races, may be clearly traced, according to the celebrated Russian historian, Kostomarov, from their first appearance in the history of the world. Already at that time a tendency manifested itself to form permanent social organisations, to conquer neighbouring countries, to rely for support on the masses that were slavishly devoted to the Government, and to assimilate them with the nation ; as also the religious intolerance, the contempt for other nationalities and the self-respecting conviction that the people of Great Russia were the chosen race. In the subsequent course of their history these characteristics assert themselves with increasing clearness, and the chauvinism of the people of Great Russia—if we may be permitted this anachronism, and designate ancient occurrences by a modern catch-word—assumes true Asiatic forms. Travellers who visited Moscow in the fifteenth, sixteenth and seventeenth centuries unanimously assert, observes Kostomarov, that the Muscovites despise foreign religions and foreign nations. Even the Tzars, who in this respect were not so fanatically inclined as the masses, washed their hands after touching the ambassadors of heterodox States. The Germans who had settled in Moscow were despised, and the clergy condemned all intercourse with them. The Patriarch of Moscow having accidentally blessed some Germans demanded that they should be compelled to distinguish themselves from the orthodox by a particular dress, so as to enable him in future to avoid such errors.

When, however, Peter the Great determined to render the blessings of West-European culture accessible to his people, he was obliged to invite aliens to instruct his subjects. Immediately a reaction set in among the higher classes. There was quite a craze for everything foreign ; and foreigners, especially Germans, attained—almost exclusively—to the highest dignities in the State. Prince Menchikov, who was a celebrated wit, even prayed the Emperor Nicholas to raise him to the rank of a German. This was, certainly, a long time ago! Now, for instance, it is the very reverse of advantageous in Russia to be a German. Neither the Tzar Alexander III. nor his people are enthusiastic about foreigners. The party which derides the "decaying" West, fosters national chauvinism, and despises foreign nationalities, has at present the upper hand, and believes, as do also the lower classes, that the Russians are the chosen people.

The inclination to conquer neighbouring countries and to expand in all directions, has been peculiar to the people of Great Russia in all ages. Even during the time of the Mongolian yoke, the Grand Dukedom of Moscow increased in size, although its rulers as representatives of the Khan of the Golden Horde collected tribute for the latter. The Tzars inherited from the Mongolians the true Asiatic view of their own position. Like the Emperor of China, the Shah of Persia, and the Khan of the Golden Horde, the Tzar looked upon himself as the king of all kings, the foremost among rulers. This view took deep root among the people, and even at the present day it is reported in Russia that in 1854 the Frenchman and the Englishman revolted against the Tzar. This view leads, however, to the idea of universal empire; an idea which for a long time past, even if unconsciously, has prevailed not only with the Russian Government, but with the Russian people as well. To it must be ascribed the intuitive desire for conquest which has displayed itself both among the Cossacks and the various other "tools" which executed the orders of the Central Government on the confines of the Empire. The Government has always supported the successful enterprises of its subordinates, even when they were contrary to instructions. The idea of universal empire determines the political ideals of the Russians. In Europe they aspire above all to the conquest of Constantinople, the East Roman seat of Empire. In Asia they look upon themselves as heirs and successors of the great conquerors and rulers of the world, Chingis Khan and Tamerlane.

In the following pages we shall not, however, consider Russia's aspirations in Europe, which are beyond the scope of the present treatise, but shall confine ourselves exclusively to the discussion of Russia's aspirations in Asia.

Every one who wishes to understand Russia must gain a conception of the great influence which Asia has exercised upon her from time immemorial. Russian writers, even their official historians, such as, for instance, Karamzin the historiographer of the Tzar Alexander I., and Ilovaiski whose "History of Russia" has long been used as a handbook for Russian schools, are obliged to admit this, inasmuch as in the ninth century only seven of the thirty-six Governments of Russia in Europe, which are at present almost exclusively inhabited by natives of Great Russia, were peopled by Sclavonic races, the people of Great Russia springing from a mixture of Sclavonian, Finnish, Turkish and Tartar races. Stchapov states in his "History of Russia's Intellectual Development," that up to Peter the Great's time, Byzantine civilisation was based exclusively on the Russian people's Oriental conception of the world. The Russians only travelled to Constantinople, Mount Athos, Jerusalem, and India. Lastly, Schashkof in his "History of the Russian Woman," harks back repeatedly to the influence of Asiatic civilisation on Russia. "The influence of Asiatic

RUSSIA ASPIRES TO POSSESSION OF INDIA 69

nations on Russia," he says, "cannot be denied. Long before Russia was conquered by the Mongolians, we find there Turks, Berendiei, Polovces, and other Asiatic races. They intermarried with the Russians, mingled their blood with the Sclavonic blood, and influenced our character, our language, our manners, our customs, and our ideas. The Mongolian rule of two centuries confirmed this influence. After we had shaken off the Mongolian yoke, we took Kasan, Astrakhan, Siberia, the Caucasus and the Kirghiz Steppe. Everywhere we came into contact with Asiatic peoples, and from the intermixture of races which resulted, there sprang a new race, whose development was arrested, and is still arrested, by the continual admixture of Asiatic blood, as well as by the influence of Asiatic ideas and manners. This influence is by no means confined to the lower classes of the population; the majority of our nobility is of Asiatic extraction."

The nations of Central Asia regarded an Indian campaign as a means of enrichment, and the possession of India as the acme of power. Every Central Asian ruler has raved about an Indian campaign, and has marched to India as soon as his circumstances permitted it. This explains the numerous invasions of India. True to Asiatic traditions, the Russian people, too, rave about the conquest of India, the possession of which signifies universal empire to Asiatics. Even the Tzars, the successors of the Asiatic conquerors of the world, allow themselves to be allured by Asiatic traditions; cast longing looks on India, and are eager about its conquest.

As a young man, says the Russian historian Soloviev, Peter the Great was keenly interested in the discovery of a water-route to China and India by way of the

North Sea. Shortly after he was convinced of the impracticability of this dream, but took every opportunity of ascertaining the fullest particulars regarding India, and the routes leading thereto. When, in 1716, he gave orders for the expedition to Khiva, he instructed Prince Bekovitch-Cherkassky who was placed in command, to send Lieutenant Kozin and two merchants from Astrakhan to India. Kozin was to find out all particulars concerning the water-route, and to use it as far as possible. Should he hear of a better and more convenient route from India to Russia, he was to return by it. A few months later the Tzar commanded Prince Cherkasski to send a man of experience and tact, and conversant with the languages of the countries, by the Persian route to India, with instructions to return through China and Bokhárá. Peter I. gave both messengers letters of recommendation to the Khan of Khiva, the Khan of Bokhárá, and the Great Mogul. Soon after he commanded his envoy in Persia, Artemius Volynski, to send off the Tartar Tevtelev, who subsequently became a Russian Major-General, to India through Persia, with instructions to return by way of China. Clinging to his youthful dreams, the great Tzar wished to restore the old trade-route from India *viâ* Bokhárá and Moscow to the Baltic Sea, and with this view he established custom-houses at Orenburg, Troisk, and Petropavlovsk, where at that time all the trade-routes leading from Central Asia into Russia converged.

His successors had enough to do in Europe, and applied their chief resources to the furtherance of European policy. This did not, however, prevent them from constantly collecting information regarding Asia, nor from availing themselves of every suitable opportunity for fresh Asiatic conquests. But, above all, the remote, mysterious country, in which the popular imagination pictured an accumulation of all sorts of riches, and whence hailed the most wonderful fabrics and the most costly precious stones, occupied the minds of all. To get to India was the dream of every enterprising merchant or statesman whose sphere of activity was in Asia. This impulse was, it is true, an unconscious one with most; but with many an one, rooted as it was in aims whose scope was well defined, it assumed more tangible shape. In 1800 the Tzar Paul I. planned a campaign[1] against India, and invited General Bonaparte to join in the undertaking. According to this plan Russia and France were each to provide 35,000 men and to transport them across the Caspian Sea to Asterabad. Thence the combined armies were to march through Persia, Afghanistan, and the Punjab and attack the British possessions in India. General Bonaparte considered this plan impracticable. A few years later the Emperor Napoleon proposed to the Tzar Alexander I., in Tilsit, that they should make a joint attack on India, in order to undermine the English power. In the course of 1807 and 1808 the two

[1] This plan is given verbatim in the "Deutsche Revue" of May, 1888. It is true Lieutenant-Colonel Batorski in his book, which appeared in 1886, entitled, "Plans of Campaigns against India submitted by Napoleon Bonaparte to the Tzar Paul I. in 1800, and to the Tzar Alexander I. in 1808," attributes this plan to the First Consul. As, however, General Bonaparte raised serious doubts as to the feasibility of this plan, which doubts the Tzar Paul I., in his reply, endeavoured to invalidate, and as the latter shortly after, on 12th January, 1801, gave the order to Prince Orlov-Denissov to march at the head of the Don-Cossacks by the Khiva and Bokhárá route to India, it appears to us much more probable that the Tzar Paul I. himself planned the campaign against India.

Governments discussed this proposal, and General Gardanne, French Ambassador at Teheran, endeavoured to secure Persia's co-operation as ˙.well. Neither Nicholas I. Alexander II., nor the present Tzar Alexander III. have, as far as we know, made any plans to invade India ; but their entire policy in Central Asia proves that India was and is not indifferent to them. On the other hand, several of their subjects have occupied themselves with the idea of an invasion of India. A writer who was intimately acquainted with Count Perovski, Governor-General of Orenburg, and a personal friend of the Tzar Nicholas I., informs us that his eyes sparkled, his face flushed up, and he went into ecstasies when he spoke of a campaign in India. A fortune-teller predicted of Prince Bariatynski, an intimate friend of the Tzar Alexander I. in his youth, that he would perform great deeds in the Far East. When he was appointed Governor of the Caucasus, and found himself at the head of a large army experienced in war, he thought his time had come. He worked out a detailed plan of campaign. His army was to consist of three divisions, two of which would be furnished by the Caucasian army. He caused such a thorough inspection to be made of the route from Asterabad by way of Herat and the valleys of the Farah Rud and Helmund to Kelat, whence he proposed to reach the Indus, that he was enabled to append a line of march to his plan of campaign. Relying on his personal intimacy with the Tzar, and the confidence reposed in him by his sovereign, he submitted his plan at St. Petersburg, and it was approved of. The Prince was requested to make a further reconnaissance of the country between Herat, Kelat, and the Indus. It was, however, deemed advisable to await a more favourable opportunity for the execution of his plan.

The plans of campaign against India in the archives of the Russian Chief Staff may be counted by hundreds, and every year fresh ones are sent in. And though the majority of them have no special value, and many, such as the plan of General Chrulov, one of the heroes of Sebastopol, appear fantastic, yet at any rate they are significant of the wishes and inclinations of the people, as well as of the tendency of public opinion in Russia.

One of the most popular men in Russia, General Skobelev, who died a few years since, and who through his sister was connected with the Russian Royal family, also drew up a plan of campaign against India, which was discussed in the English Parliament on the 13th March, 1888. According to this plan, said the Hon. member, General Sir Edward Hamley, Russia is to march into Afghanistan and to take as her base of operations the country between Cabul, Herat and Candahar.

For some decades past interest in India and in the countries by which it can be reached, has been increasing in Russia. This is very evident from the number of books and newspaper articles which appear on Central Asia, Afghanistan, Kafiristan, Persia, and India. It would occupy too much space to enumerate all the works of this kind, and we therefore confine ourselves to a statement of the one fact, that in the course of 1887 three works on India have appeared in the organ of the Russian Head-Quarter Staff; they are:

1. "Invasions of India," by General Sobolev, Chief of the Asiatic Department of the Head-Quarter Staff;

2. "A Military-Statistical Sketch of India," by Thysenhauzen; and

3. "Travels in India," by an officer who was deputed to attend the great manœuvres at Delhi.

The publication of these works leads us to the conviction that, though the attraction towards India was an unconscious one at the beginning of this century, this is now no longer the case. The two principal wishes of the Russian people, and the two principal aims of the Russian Government are: to possess Constantinople in Europe, and India in Asia.

That Russia aspires to the possession of India her action in Asia during the nineteenth century proves clearly enough.

In a memorandum on the Euphrates Valley Railway written in 1858, the subsequent commandant of the Third Army Corps in Gratz, Master of the Ordnance Baron Kuhn observed that in future Russia would most probably advance mainly on the Asiatic side to the sea—the civilising medium—so that from her Caucasian base she might gain access on the one hand to the Persian Gulf, and on the other hand through Armenia and Asia Minor to the Mediterranean; since her advance on the European side would be opposed by Austria. Were this in reality Russia's intention, her policy in Central Asia during the last sixty years must necessarily have been a very different one. Russia, as we know, is wont to pursue her objects with great energy and recklessness. If she therefore intended to reach the Persian Gulf, she would surely have found many an opportunity since 1828, *i.e.*, since the date of the conclusion of the treaty of Turkmantchai, for a war with Persia, inasmuch as Russia does not readily surrender what she has once possessed. Now Persia has hitherto retained possession of the provinces Ghilan, Mazanderan, and Asterabad, which Peter the

Great acquired in the year 1724, and his successors restored to Persia in 1734. Russian diplomacy is unsurpassed in the art of creating agitation and anarchy amongst neighbours on whom she has designs. And although Persia is in a state of political and military decadence, yet Russian diplomacy rests satisfied with opposing English, and strengthening Russian influence at Teheran. Lastly, the Caucasian army has since 1864, *i.e.*, since the pacification of the Caucasus, been available for employment elsewhere, and would be capable, even without the co-operation of other troops, of conducting a successful campaign against Persia, and compelling the Shah to cede some of his provinces to Russia. We say some, as we know that Russia usually prefers to weaken her neighbours internally in the first instance, with the ulterior view of conquering their territory piecemeal. If, therefore, Russia contemplated the conquest of Persia in order to reach the Persian Gulf, her action in Persia would have been totally different.

In our opinion the other assertion of the Austrian General is equally unconfirmed by facts, *i.e.*, that Russia would endeavour to reach the Mediterranean by way of Armenia and Asia Minor, because, as he himself states, Austria might oppose Russia's advance on the European side.

Russia cannot relinquish her aim of reaching Constantinople from Europe, unless she renounces Pan-Slavism. And that she is at the present day less than ever inclined to do this all who have any acquaintance with the prevailing currents of thought in Russia are aware. Austria did not prevent Russia in 1877-78 from using her main resources in Bulgaria instead of Armenia. Even after victorious campaigns Russia evinced but a moderate interest in Asia Minor in her treaties of peace. In 1829 she acquired, by the treaty of Adrianople, Akhaltsikh, Akhalkallaki, Anapa, and Poti ; and in 1878, by the peace of San Stefano, Kars and Batoum. If we consider, however, that Turkey, both in 1829 and 1878 was completely vanquished, and compelled to accept the conditions of peace dictated to her by Russia, we must admit that the latter's demands in regard to Turkey in Asia were moderate; which cannot be said of her stipulations in regard to Turkey-in-Europe. This leads us to the inference that the St. Petersburg Cabinet attaches no particular importance to the possession of Asia Minor.

We are far from wishing to assert that Russia will for ever forego the possession of Persia and Turkey-in-Asia. We content ourselves with affirming that she manifests far greater activity both on the Balkan Peninsula and in Central Asia.

Several politicians are of opinion that there is room enough in Asia for both Russians and English. Lord Salisbury lent the whole weight of his authority to this view, which he enunciated in the English Parliament in the summer of 1887. We know, however, that the noble lord was not always of this opinion, that he had already expressed himself on several occasions very decisively regarding Russia's policy in Asia, but that, so soon after successfully effecting a settlement of the North-West frontier of Afghanistan, he could not speak otherwise, both in view of his position and the political relations of the two Empires.

From the English stand-point there would be no objection to the division of Asia between England and Russia. England is in possession of a rich, densely populated country of inestimable value, and can therefore be satisfied with her share. On the other hand, Russia's possessions in Asia generally, and in Central Asia in particular, represent but a very small value. In a lecture on "Russia's Progress in Central Asia," General Kuropatkin stated in 1885 that Russia had, in the course of the last forty years, annexed a country with an area of about 30,000 square miles and with 3,500,000 inhabitants. This country produced from 1868 to 1878 a total revenue of only 32,000,000 roubles, whereas the total expenditure amounted to 99,000,000 roubles. The deficit for the ten years consequently amounted to 67,000,000 roubles, or 6,700,000 roubles per annum. In this country about 2,000,000 dessiatines, *i.e.*, one-fiftieth part of the total area, is cultivated, about 40,000,000 dessiatines are used as pasture-land, whilst the remaining 60,000,000 dessiatines consist of deserts which are useless for grazing even the hardiest animals. In this country there are tracts in which camels can only be watered twice in 390 miles. Now, does such a country represent a possession which will repay the sacrifices of blood and treasure which it has entailed? This question can only be answered in the negative. No wonder, then, that the English, who estimate everything at its true value and are aware that Russia could conquer something much more valuable with such an expenditure of means and power combined with such energy and perseverance, regard with the greatest uneasiness the approach of the Russians to the confines of India. What more natural than that they should suspect them of evil intentions in thus continually advancing towards India? In England the masses feel this instinctively, and the highest authorities on Asiatic affairs frankly admit it. Thus in 1874 the English General Sir Henry Rawlinson, formerly envoy and minister at the Court of Persia, late President of the Royal Geographical Society, and member of the Council of India, wrote in his celebrated work, "England and Russia in the East," second edition, page 350, that "the continued advance of Russia in Central Asia is as certain as the succession of day and night. Russia will continue to push on towards India until arrested by a barrier which she can neither remove nor overstep. If this programme be correct, it means of course contact and collision, and such I believe, as far as my own means of observation extend, to be the inevitable result in due course of time." The English ex-minister and statesman, Sir Charles Dilke, in his much-talked-of articles on the British Army, which appeared in the *Fortnightly Review* towards the close of 1887, considers a war between England and Russia inevitable, and asserts that General Roberts, Commander-in-Chief in India, had declared that an Anglo-Russian war for the possession of India would have to be fought out at no distant date. After a minute study of Russian traditions and aspirations, we coincide with these views, and believe we may affirm with absolute certainty that Russia aspires to the possession of India.

III

CAN ENGLAND ARREST RUSSIA'S ADVANCE IN ASIA?

ENGLAND'S insular position and her powerful fleet secure her against invasion. The same holds good with regard to the great majority of her colonies, which the European military powers could only reach by sea. Hitherto, remarks the Russian writer Juchakov, England has kept her hold on India—her most precious possession—under advantageous circumstances; but now, by Russia's advance in Central Asia, India's security is threatened. Should England lose this advantage of position she must submit to the inevitable necessity of making adequate preparation, while at the same time risking, in common with other continental powers, the miserable consequences of a disastrous campaign. This explains the intense agitation created in England by Russia's approach to the confines of India.

At the close of the eighteenth century General Bonaparte's Egyptian expedition roused the apprehensions of the Marquis of Wellesley, Governor-General of India. To frustrate a probable invasion by the French, he entered into negociations with Persia, through which country the road to the Indus lay, and his representative, Captain Malcolm, in 1800 concluded with the Shah an offensive and defensive alliance, which provided that both powers should act conjointly against a French army in Persia. The ill-success of the French in Egypt quieted the English indeed for the moment; but shortly after, the Tzar Paul I.'s designs on India; the war of 1804-1806 which resulted in the cession to Russia of certain Persian provinces including Baku, notwithstanding the Anglo-Persian treaty; then the negociations of Napoleon I. with the Tzar Alexander I. and the Shah of Persia regarding a joint expedition to India, justly gave rise to more serious apprehensions. Thereupon the British Ministry sent out Sir Harford Jones, whilst the Governor-General of India, Lord Minto, simultaneously despatched his own nominee, Major-General Malcolm, on a mission to Persia. General Malcolm was the first to arrive, and scattered gold, to which the Persians are so extraordinarily susceptible, broadcast. In spite of this, he failed to paralyse the influence of General Gardanne, who held out to the Persians the prospect of a restoration of the provinces lately taken by the Russians through Napoleon's intervention—and he found himself obliged to quit Persia. Shortly after, Sir Harford Jones, who was impatiently awaiting the result of General Malcolm's negociations, arrived at Bushire. As Envoy of the King of England, he proposed to the Shah to protect and support Persia against Russia. As by this time the opinion had gained ground at Teheran that France could not be of much assistance to Persia, the British Envoy's proposal was gladly accepted. Sir Harford Jones' journey from Bushire to Teheran resembled an ovation. General Gardanne quitted Teheran without awaiting his arrival, and the negociations were conducted with such rapidity, that by the 12th March, 1809, a preliminary agreement was concluded. By its provisions Persia engaged to oppose the passage of any foreign army towards India, and to defend India, should it be attacked by the Afghans or any other power, with an army, the strength of which was to be fixed in the definitive treaty. England engaged in return to support Persia against any European power, and for this purpose she was to place at the Shah's disposal, until the expulsion of the enemy, an army, war *matériel*, and a number of officers, as well as paying a proportionate subsidy.

In pursuance of this treaty, the English Government sent out officers who drilled the Shah's troops in European fashion. Shortly after, a war broke out between Persia and Russia, and the English officers led the Persian troops to many a victory; in the end, however, the operations were unfavourable to Persia. In 1812 England became reconciled with Russia, recalled her officers, and on the 12th October, 1813, through England's mediation, a treaty of peace between Russia and Persia was signed at Gulistan, in the Russian camp on the river Seiwa. Persia surrendered Grusia, Imeritia, Mingrelia, Abkasia, and the Khanates of Karabagh, Shekee, Shirwan, Derbend, etc. The new frontier-line between these countries was determined by the Araxes for the greater portion of its course. Lastly, Persia relinquished the right to retain ships of war on the Caspian Sea. Thus for the second time in the course of twelve years, *i.e.*, since the conclusion of the first offensive and defensive alliance between Persia and England, England's aid proved unavailing to protect Persia against Russia.

The Shah, however, by no means regarded the treaty of Gulistan as final, as he could not reconcile himself to the idea of losing so many provinces. Consequently soon after the ratification of the Gulistan treaty he concluded with Sir Gore Ouseley, the English Ambassador Extraordinary, a treaty on the basis of the preliminary agreement of 1809, which was signed by Mr. Henry Ellis at Teheran on 25th November, 1814. By this treaty Persia engaged to prevent the passage through her territory of any European army marching towards India and to use her influence to induce the rulers of Khiva, Bokhárá, and Kokand to oppose in like manner the march of an invading army towards India through their countries. Henceforth "the limits of the two States of Russia and Persia were to be determined according to the admission of Great Britain, Persia, and Russia." In the event of war Great Britain and Persia were mutually to aid one another. Instead of providing an army, England paid an annual subsidy of 200,000 tomans (£83,000 sterling). In the event of war between England and Afghanistan the Shah placed a Persian army at the disposal of the English. In a Perso-Afghan war, on the other hand, England engaged not to interfere, and only to use her good offices at the request of both belligerent States.

It may be observed that it was injudicious on the part of the English to embody in the treaty the article, whereby the Shah engaged to use his influence with Khiva, Bokhárá, and Kokand to induce these States to oppose the march of an invading army towards India. An army which could reach India in such force as to be dangerous to English authority would easily overcome the resistance of Khiva, Bokhárá, and Kokand.

With the conclusion of the Treaty of Teheran in 1814 commenced the period of England's exclusive influence in Persia. England pursued two objects: In the first place, she desired to raise the military strength of Persia, and to this end sent officers, who built arsenals and disciplined the Persian army. These officers acquitted themselves in all respects beyond expectations, and we owe it to them, as Sir Henry Rawlinson remarks, that the Englishman at the present day still commands esteem and respect in any part of Persia. In the second place, England endeavoured to gain a commanding influence in Persia, in which she was equally successful. The Prince Royal was particularly partial to the English language, and Persia gave England many tokens of the warmest sympathy. This of course roused the jealousy of Russia. True to her traditions, she began to treat Persia with contempt and disregard, whilst on the other hand she endeavoured to inveigle the Shah into a war with Afghanistan, and urged him to take Herat. As Persia refused to comply, on the ground, as the Shah openly said, of not wishing to incur England's enmity, Russia started a point of controversy which led to war. This broke out in 1826 and ended in 1828 with the peace of Turkmantchai, by which Persia was compelled to cede to Russia the Khanates of Erivan and Nachitchevan, and to pay five millions of tomans, *i.e.*, 20,000,000 roubles. For the third time in the short space of twenty-four years, *i.e.*, since the outbreak of the Russo-Persian war in 1804, Persia satisfied herself that England's friendship and promises were of little avail in a pressing emergency. It is not surprising, therefore, that the Shah's sympathies turned to Russia, and that England's influence in Persia rapidly declined. England availed herself of Persia's financial difficulties to obtain a release from the further payment of subsidies for a sum down of 200,000 tomans, which was by no means calculated to increase the regard for England in Persia.

Since 1828 Russian influence has been predominant at Teheran.

When England relinquished the idea of making Persia a barrier to Russia's advance in Asia, she turned her attention to Afghanistan, and the Khanates of Khiva, Bokhárá, and Kokand. English statesmen believed that these Khanates, separated from Russia by extensive deserts and inhabited by warlike tribes, would be able to arrest Russia's progress, provided they became reconciled with one another, concluded offensive and defensive alliances, and were furnished with arms, ammunition, and instructors. A number of English agents endeavoured to accomplish this. Our readers know the internal condition of the Khanates, and are consequently aware of the impracticability of this scheme. This was impressed upon the English by a tragical event. In 1840 the Amir of Bukhárá, Nasr-Ullah, had the English agents Stoddart and Conolly arrested, and shortly afterwards beheaded. England was not even able to avenge their death! Regarding England's endeavours to make Persia a barrier against Russia, Sir Henry Rawlinson says: "We had been building on a quicksand." These words might be still more appropriately applied to England's plans in regard to the three Khanates.

At that time Russia's frontier was still very distant from Afghanistan, and the latter lay exclusively within reach of England's sphere of power. England therefore endeavoured to enter into closer relations with Afghanistan. Afghanistan had, however, less cohesion and stability than Persia. It consisted of a collection of loosely connected Khanates, such as Cabul, Candahar, Herat, Balkh, etc., which Dost Mahommed first succeeded, towards the close of the thirties, in drawing more closely together; and possessed neither an old dynasty, nor fixed territorial limits, and not even a homogeneous population. North of the line Cabul-Herat the inhabitants are not Afghans, and so-called Afghan Turkestan comprised Khanates which at one time were independent, then were conquered by the Amir of Bokhárá, and finally by the Amir of Cabul. The Afghans themselves occupy barely half of the entire country, and are divided into Eastern (upper) and Western (lower) Afghans. They are characterised by a strong love of individual liberty, and the general tendency with them is not towards centralisation, but rather to the widest possible independence. According to Russian statements, the Afghans are divided into five races, which again are subdivided into four hundred and five tribes, each of which is split up into numerous families. As with most Muhammadan States, internal conflicts break out between the Amir and the pretender, on the throne becoming vacant; and lastly, individual tribes revolt from time to time, as was the case with the Ghilzais in 1887. Hence it is apparent that the idea of making Afghanistan a barrier to Russia's advance was impracticable.

Russia availed herself of her influence with the Shah to make of him a medium whereby she could interfere in Afghan affairs. The possession of Herat has ever been the heart's desire of the Persians; but even at the time of their preponderating influence at Teheran the English would not help them to its attainment. In order to create a lasting antagonism between England and Persia, the Russians induced the Shah to take possession of Herat. The English agents succeeded indeed in 1832 in arresting a Persian expedition against Herat, but as soon after as 1833 one actually set out under the command of the Persian heir-apparent. The latter was obliged, in consequence of Shah Abbas Mirza's death, to raise the siege of Herat, but vowed to return again. Both in 1838 and 1853 Persian armies again marched against Herat. On both occasions English officers conducted the defence, English intervention compelled the Persians to beat a retreat, and Persia engaged not to send troops on any consideration into Herat territory.

[margin note: A Russian cav commanded Hera attack.]

The reply of Russian diplomacy to the despatch of English agents to Khiva and Bokhárá was the mission of Vitkevitch to Cabul. This roused the English to the highest pitch of excitement, and as Dost Mahommed maintained a tolerably reserved attitude towards England, in January 1839 the first Afghan war broke out. In a very short time nearly the whole of Afghanistan was conquered by British troops, and Shah Sujah was installed with great pomp at Cabul. In November 1841 a revolution broke out. Shah Sujah was dethroned, and most of the English garrisons were massacred. In the following year these massacres were avenged, and the British troops then retired from Afghanistan. For some years the English held aloof from Afghan affairs, but subsequently were reconciled "perpetually" with the Amir Dost Mahommed, and engaged to pay him a yearly subsidy of £200,000 sterling.

Our readers will probably have been struck by the difference between the Russian and English methods of dealing with Central Asian countries. The former endeavour to weaken and undermine them, whereas the latter desire to strengthen, civilise, and consolidate them. These different methods of treatment correspond, moreover, to the objects at which each of the civilising powers aims. Russia is continually extending her frontier. A territory incorporated by Russia in the empire is at once regarded as a Russian province and is colonised by Russians. The Government employs all the resources at its disposal to secure the gradual adoption by the new citizens of Russian manners and customs, the Russian language, and even religion, so that after a term of years they may become absorbed by the Russian nation. Consequently, from their point of view, a Central-Asian State can never be too weak, nor its internal condition too unsettled. England, on the other hand, possesses the most valuable portion of Asia and knows that it must be regarded as a conquered country, and can never under any circumstances be amalgamated with Great Britain. "India," says Sir Henry Rawlinson, "is a conquered country, where a certain amount of discontent must be ever smouldering which would be fanned into a chronic conflagration by the contiguity of a rival European power." It is on this account that England is so apprehensive of Russia's approach towards India, and would have the Central-Asian States as strong as possible, so that they may check Russia's progress. She therefore spares no sacrifices in order to render them capable of resistance.

To carry out a policy systematically in England, the general popular sentiment must first be enlisted in its favour. This is, however, especially difficult with questions of foreign policy, because with them, as an English statesman observes, the egoism, incredulity, ignorance and indifference of the public in general have to be overcome. This difficult task was accomplished by three talented men: John McNeill, David Urquhart, and Baillie Fraser. The ill-success of English policy at

Teheran, and more especially the Treaty of Unkiar Skelessi, concluded in 1833 between Russia and Turkey, alarmed the English. Then came McNeill from Teheran and David Urquhart from Constantinople, where they held subordinate diplomatic posts, and in conjunction with Baillie Fraser inaugurated a press campaign. Not only the daily papers, but monthly and quarterly reviews as well, entered zealously into the contest. In addition, the above-named started a special organ, the celebrated *Portfolio*. In 1836 McNeill was appointed Envoy at Teheran ; Urquhart Secretary of Embassy at Constantinople ; and Baillie Fraser remained in London to continue the conduct of the campaign from Downing Street. They described most ably the dangers to which Russia's procedure might expose England both in Europe and in Asia, and under their influence the waves of Russophobia mounted high and reached their culminating point at the close of the thirties of the present century, on the outbreak of the first Anglo-Afghan war, which McNeill ascribed to Russian intrigues. The wide-spread Russophobia in England since that time must be regarded as one of the principal causes of the Crimean war. It redounds to the permanent credit of these excellent men, that they opened the eyes of the English, and directed their attention to the dangers of Russia's advance. Unluckily for England, they confined themselves to answering the question what was to be aimed at, without discussing how the desired object was to be attained. To the present day hazy notions prevail on this point in Great Britain. And yet the English might perceive from the experience gained in the first half of the nineteenth century, that the policy they have hitherto pursued has been a failure, and that they are unable to undermine Russia's influence in Persia and Central

Asia, or to check Russia's advance. The reason of this is not far to seek.

From the study of the science of physics we know that the intensity of light, as well as of sound, is in an inverse ratio to the square of the distance of the object which produces the light or sound. A similar law might also be applied to politics, namely, that the influence of two powerful rival states upon a third weaker one decreases in proportion to the square of the distance. But if the correctness of this law be admitted, it will be perceived that England is so unfavourably situated as compared with Russia both in Persia and in Central Asia, that she must always come off second best. This can be easily proved. Russia borders on Persia, and can at any time march into that country an army which, as the Persians know from experience, is far superior to theirs. England, on the other hand, can only attack Persia from the sea, which would necessitate extensive preparations on her part, and on landing she would still have a long and fatiguing march to accomplish before reaching Ispahan, let alone Teheran. England cannot protect Persia against Russia. With the best will in the world the English are not in a position to place a sufficiently strong army on the northern frontier of Persia in time to arrest Russia's triumphal march, and to force her to treat for peace. In spite of England's guarantee, Russia several times forcibly took Persian provinces. And when Russia acquires a Persian province, she is also in a position to retain it permanently, whereas England could only occupy and permanently retain a Persian island, or at most a seaport town. Lastly, Russia being a neighbour, can make herself far more disagreeable than England, should the Government of the Shah prove not sufficiently docile. For these reasons English influence at Teheran was purchased by bribes, subsidies, gifts of arms and the loan of instructors, as well as by promises to protect Persia against Russia; whereas Russian influence mainly depended upon the fear of Russian power.

England's position in Central Asia was still more disadvantageous. Remotely situated both from England and India, the countries there were secure from any exercise of England's power. She was therefore unable to protect the Central-Asian States against Russia. The influence of the English in Central Asia may consequently be taken as *nil*.

From this brief survey we see that the English cannot compete with the Russians either in Persia or Central Asia on equal terms. This was already apparent before the Eastern campaign of 1854–1856. At that time the English had already gained considerable experience in Persia, and the Russians had already crossed the Kirghiz Steppe and established themselves both on the Sea of Aral and the Jaxartes. Had the British Government been cognisant of this, it must have admitted that the object of checking Russia's advance on India could not be attained by its policy in Asia. It must consequently have decided, either to allow Russia to advance unhindered, or to check her at any cost in some other way. In the former case, England should have cared as little for Russia's progress in Asia, as Russia herself cares for England's progress in India and Afghanistan. At the same time, she might have consoled herself with the thought of the great distance which separated Russia from India, and of the difficulties which the Circassians and the Turcomans, as well as the vast tracts of arid desert, presented to Russia's advance. In the latter case, more effective measures should have been resorted to, to check the Russians in Asia. A glance at the map of Asia must convince any military expert of the eminent strategical importance of the Caucasus. Were the Russians to lose the Caucasus, they must simultaneously forfeit all influence in Turkey-in-Asia and in Persia, besides their supremacy on the Caspian Sea; and their further advance in Central Asia would be well nigh impossible, or in any case be rendered very difficult. The deliverance of the Caucasus from the Russians should therefore have been the chief aim of English policy during the Crimean war.

Strange to say, even at the present day England misapprehends the real state of affairs, and at every fresh success of Russia in Asia both newspapers and serious military and political writers break out into a storm of indignation against the Government, which by its weakness, want of determination, a policy of surrender and ineptitude, has failed to prevent this or that encroachment of Russia. Sir Henry Rawlinson would, even at the risk of a war with Russia, keep her at a certain distance from India, and regain the lost influence in Persia. Our readers are aware that this programme is impracticable. Lieutenant Yate, of the Bombay Staff Corps, took part in the labours of the commission deputed to settle the Russo-Afghan frontier in 1885. At a distance of over 600 miles from the Indus, and several thousand miles from the mother-country, he was able to appreciate the precarious position of General Lumsden, who had only his escort of 1,000 men to rely upon, and could not keep up communications with either India or England; whereas General Komarov could in a short time double or treble his forces if he chose. In spite of this,

Lieutenant Yate failed to comprehend that England's power cannot extend to such a distance, and attributed "Russia's successes to the able and resolute policy of the Tzar and his ministers." In like manner the distinguished Oriental scholar, Professor Vambéry, in his well-known work, "The Coming Struggle for India," ascribes all Russia's success to the ineptitude and incompetence of the English Government. His book teems with such expressions as : "If the Government is unable or unwilling to give the requisite support to the endeavours of its representatives ! "

"As, however, the Ministry on the Thames only accorded him (Sir Henry Rawlinson) a very insufficient degree of support, his statesmanlike tact led to no result."

"In view of the extreme danger to which this indecisive and effete policy threatens to give rise, the statesmen of Great Britain must resolve to look coming events boldly in the face," etc.

Unluckily for England, her leading statesmen share these incorrect views. As we have described the moves of Russia and England during the first half of the nineteenth century, and are now about to discuss the Crimean war (1854–1856), we here quote the views of Lord Palmerston, who was one of the leading English statesmen before and during that war. In a letter of the 18th July, 1851, to Lord Clarendon, the English Premier wrote : "The policy of the Russian Government has always been, to proceed with its conquests as rapidly as the apathy or want of firmness of other Governments permitted, but to retire if it encountered determined opposition, and then to await the next favourable opportunity to renew the onslaught on its intended victim." Under the influence of the false impression that Russia always retires when she meets with determined opposition, and that England was able by a policy of energy and tact to check Russia's progress, the plan of the Crimean war was originated.

As is well-known, France and England allied themselves to protect Turkey-in-Europe permanently from Russia. Well-informed people maintain that the Emperor Napoleon III. was bent upon making the war a decisive one, and attaining great objects. Though he did not succeed in gaining over England to his views, he still decided for war in the hope of being able to persuade his ally in the course of the campaign to extend the original plan in proportion to the sacrifices entailed. The British Government, however, remained true to its original resolve. On the 2nd June, 1854, the Premier, Lord Aberdeen, made the following remark in the House of Lords: "The war was undertaken to protect Turkey, but not to divide Russia"; and until the close of the war the British Government adhered to its original programme. Lord Palmerston observed to General Zamoiski: "The Allies do not contemplate a war à *outrance*. Russia must be compelled to renounce her designs on Turkey and the Black Sea, without forfeiting her territory." Some months later he said quite frankly to General Chrzanovski, who was then in the English service: "Nous ne voulons pas le démembrement de la Russie." And yet Lord Palmerston was precisely *the* statesman who displayed most energy during the Crimean war. When, in January 1855, Lord Aberdeen's Ministry, of which he was a member, was accused of too lax a conduct of the war, Lord Palmerston succeeded to the premiership. The Tories were not inclined either to go any further than he was, and Disraeli, the then leader of the party in the House of Commons, even reproached the Government with not having laboured zealously enough for the restoration of peace on the fall of Sebastopol. When such feelings prevailed, it is not to be wondered at that England failed to turn the opportunity offered her to better advantage.

And yet the political situation was such, that England had merely to express a wish in order to secure her interests both in Europe and Asia permanently against Russia's aggression. At the beginning of 1854, the Allies, and particularly France, endeavoured to gain over Austria and Prussia to their side, and submitted to them the draft of a treaty. Austria considered it too moderate, whilst Prussia declined to assume a hostile attitude towards Russia. A few months later negociations were resumed between France, England, and Austria, and as we learn from a tolerably reliable source, Austria laid stress on the fact that as a neighbour of Russia she was at any time exposed to her revenge. She could consequently only take part in a war which had in view great objects, the attainment of which would render Russia innocuous to Austria. To this, however, England would not consent, and assumed an attitude of reserve, as did also the Emperor Napoleon, who in a note dated 26th March, 1855, drew the attention of the London Cabinet to the state of the Kingdom of Poland as being contrary to the treaties of 1815, and described the dangers which might arise therefrom to Europe.

It is then clear that England, who of all others had much more reason to fear Russia's progress both in Europe and Asia than France, hung back from enlarging the scope of the war. In the face of this, Sir Henry Rawlinson's reproach that France's envy prevented the English from acting energetically in Asia, aiding Shamil, and expelling the Russians from the Caucasus, appears to us unjustifiable. France had no interests in Asia, and consequently did not feel disposed to transfer the military operations to Asia. If, however, England had wished this in good earnest, she could, with the aid of Turkey, whose army would have held Russia in check on the Danube, and with Persia, who wished to regain her lost provinces, have operated in Asia ; whilst France and Austria would have acted in Europe. Had Russia been driven beyond the Dnieper, Turkey in Europe would have been rendered perfectly secure, and the seizure of the Caucasus would have probably made Russia's further advance in Asia impossible, and in any case very difficult. "Had English statesmen," says Master of the Ordnance Kuhn in his treatise on the Euphrates Valley Railway, "more fully realised these circumstances, they would, in the last war with Russia, have landed their troops to their infinitely greater advantage on the East coast of the Black Sea, instead of at Sebastopol."

The foreign policy of a country is not, however, always guided by a Cavour or a Bismarck. The powers of the majority of statesmen hardly suffice for the performance of commonplace tasks, and they esteem themselves fortunate if they secure a few years of rest to the State which they rule. Lord Palmerston consequently contented himself from 1854–1856 with rescuing Turkey, and did not avail himself of the favourable opportunity to secure England, both in Europe and Asia, from Russia's encroachments.

Russia, on the other hand, rightly understood the situation. The expedition of the Allies to the Sea of

Azov, which took place in May and June, 1855; the occupation of Kertch, Yeni Kale, and Anapa; and the expedition of Omer Pasha to Sukhum Kale a few months later, were watched with the utmost suspense. There was a full appreciation of the extent of the danger, and of the consequences which the loss of the Caucasus would have for Russia. General Fadieiev, who was Governor of the Caucasus during the Crimean war, describes very vividly in his Caucasian letters, published in 1861, the state of mind which then prevailed. If Omer Pasha, the General opines, had been supported by the Allies, the position of the Russians would have been desperate. They had to hold lines 720 miles in length, and could not get together a larger army. A battle lost would have been the signal for a general rising of the warlike, half-subdued mountaineers, who might soon have made an end of Russian rule. It was a critical moment, and was let slip. The Caucasus in the hands of the Western Powers would have been an insuperable barrier to Russia's advance in Asia, and would have secured the influence of the Western Powers in the East, since whoever has a firm hold on the Caucasus dominates Persia, Turkey in Asia, and Turkestan. It was known, too, in St. Petersburg, that a railway from the coast of the Black Sea to Baku would convert Asterabad into a European port; and then there was the possibility that English and French ships would appear in the Caspian Sea, and menace the Russian inland governments. And even if the Western Powers had not utilised to its full extent the political value of the Caucasus, the situation in the East would have been completely changed, and the further advance of Russia in Central Asia would only have been possible under much more difficult conditions.

The Russian Government perceived the danger that threatened, and on the conclusion of peace immediately applied itself with all energy and recklessness to the final conquest of the Caucasus, and the removal of the Circassians to other quarters. Public opinion approved these measures, for "it was a question," as a Russian writer says, "of Russia's existence, which was in the utmost peril."

If, as far back as the sixties, ideas were so openly exchanged in Russia regarding the value of the Caucasus, how is it that the English showed so little appreciation of the discussions of Russian writers, as is apparent from their subsequent line of policy?

The English, according to their own report, are above all things practical people and not, like the French, disposed to sacrifice themselves for humanitarian objects. Consequently, they left both the Poles and Circassians to their fate. They hoped that the tenacity and patriotism of the Poles would create difficulties for the Russians for long years to come; and that the savage courage, fanaticism, and love of home of the Circassians would enable them to defend their inaccessible mountains. Lastly, they hoped that the Russians would not be able to cross the extensive, arid Kirghiz and Turcoman deserts. In so doing, they overlooked the fact that the result of an unequal contest must prove disadvantageous to the weaker, if the stronger has time enough to complete his preparations unmolested. The English regarded Poland as a ball at Russia's feet. The resistance of the Poles may possibly act as a hindrance to Russia's internal development, but it is of no importance to the external policy

H

of the Tzar's Empire. The Poles paid their taxes just like the Russians, and fought under the Russian flag both in Europe and Asia, just as they fought in France under the German flag in 1870. The resistance of the Circassians was overcome, and on their refusing to migrate to the country allotted to them, the great majority of them were expatriated, and the Caucasus lost to its heroic defenders. The Russians succeeded at length with great perseverance and small expenditure of power in possessing themselves piecemeal of the deserts of Central Asia. But a few years have elapsed since the Peace of Paris which ended the Crimean war, and England's position confronting Russia in Asia has become a much more difficult one.

A further motive for England's policy is to be found in the mistaken idea that Russia is very weak in Asia, and in the exalted opinion of the defensive power of the Mahommedan races. The small force with which Russia operated against Persia both in 1811 and 1826, gave rise to the opinion that she was unable to place larger armies in the field in Asia. In forming this opinion, the fact was overlooked (1) that since the beginning of the nineteenth century Russia's forces in the Caucasus have continually increased. They amounted in 1800 to 3,000, in 1804 to 15,000, and in 1853 to 280,000 men ; (2) that Russia retains the bulk of her troops in Europe in readiness for objects of European policy, whilst in Asia she endeavours to do with forces numerically as small as possible, though in an emergency she can considerably increase them ; (3) and lastly, that after the conquest of the Circassians, the Caucasian army must become available for employment elsewhere. Further, the defensive power of the Mahommedan races was judged by that of the Circassians and Algerians. It must, however, be observed that the military value of Asiatic races varies very considerably. The English themselves rule over more than fifty millions of Mussulmans in Asia who are far from being a match for either Circassians or Algerians. And even these latter only rouse themselves to any considerable exhibitions of strength when led by able men. Shamil invested the resistance of the Circassians, and Abd-el-Kader that of the Kabyles, with an unusual lustre. As a whole, the races of Central Asia are addicted to anarchy and are quite incapable of offering any serious resistance to a European power. It is consequently surprising that one with such an accurate knowledge of matters relating to Asia as Sir Henry Rawlinson should assert that Russia would be unable to conquer Persia, because every range of mountains would constitute a fresh Caucasus; or that a defensive alliance between Khiva, Bokhárá, Kokand, Persia, East Turkestan (Kashgaria), and Afghanistan would be unassailable by Russia!

Although the hopes entertained of the defensive power of the races of Central Asia proved quite fallacious, and Russia daily became more dangerous to India, England's policy underwent no change. She did not even endeavour to utilise the favourable opportunities which presented themselves in 1863 and 1877 to retrieve her shortcomings in 1854. We can only explain this by the total lack of comprehension of military problems both in the Cabinet and in English society itself. "The Government is a civil Government, and answerable to citizens," said the Marquis of Salisbury on 14th May, 1888. Surely it is the same on the continent. There too the Ministers, excepting those of War and Marine, are almost exclusively civilians, and the representative bodies for the most part also consist of the same. There is this difference, however, that Generals and Admirals are almost invariably entrusted with the management of the army and navy. They have a seat in the Cabinet, where they represent the military interests of the State, and view all questions from the military stand-point; whereas in England the Secretary of State for War and the First Lord of the Admiralty have had just as little military education as the rest of their colleagues, and have not learned to think with a military mind. That, however, a military is quite as necessary as a legal mind, hardly any one will wish to dispute. And in the same way as a lawyer has to decide whether or no contracts concluded by a bank or a railway company are illegal, the foreign policy of a State should be tested as to whether or no it transgresses military considerations. This is unfortunately not the case in England. Lord Wolseley, Chief of the Staff of the English army, confessed in the House of Lords that he was not admitted to the secrets of the Cabinet. Yet it is impossible to form a judgment on current questions of foreign policy without an accurate knowledge of all the details. Any other more or less well-informed person can only form a judgment on the course of foreign affairs after a certain lapse of time, and even then only on questions that have been disposed of.

We do not doubt the Marquis of Salisbury when he says that the British Government lays great stress on the opinions of experts. An expert, however, only gives his opinion when requested to do so, and only answers the questions put to him, whereas a member of the Cabinet speaks as often as he deems necessary. The Minister can gain a hearing for his opinion by bringing it forward in the proper place, in good time, before a decision is arrived at, and becoming personally responsible for it; whereas an expert, should his opinion be asked, can only state his views in a report or a committee of inquiry. The report is submitted to the Minister of the Department, who probably also reads or looks through it; the shorthand notes of a committee of inquiry may be communicated in the form of a Blue Book to the members of the Cabinet, and to both Houses of Parliament; but no one, Lord Wolseley says, takes the trouble to read a Blue Book on military subjects. This assertion of the noble lord received a striking confirmation in the course of another sitting of the House of Lords. Lord Wolseley appealed to a statement of his views on England's military position made before a Royal Commission in 1886. Lord Salisbury, who had already assumed office in 1886, was obliged to confess that he had no knowledge of Lord Wolseley's statement. Yet Lord Wolseley is the first military authority in England, and Chief of the Staff of the English army!

We readily believe that experts are employed in the solution of all military problems of a technical nature, or of those affecting army-organisation, and that due regard is paid to their opinions. In questions of foreign policy, however, every one, and especially every statesman, considers himself an authority. It is, therefore, altogether improbable that the Cabinet appeals to military authorities in such cases, especially as it would have to initiate them into several secrets of foreign politics to enable them to give a competent opinion. As, however, persons of military education have no seat in the Cabinet, England's foreign policy is not tested from the military stand-point, and, what is more, a political precedent is created without the co-operation of military talent. The foreign policy of a country should be judged from a military, no less than a diplomatic stand-point, and the neglect of military considerations may in time be productive of very evil consequences.

The want of persons of military education in the English Cabinet is the more palpable, because since 1837 a Queen, who as a woman holds aloof from military questions, has ruled England ; whereas in most of the other monarchical States of Europe the head of the State is versed in military matters, and in closest contact with military circles.

English society is, moreover, not so well informed, by far, on military topics as other European societies. The educated youth of the continent is obliged, even if pursuing some other vocation, to serve for a year, and to pass the examination for an officer of the reserve. For the last twenty years a far higher standard of knowledge has been required of officers by profession, than is the case in England even at the present day. English military literature is not on a par with the military literature of first-class European powers. Suffice it to say that Lord Wolseley was the author of the first "Soldier's Pocket-book for Field-Service," whereas in every first-class European State, Pocket-books for officers of the line, engineers, artillery and Staff have been in existence for several years past, and no Chief of the Staff of any continental army would think of undertaking such a task himself. The degree of military knowledge possessed by English society is therefore by no means adequate to qualify it for co-operating with success in the elaboration of a traditional policy which would be in harmony with military considerations, or to compensate for the want of military culture obtaining in the Cabinet.

Shortly after the termination of the Crimean war, public opinion in England became alarmed at Russia's progress in Central Asia, and since then the Central Asian question is the prevailing topic. In regard to it the most divergent views are held. Mr. Gladstone said in the House of Commons, on the 27th November, "I myself do not in the least, or in any wise fear Russia's territorial aggrandisement; indeed I regard all such talk as old women's tales." The Duke of Argyll wrote in his work, "The Eastern Question," "We ought not to regret Russia's progress in Asia, as it is of service to the interests of humanity." Sir Henry Rawlinson, on the contrary, maintains that Russia must be checked at any cost, and, as already stated (page 78), General Roberts was of opinion that a contest between England and Russia for the possession of India was within measurable distance.

The Tories, who display on the whole more taste for foreign politics than the Whigs, perceived more clearly the approaching danger. In spite of this, their policy differed from that of the Whigs only in Afghanistan. Both parties endeavoured to check Russia by diplomatic means, and although they have had frequent opportunities in the course of the last three decades of satisfying themselves as to the futility of the means hitherto employed, yet as often as English public opinion was alarmed by fresh Russian annexations or expeditions, each Cabinet in turn, whether Conservasive or Liberal, made inquiries of the Russian Foreign Office, and opened negociations. These did not retard the advance of the Russian columns for a single day, nor did they save a single Khanate, if its conquest was decided on at St. Petersburg, or if a favourable opportunity for the purpose presented itself. To Russia they could not but be welcome, as they afforded her the means of exerting pressure on England in European affairs, without allowing herself to be in any way disturbed in Asia. The steps of the London Cabinet assisted rather to enhance the lustre of Russia's success.

The question obtrudes itself upon us : How is it that the English people do not perceive the truth of the Duke of Argyll's remark, that "it is alike useless and undignified to keep on protesting against Russia's advance, when you are unable to prevent it"? This may be explained by the fact that the English are not addicted to fatalism, and that it is essentially contrary to their character calmly to await approaching dangers. Hardly any one probably is capable of enthusiasm for a negative programme (and the noble duke's advice is, surely, nothing else), and English popular sympathy cannot easily be enlisted in its favour; a positive programme, on the other hand, is hard to plan, and harder still to carry out. For this reason, every Government prefers to negociate. It thus has the appearance of doing its utmost to check the Russians, and at the same time appeases popular opinion. For these several reasons no party, no group of talented persons, enters a sufficiently vigorous protest against these futile negociations.

As we have fully described Russia's advance in Central Asia in the first chapter, we can now confine ourselves to a cursory sketch of the Anglo-Russian diplomatic negociations bearing upon this subject.

The settlement on the Sir Daria (Jaxartes), the menacing of the three Khanates whose independence was considered indispensable for the security of India, the advance on Kokand and the occupation of Chemkent occasioned such uneasiness in England, that Prince Gortchakov decided to allay it by issuing an exposition of the motives, intentions, and aims of Russian policy. In a "Circular Note" of the 21st November, 1864, he stated that Russia's position was compulsory. Like every civilised country which comes into contact with half-savage races, she was compelled to check incursions and brigandage. To put a stop to these she was obliged to reduce the population on the border to a more or less complete state of subjection. In course of time the border peoples adopted quieter habits. Then they in their turn were exposed to the attacks of more distant tribes. The State was bound to protect them, and to undertake costly expeditions to remote regions, in which ambition had far less share than imperious necessity, and the most difficult task of which was to stop at the right moment. The Imperial Government had established itself on the one hand on the Sir Daria, on the other hand on the Issik-Kul, in the hope of restoring the peace indispensable for its frontiers. In this it had not succeeded, as between the extreme points of this double line there remained a vast unoccupied desert-tract, in which the incursions of marauding tribes rendered colonisation and caravan-trading impossible. The Imperial Government consequently found itself compelled against its wish to connect the two frontier lines, one of which extends along the Chinese frontier to the Issik-Kul lake, and the other from the Sea of Aral along the course of the Sir Daria, by fortified posts; and in order to avoid the almost inevitable danger of having to proceed from reprisal to reprisal, which might lead to endless extension, "*to adopt these lines as its final limits.*" "The new line traverses a fertile, well-wooded region watered by numerous streams ; it offers advantages for colonisation, and for provisioning our garrisons. On the other hand it gives us as immediate neighbours the settled agricultural and trading population of Kokand. We confront a social population which is more reputable, more compact, less nomadic, and better organised ; and this consideration designates with geographical precision the limit to which "*interest and reason advise us to proceed, and at which they bid us halt.*"

Scarcely had this "Circular Note" been remitted to the foreign Courts, when hostilities were resumed in the Sir Daria valley. In 1865 Tashkend was occupied and in 1866 Khojend and a large portion of the Khanate of Kokand. This again occasioned great excitement in England. In a note dated 31st July, 1865, the Chief of the Foreign Office, Lord John Russell, instructed Mr. Lumley, English Chargé d'Affaires at St. Petersburg to inform the Russian Government that he regarded the fears of a conquest of India as purely chimerical. Nevertheless, to appease the resentful feelings roused in England by the Russian conquests, and to obviate future misunderstandings, Lord Russell proposed an interchange of diplomatic notes regarding the respective positions of Russia and England in Central Asia. Prince Gortchakov replied that as his Majesty the Tzar had notified his intentions regarding the new acquisitions in Asia, he considered a further declaration superfluous. In view of the apprehensions of the British Government the Tzar Alexander II. declared two months later to the British ambassador that " his Government in Central Asia had no ambitious designs whatever ; that the language of his Government on this subject was perfectly free from all reserve, or *arrièrepensée.*

Lastly, Prince Gortchakov repeatedly assured England's representative that the interests of trade, and the necessity of securing peace in the territorial acquisitions in Asia, would continue to be the final aim of Russia's policy.

In spite of these assurances, Russia developed great activity in Central Asia in the sixties. The English Government remained satisfied, notwithstanding, with these declarations, which were controverted by facts. On 26th December, 1867, Sir Stafford Northcote, Secretary of State for India in Lord Derby's Conservative Administration, wrote to the Viceroy of India: "Her Majesty's Government perceives in the progress of the Russian arms in Central Asia no ground whatever for apprehension or envy. The conquests which Russia has already made, and which in all probability she will still make, appear to the British Government as a natural consequence of the circumstances in which Russia found herself placed, and do not afford the smallest pretext for remonstrances which might engender suspicion or fear in regard to this country."

The English people by no means shared the Olympian repose of its Government. Articles on the Central Asian question appeared daily in the English papers; from day to day the apprehension of English public opinion regarding the fate of India increased, and when in 1868 Russia defeated the army of the Amir of Bokhárá, and annexed Samarkand, the British Government felt obliged to demand further explanations from the St. Petersburg Cabinet.

At the same time Sir Henry Rawlinson handed in to the British Government a "Memorandum on the Central Asian Question." The ideas evolved in this Memorandum created a tremendous sensation, and were circulated in every possible way. The well-known Russian authority on international law, and Foreign Office official, F. Martens, calls this Memorandum a historical document, as it influenced the policy of the British Government very considerably. The influence of this Memorandum, the Russian scholar opines, is visible both in the policy of the "scientific frontier," and in Lord Beaconsfield's Afghan policy.

In view of the importance of this Memorandum, we must become acquainted with its leading ideas.

In his opening remarks Sir Henry Rawlinson affirms that Russia in the Crimean war had suffered a grievous blow in Europe, but she had escaped a still greater calamity in Asia. If England had taken steps to utilise the co-operation of the Circassians, Russia might have lost all her Trans-Caucasian provinces. To obviate the possible recurrence of such a danger, Russia devoted all her energy to the war in the Caucasus. The Circassians were vanquished, and preferred expatriation in Turkey to submission. The importance of this extinction of Circassian nationality in the Caucasus was not recognised at the time in England, and has not been recognised at the present day; yet it was the turning-point of Russian Empire in the East. The Circassians formed a barrier to the tide of onward conquest. When they were once swept away, there was no obstacle to the continuous march of Russia from the Araxes to the Indus.

After these prefatory remarks Sir Henry Rawlinson describes Russia's progress in Central Asia since the Crimean war, and concludes his description with a forecast of coming events, of which the following is an epitome:—

In ten years' time Turkestan will be connected by a

railway or canal with the Caspian, the Caucasus, and hence with St. Petersburg. The Uzbek governments will have ceased to exist. Trade and cultivation will increase. Russia will be established on the Oxus, and the garrison of Turkestan will number at least 40,000 men. As long as Russia confined her attention to consolidating her acquired territory on the Oxus, we should have no occasion to complain of her neighbourhood. The danger was, therefore, not an imminent one. But Russia would not maintain this passive attitude. Entrenched upon the Oxus, she can exercise an influence on Afghanistan, and the close connexion between Bokhárá and Afghanistan, the existence of which is not generally known in England, will be of assistance to her for that purpose. The two provinces march with each other for many hundred miles. Balkh, Khulm, and Kundúz have for the last thirty years been held by the Afghans, but belong properly to Bokhárá. Maimana, Sar-i-Púl, and Andkhui are in dispute between the two States. Russia, therefore, in possessing herself of Bokhárá will inherit a multitude of Afghán grievances. The political relations of the two countries are equally intimate, and for the last thirty years Bokhárá has largely influenced the fortunes of Cabul. In 1839 Dost Mahomed took refuge in Bokhárá, and it was thence that he returned in 1841. His son returned from Bokhárá in 1842; and in all the Afghán revolutions Bokhárá has played a prominent part. In 1865 Abdur-Rahman Khán expelled his uncle Sher Ali Khán by means of an Uzbek contingent, and Bokhárá has since swarmed with Afghán refugees. Russia has consequently an Afghán contingent in her service commanded by a grandson of Dost Mahomed. She is mistress of a land which exercises great influence on Cabul. *If we remain inactive* she can at her discretion exercise a dominant influence there, or merely confine herself to the cultivation of friendly relations.

Sir Henry Rawlinson does not fear the intimate relations of Russia and Cabul on the score of an invasion. He characterises the idea of an invasion by way of Cabul as chimerical, and opines that a hostile army could only advance by way of Herát and Candahar, and not by way of Cabul and Pesháwur. Russia's influence will, however, make itself felt in a not less effective way. He notices that the Maharajah of Cashmere was said to have been negociating with the Russian authorities of Tashkend. And if Russia from her strong position on the Oxus exercises a dominant influence in Afghanistan, then every native of India who fancies he has cause for discontent will turn to Russia. The natives of India have not, indeed, any particular affection for the Russians, nor do they believe that Russian rule would be more beneficial than English. But the approach of a rival European power agitates men's minds, and change is always agreeable to Asiatics. Now the agricultural populations of India are contented with our administration. But there are, according to the report of Sir Richard Temple—who has had great experience of India—four classes "who are necessarily our enemies, and are not open to any conciliation we could reasonably use. These are—

" 1st. The priestly class, whether Hindoo or Mohammedan.

" 2nd. The military and political class.

" 3rd. The native princes and chiefs whom we have superseded ; and,

"4th. The mob, the *canaille*, the blackguardism of the whole population."

"Now if this statement be correct—and there seems no reason to doubt it—it may truly be said that we are living upon a volcano in India, which at any minute may explode and overwhelm us, and the class which would be first exposed to Afghán intrigue, set on foot by Russian propagandists, is of all others the most inflammable and virulent."

These reflections, however, by no means exhaust the subject. Russia's advance in Asia bears a striking resemblance to siege tactics. The first parallel would be the Russian frontier in the forties. Considered strategically, this was a mere line of observation. The line which Russia is now preparing to take up would constitute the second parallel, which we might call, as Sir Henry Rawlinson observes, her line of demonstration. According to General Romanovski's plan, it would be drawn from Krasnovodsk on the Caspian, south of Khiva to the Oxus, and along the course of that river to the Pamir plateau. This parallel is above 1,000 miles in advance of the first line, but it does not directly menace India, inasmuch as the intervening Afghán mountains constitute a strong military defence.

The third parallel, lastly, which Russia, if she survive revolution in Europe and catastrophe in Asia, will attempt, would be drawn from Asterabád along the Persian frontier to Herát, and from thence through the Hazáreh highlands to the Oxus, or possibly by Candahar to Cabul. Should Russia establish herself upon such a line, her position would indeed be formidable. Troops and stores might be concentrated to any extent at Asterabád. The country between the Caspian and Herát is open and admirably supplied.

Herát has often been called "the key of India," and deserves the name. It is no exaggeration to say that if Russia were once established in full strength at Herát, and her communications were secured with Asterabád, Khiva, Bokhárá, and Tashkend, all the native forces of Asia would be inadequate to expel her from this position.[1] If Russia were to possess herself of Herát, she would have the means of seriously injuring us, inasmuch as she would have the resources of Persia and Afghanistan at her disposal.

"It is not in general sufficiently considered, that in a political struggle with Russia of this nature we should not engage her upon at all equal terms. We have no natural claim on the affections or allegiance of the Persians or Afgháns, and can offer them no inducement to prefer our alliance to that of the Russians; whereas Russia has only to point to India as the traditional plunder-ground of Central Asia, to enlist their sympathies at once. The pleasant memories of the sack of Delhi by Nadir Shah, and of Ahmed Khán Abdalli's successful campaign against the Mahrattas have hardly faded. Such visions possess irresistible attractions for Asiatics, and would always incline them to side with the invader rather than the invaded. It is thus quite within the bounds of possibility that some years hence, in the event of a European war between Russia and England, Russia might launch upon India from her Herát base a force of 50,000 Persian 'Sirbaz,' disciplined and commanded by Russian officers, and fully competent to cope with our best native troops; supporting such a force with 20,000 Turcoman and

[1] It must not be forgotten that since the above was written by Sir Henry Rawlinson the communications referred to have been perfected by the construction of the Trans-Caspian railway.—ED.

Afghán horse, the best irregular cavalry in the world, and by a small body of Russian troops to give strength and consistency to the invading army. An invasion of this nature might, it is true, not jeopardise our hold on India, for our garrisons, reinforced from England, would probably be equal to the emergency; but, at any rate, we should have to fight for our lives, for our existence, and should be quite powerless to strike a blow against Russia in return."

No wonder this Memorandum created a tremendous sensation. The accurate knowledge of the circumstances, the fine talent of observation, and the great descriptive power of the author were still further enhanced by his personal authority. Twenty years have since elapsed, and part of his predictions have been literally verified. A few years after, Russia took up the line which Sir Henry calls the second parallel; now she has already established herself along the greater portion of the so-called third parallel, and it will not be long before she possesses herself of the entire line so minutely defined by Sir Henry Rawlinson. Lastly, the description of the dangers which Russia's advance in Central Asia conjures up for England's hold on India is so clear and precise, that little can be added to it at the present day. It is, moreover, perfectly free from exaggeration. It is evident that the author of the Memorandum endeavoured to appeal to the reason of his fellow-countrymen, and not to affect their fears. Thus, for instance, he describes the danger of a Persian invasion which would be led by Russian officers. Any one who reads the Memorandum attentively can easily perceive that Russia, if in possession of Herát, could also move forward a strong Russian force, inasmuch as, according to Sir Henry, troops and material can be concentrated to any extent in Asterabád, and the country between that port and Herát is rich and open. And that a Russian invasion, supported by Persian and Afghan troops, would represent a danger of a totally different description to a Persian one, no one probably would dispute. The sober statement of facts in this Memorandum accounts for the lasting impression which it has created.

Though Sir Henry Rawlinson claims our admiration as a thorough Asiatic expert and a subtle observer, yet, as a statesman, we cannot accord him so high a rank. His advice is not that of the sober politician, who thoroughly weighs the difficulties of the task which he has set himself, but rather of the optimist who allows himself to be only too easily persuaded of the possibility of that which he desires. Thus, for instance, he believes that a confederacy of the Uzbek Khanates, Kashgar, Persia and Afghanistan would be unassailable. We look upon this assertion as chimerical. Further, he assures us that without Persia's co-operation Russia can never establish herself in Herát and keep up her communications with Asterabád. To deprive Russia of Persia's co-operation, he would regain the lost ground in Persia, and strengthen ·English influence at Teheran. As former Envoy and Minister at the Court of Persia, he should, however, know that Persia relying on England for support would be a challenge to Russia, and, thrown upon her own resources at the critical moment, would be no more capable of opposing a Russian army than she was in 1804, 1811, and 1827. Lastly, he advocates the adoption of Lord Auckland's policy of making Afghanistan a strong and friendly power; criticises the policy of "masterly inactivity" pursued by Lord Law rence, and recommends the completion of the communications with Afghanistan, more especially the construction of the railway from Lahore to Pesháwur, and the occupation of Quetta beyond the Bolan Pass. No objection can be taken to the completion of the communications or the occupation of Quetta ; but this is not Sir Henry's chief solicitude. It is probable, he opines, that the Afghán tribes might regard the erection of a fortress above the passes as a menace. In that case the idea should be abandoned, as it would not be worth while risking the rupture of our friendly intercourse for so small an object. We cannot, Sir Henry says, permit Russia to advance to Cabul or to represent herself there as a friendly power prepared to protect the Afgháns against the English, if we would not jeopardise India. England must obtain a dominant position at Cabul. Afghanistan must become a strong and friendly power. If, however, we remain inactive, Russia will secure her position at Cabul.

This would be all perfectly correct, if Afghanistan possessed the elements essential to the formation of a strong power, and if perfect reliance could be placed on her. We know, however, that up to the thirties Afghanistan consisted of a collection of disunited and independent tribes, which were first drawn more closely together by Dost Mahomed ; that it possessed neither an old hereditary dynasty, nor a homogeneous population, and that the dominant race of Afgháns is split up into numerous tribes and clans animated by a love of individual liberty, and inclined to revolt whenever a change of rulers takes place, or on any other like occasion. It is therefore hardly to be supposed that under such circumstances Afghanistan can become a strong and reliable power.

As long as Russia was separated from Afghanistan by independent states, Afghanistan lay exclusively within the sphere of England's power. The situation becomes a totally different one, however, now that Russia has moved her boundary pillars up to those of Afghanistan, especially if she organises her newly-acquired territory and firmly establishes herself in it. Afghanistan, which is too weak to oppose either Russians or English, will now be between hammer and anvil. If the Amir seeks the support of England, Russia can create anarchical disturbances in Afghanistan. We need only refer to what Sir Henry Rawlinson tells us in his Memorandum of the Afghán revolutions, the intimate relations of Bokhárá with Cabul, and the Afghán refugees in Bokhárá. Little reliance can, moreover, be placed on Afghán friendship. In Sir Henry's words (which we quoted before) : " We have no natural claim on the affections or allegiance of the Afgháns, no inducement to hold out to them, which should lead them to prefer our alliance to that of the Russians ; whereas Russia has only to point to India as the traditional plunder-ground of Central Asia, and she at once enlists their sympathies in her behalf! " This is perfectly correct, and we have therefore, we think, proved from Sir Henry Rawlinson's own statements that in a serious emergency, when most needed, Afghanistan will not be found sufficiently strong or reliable.

The British Government recognised this fact as little as Sir Henry Rawlinson. Both believed that a skilful policy in Asia would suffice to protect India, and made no endeavour to avail themselves of the opportunities for weakening Russia which occurred from time to time.

"Sir Henry Rawlinson's Memorandum," observes M.

Martens, "created such a powerful impression, that the feeling of uneasiness and mistrust which predominates in the Memorandum has ever since been apparent in the diplomatic intercourse of the two powers."

At the beginning of 1869 Lord Clarendon put the following question to the Russian Ambassador, Baron Brunnow: "How public opinion in England could be appeased, and complications avoided between the two Governments respecting Central Asia." The English Minister proposed that a "zone preventing any contact" should separate the Asiatic possessions of the two countries. In his despatch of 7th March, 1869, Prince Gortchakov instructed Baron Brunnow to inform the British Government that nothing could coincide more exactly with the Tzar's thoughts. Further, he was to invite the British Government to forsake all its old prejudices; and lastly, to repeat the positive assurance "that His Imperial Majesty regarded Afghanistan as quite outside the sphere within which Russia might be called upon to exercise her influence. He meditated no interference or interposition which might militate against the independence of that country."

England would not, however, recognise Afghanistan as neutral territory, and proposed the Oxus as the ideal line which should divide the possessions of the two countries. Russia, for her part, would not accept the Oxus-line. Lengthy negociations on this question ensued, and the respective foreign Ministers, Lord Clarendon and Prince Gortchakov, even discussed the matter when they met at Heidelberg in September, 1869, but without coming to an agreement.

Shortly after, in May, 1870, the British Government opened negociations with the St. Petersburg Cabinet regarding a delimitation of the frontiers of Afghanistan, adopting as a basis for its action the Russian assurance that Afghanistan lay outside the sphere of Russian influence. These negociations lasted nearly three years. Russia disputed the Amir's claims to Maimana, Andkhui, Balkh, Kunduz, Badakhshán and Wakhán, and eventually agreed to the line proposed by England, thus affording "a fresh proof of her amicable and conciliatory disposition." On 12th January, 1873, Prince Gortchakov signified his concurrence that the Amu Daria (Oxus), from the junction of the Kokcha river as far as Khoja Saléh should form the Northern limit; that the provinces of Badakhshán and Wakhán should be incorporated with Afghanistan, and a line from Khoja Saléh to the Persian frontier be determined by which Andkhui and Maimana would be included in Afghanistan, whilst Merv remained outside the frontier. Finally, Russia agreed to the complete independence of Afghanistan both as regards internal and external affairs.

At first sight, says General Haymerle in "Ultima Thule," it appears remarkable that Russia accommodated herself so completely to England in a question of such importance as this. A thorough investigation, however, of these apparently large concessions reveals the fact that Russia gave next to nothing. She retained perfect liberty of action in Central Asia, and as to Afghanistan, she had already proposed in 1869 to recognise that country as neutral territory. In the settlement of 1873 she treated this question of independence as involving a principle, well aware that, at the time, this would only embarrass the English. Russia was, in fact, fully occupied with Khiva and Turkestan, whilst England had many questions to settle with Afghanistan; and in the event of England's violating the independence of Afghanistan, Russia could declare that she considered herself in consequence released from her engagements. M. Martens, who is in a position to know the intentions of the St. Petersburg Cabinet, stated in 1880 that as Afghanistan had become subject to England the agreement of 1873 had now merely a historical and theoretical value. Finally, a portion only of the North-East frontier of Afghanistan was demarcated, and even the line east of the junction of the Kokcha with the Amu Daria was not definitely fixed. It is therefore easily conceivable that Russia, engaged in preparing for the expedition against Khiva, should have made these apparent concessions to political expediency.

England seemed perfectly satisfied, but this satisfaction was not to be of long duration. Shortly after, Russia undertook an expedition against Khiva which ended in the conquest of that Khanate and the annexation by Russia of part of the country. The Khan of Khiva was compelled to declare himself "the obedient servant of the Emperor of All the Russias," and "to renounce the right of entertaining direct relations with neighbouring sovereigns and Khans."

These conditions of peace evoked expressions of indignation in England, and contributed very largely to the development of distrustful and hostile feelings between her and Russia, inasmuch as they were in direct contravention of the declarations which Count Schouvalov had made to the London Cabinet in January, 1873. Count Schouvalov had, namely, been sent on a special mission to pacify England in regard to the expedition against Khiva, and had then declared that "not only was it far from the intention of the Emperor to take possession of Khiva, but positive orders had been prepared to prevent it, and directions given that the conditions imposed should be such as would not in any way lead to the prolonged occupation of Khiva."[1] The English therefore taxed Russia with having wilfully broken public faith, and unmistakable engagements, and complained that even the Tzar's word had not been kept. Russia's friends replied to this that "communication of an intention did not amount to an absolute promise. A declaration or an assertion with reference to political matters was not necessarily an engagement."

We have no intention of discussing the question which of these two views is the correct one. We merely wish to state that in this case English diplomacy honestly fulfilled its duty. Since 1869 it had kept a strict watch on the proceedings of the Russian Government and had persistently inquired whether an expedition against Khiva was decided on. In the course of 1870 and 1871 the interpellations of the British representative increased in urgency, and the Russian Foreign Office had the civility to inform the British Ambassador of Russia's communications with the Khan of Khiva. In March, 1872, Lord Loftus wrote to his Government that the expedition against Khiva appeared to be fixed for the spring of 1873. At length English diplomacy succeeded in securing the despatch of Schouvalov's mission, and in eliciting positive declarations from the Tzar. The British Government cannot therefore be reproached with having maintained an apathetic attitude in this instance. On the contrary it exhausted all the expedients of diplomacy, and its labours even met with marked success. In spite of this the Khivan expedition was not suspended, the Khan of Khiva lost his independence and was compelled to cede part of his country to Russia.

[1] "England and Russia in the East," p. 317.

This incident should surely have sufficed to convince the British Government that England is powerless to arrest the advance of Russia in Central Asia by means of diplomacy. Strange to say, several politicians and political writers retain the opinion even to the present day that Russia may be checked by a determined and skilful policy. Lord Granville also derived a false impression from his ill-success in the Khivan incident, and no later than the 7th January, 1874, instructed the British Ambassador at St. Petersburg to direct the attention of the Russian Government to the dangers which threatened the friendly relations of the two Governments in consequence of the altered situation resulting from the conquest of Khiva in Central Asia. Further, he deemed it his duty to acquaint the Russian Government with the apprehensions which had arisen in Afghanistan and India from the reports circulated concerning a Russian expedition against Merv, and the savage tribes of that region, and expressed a fear that if Merv were occupied, a collision between the Amir of Afghanistan and the Russians would be almost unavoidable. Lastly, he declared that the British Government regarded the independence of Afghanistan as a condition of the highest importance for the welfare and security of British India, and the peace of Asia.

In his reply of 21st January, 1874, the Russian Chancellor reiterated Russia's intention to regard Afghanistan as outside her sphere of action. Regarding Merv, however, which was far from the frontier awarded to Afghanistan, the Chancellor could perceive no just ground for the claim of England to constitute herself the privileged protector of that spot which had hitherto served as a refuge to a race of brigands known as Turcomans.

This reply caused a great deal of bad feeling in London, as it intimated, observes M. Martens, that Russia was not disposed to give in to all the representations and protests which the British Government might make in regard to her relations with the independent States of Central Asia. Nevertheless, the London Cabinet assailed the Russian Government with such frequent inquiries as to its intentions regarding Merv, and the interest in Merv increased throughout England to such an extent that thenceforward, as the Duke of Argyll says, a very tenacious propensity for a thing or person might be designated by the word "mervousness."

In February, 1874, Disraeli's Ministry came into power. True to Tory tradition, it supported Turkey as far as possible, and according as the crisis in the East increased, the relations of Russia and England became more strained. The negotiations on the Central Asian question were, however, diligently carried on, and the English representative, to quote M. de Martens, "never tired of demanding explanations regarding supposed expeditions against this or that place."

"To put an end once for all to England's claims—to control every step taken by the Russian troops in Central Asia and every measure adopted there by the Russian authorities—the Imperial Government decided to draw up a continuous and detailed statement of the diplomatic negociations regarding Central Asia. The Memorandum compiled for this purpose, dated 17th April, 1875, was communicated to the London Cabinet in a Despatch signed by Prince Gortchakov of the same date."

After an introductory recapitulation of the negociations with England, the Memorandum protests against the assumption that the Russian Government had entered into any positive engagements, the fact being that it had merely made a voluntary and amicable communication of its intention not to pursue a policy of annexation or conquest in Central Asia. Russia had indeed deviated in some measure from this programme, circumstances having compelled her to do so against her wish. But for the future also the Emperor of Russia had no intention whatever of extending the frontiers of his dominions on the side of Bokhárá, Krasnovodsk, or the Atrek.

These intentions could not, however, be taken as formal promises, and "it had always been agreed that both parties should retain liberty of action and judgment respecting the measures necessary for their own security." Further, the following fundamental principles were agreed to :—

1. "That an antagonism in those regions between the two Governments would be contrary to their respective interests, and to the civilising mission to which each in the sphere of its natural influence is called."

2. "That to this end it is desirable to establish an intermediate zone, to avoid direct contact."

3. "That Afghanistan must form this zone, provided the independence of that country be placed beyond the reach of any encroachment by either party."

The British Government felt constrained to rectify certain expressions used in the Memorandum. The arrangements made with regard to the frontiers of Afghanistan and the intermediate zone were viewed by it in a different light. It set the highest value on the recognition of its liberty of action in regard to Afghanistan under any circumstances and in any event. Afghanistan ought indeed to remain independent, but under the influence of England. Further, Lord Derby stated emphatically that the occupation of Merv would cause a collision with Afghanistan, and thanked Prince Gortchakov for his assurance that the Emperor of Russia had no intention of extending the frontiers of his dominions on the side of Bokhárá, Krasnovodsk, or the Atrek.

In a Despatch to Count Schouvalov of 15th February, 1876, the Russian Imperial Chancellor assents to the arrangements made regarding the frontiers of Afghanistan, which country remains outside Russia's sphere of action, regards the *pour-parlers* concerning the intermediate zone as concluded, and declares that the two States, *under full reservation of their liberty of action*, will avoid as far as possible direct contact, as well as collisions between the Asiatic states that are drawn within their respective spheres of influence.

Lord Derby had no objections to make to this authoritative expression of the view which both Russia and England took of the situation. *Entire freedom of action for the future*, observes M. Martens, was now the basis of all operations in Central Asia.

Whenever a momentary advantage might be gained by it, the Russian Government was lavish of communications regarding its intentions. Thus, for instance, when the Tzar was to visit London, Prince Gortchakov communicated to the British Government that the Emperor had forbidden his Generals to undertake any expedition against the Tekkeh Turcomans in the direction of Merv. Such communications never failed of their effect, although the Russian Government had itself explained the difference between intentions and formal promises, and notwithstanding the undeniable fact that both intentions and instructions can be altered at any time.

Meanwhile Russia continued to advance unceasingly in Central Asia. In 1876 General Kaufmann annexed Kokand; and General Lomakin from his Krasnovodsk base undertook expeditions against the Turcomans nearly every year. Soon after this the Anglo-Russian relations became strained owing to the Russo-Turkish war, and Disraeli summoned some Indian regiments to Malta. Russia's answer to this step was a counter movement in Central Asia. In June, 1878, several Russian columns set out from Samarkand and Krasnovodsk for the Afghán frontier, and a diplomatic mission headed by General Stolietov came to Cabul, where it met with a brilliant reception.

Thereupon an English mission was announced to arrive at Cabul. Sher-Ali deferred his reply on various pretexts, and when at length the English Envoy, Sir Neville Chamberlain, by order of his Government advanced to the frontier fortress of Ali-Musjid, the Governor there in obedience to superior orders forbade him to proceed further.

Whilst this was occurring, the Berlin Congress put an end to the war, and Russia no longer required to exert pressure on England in Central Asia, the more so as she was too exhausted by the war with Turkey to commence at once another war for supremacy in Asia. General Stolietov, who was to hand over the ratification of the treaty at Cabul, was therefore instructed to inform the Amir, that Russia would for the present abandon warlike action against England.

Although the decision of the Russian Government was already made known to the Amir on the 8th October, and the English ultimatum requiring him to dismiss the Russian embassy, to receive a permanent Mission, and to tender an apology, was not presented to him until the 8th November, he still refused to comply. On the 21st November British troops crossed the Afghan frontier, and in 1879 peace was concluded at Gandamak.

Thereby the Amir engaged to adjust his relations with foreign States in accordance with England's advice, and to place them under her direct control. (Art. 3.)

An English envoy with a large escort was to reside permanently in Cabul as a stationary diplomatic representative, and to have the right of sending English agents to the Afghán frontiers. (Art. 4.)

The politico-commercial relations between Afghanistan and India were to be regulated by special arrangement. The valleys of Kurram, Pishin, and Sibi were handed over to England, the latter, in return, engaging to pay the Amir in cash the surplus revenue derived therefrom after deducting the cost of administration. The British Government, moreover, assumed the control of the Khyber and Michni passes. (Art. 5.)

In return, the Amir was to receive a yearly subsidy of £120,000 sterling.

In virtue of this agreement Afghanistan ceased to be an independent State. Russia looked on calmly at the course of events, and redoubled her efforts in Trans-Caspian territory. As we have already seen in the first chapter, General Skobelev took Geok Tepe in 1881 ; in 1884 Merv submitted to the White Tzar, and shortly after, his troops took possession of Old Sarakhs.

Needless to remark, the seizure of Merv produced tremendous excitement in England, and a flood of despatches. At St. Petersburg the report was at first contradicted, and on its being confirmed it was said that the Tzar was exceedingly displeased and enraged at the conduct of his generals in Turkestan. In short, the history of the treaty with Khiva repeated itself in every detail; and the explanations awaited from St. Petersburg had not yet arrived when the news of the capture of Sarakhs, the truth of which was at first denied by Lord Granville in Parliament, reached London. Soon, however, this news was also confirmed, and the London Cabinet had occasion to satisfy itself for the hundredth time of the inefficacy of diplomacy either to stay the execution of the plans laid by Russia in Central Asia, or to undo accomplished facts.

We now come to the question of the settlement of the Afghán frontier between Khoja Saléh and Sarakhs. As we know, the Northern limit of Afghanistan eastward of Khoja Saléh was definitively settled in 1873, whilst that portion from the Oxus to the Persian frontier was merely generally defined as coinciding approximately with a line drawn from Khoja Saléh to Sarakhs. Agreeably to this definition, Prince Gortchakov asserted, in a despatch of 21st January, 1874, that Merv was far from the frontier awarded to Afghanistan. Now England wished to created a neutral zone beyond Afghanistan. Russia desired that Afghanistan should serve as the intervening buffer, and in 1876 the Russian Chancellor declared "the discussion respecting the neutral zone closed, as leading to no practical result." In a later phase of the negociations the English demanded a topographical delimitation, whilst Russia insisted on an ethnographical one. Now, owing to Russia's conquests in Turkestan, the question of the frontier-settlement acquired a greater actuality, and the diplomatic correspondence on this subject became more animated. In

1882 M. de Giers reiterated the assurance that Afghanistan was outside Russia's sphere of action, and declared that he attached great importance to the settlement of the portion of Afghán frontier which had not been accurately defined. Finally, on the 29th April, 1884, Lord Granville accepted Russia's proposals, and on the 5th July of the same year it was decided that a mixed commission should meet in Turkestan on the 1st October to settle *in loco* the frontier in question, and to draw up a joint report for the consideration of the two Cabinets. The frontier settlement commission was not destined, however, to meet immediately. On behalf of Great Britain a numerous English commission appeared in the beginning of November, under the lead of General Lumsden, with an escort of 1,000 men. The Russian Government did not so much as send its commissioners to the place. The illness of General Zelenoï, who was to take part in the labours of the commission on behalf of the Russians, served as a pretext for the absence of the Russian commissioners. In February, 1885, M. de Giers sent the engineer Lessar, who had lived ten years in Turkestan and had made a preliminary survey of the railway from Askabad to Sarakhs and Merv, on a special mission to London, to negociate the question of the frontier-settlement direct with the British Cabinet.

Meanwhile both Russian and Afghán troops continued to advance nearer and nearer to the Northern frontier of Afghanistan, and occupied lands in dispute, so as to create accomplished facts. This gave rise to protests on the part of both Russians and English, and on 17th March it was arranged that Russians and Afgháns alike should remain stationary in their respective positions on the frontier. In spite of this arrangement, General Komarov, on the 30th March, attacked the

Afgháns at Pul-i-Kisti on the Kushkh river, because, as he asserted, their behaviour was provocative, and drove them from Panjdeh.

It must be admitted that although the question of the frontier settlement was negociated on Russia's initiative, the action of the St. Petersburg Cabinet in regard to it was anything but accommodating. On the whole, since the Eastern crisis, the relations of the two Cabinets had been none of the friendliest, and Russia was very glad of the opportunity to repay the London Cabinet for its attitude during the Berlin Congress. Russia's increased activity in Central Asia may also be partly attributed to the same motive, and on coming into contact with the Afgháns she acted in accordance with her traditions by endeavouring to compromise the English in the eyes of the Afgháns. She beat the Afgháns in sight of the English officers, and finally secured concessions in the delimitation of the frontier. Thereby Russia proved to the Afgháns that the English were incapable of protecting them from the White Tzar.

After the occupation of Merv and Sarakhs the relations of Russia and England became so strained that both powers proceeded to arm. The course of the negociations on the frontier settlement were by no means calculated to lessen the friction, and in March, 1885, a squadron was held in readiness to sail from Portsmouth, the Reserves and Militia were called out, and two Indo-British army corps were mobilised. We are not so accurately informed regarding Russia's preparations, as in a despotically governed State military arrangements can be kept secret, and indeed are so in Russia. At any rate, according to information received from St. Petersburg at the beginning of March, the Governor and Commander of the Caucasus—Prince

Dondoukov-Korsakov—arrived in St. Petersburg to take part in the deliberations on the Campaign in Central Asia; an army of 35,000 men was to be transported thither from Baku across the Caspian.

The English now thought it time to enter into negociations with Abdurrahman Khan with a view to a closer connection and alliance. To this end the Viceroy of India, Lord Dufferin, invited the Amir to an interview at Rawal Pindi, at which place he arrived on 30th March. A great number of troops with a strong force of artillery had been massed there. The Rajas of half India, all the notabilities of the country, among them his Royal Highness the Duke of Connaught, were present, in order to stamp the meeting as one pregnant with far-reaching significance.

Suddenly a report got abroad that on 30th March, *i.e.*, on the very day of the Amir's entry into Rawal-Pindi, a collision had occurred between Russian and Afghán troops. This news occasioned the greatest excitement both in India and England. Liberals and Tories were unanimous in their denunciation of Russia, and called loudly for war. The British Government, however, had many cares in the Soudan, in Egypt, on the Congo, in Canada, etc., and did not wish to go to war with Russia alone without allies. Russia was occupied with the Bulgarian question. Consequently it did not accord with the wishes of either the Russians or the English to bring the dispute to a head, and the two Governments endeavoured to shift the responsibility of having caused the collision on to each other's shoulders. The British Government demanded the disavowal and recall of General Komarov. The Russian Government conferred distinction on him, and maintained that the Afgháns had provoked the collision, and General

Komarov had merely done his duty. Finally the matter was allowed to drop, and the negociations on the Afghán frontier were resumed. In 1886 an agreement was arrived at regarding the portion of frontier between the Heri-Rud and Murgab rivers. Russia relinquished the Zulfikar Pass; England, in the name of the Afgháns, Panjdeh. At length the two Governments succeeded in July, 1887, in coming to an understanding in regard to the Russo-Afghán frontier from Persia to the Oxus.

This agreement gave general satisfaction in England, and resulted in a marked improvement in the Anglo-Russian relations. At that time Russia was concentrating troops on her Western frontier, and her relations with Germany and Austria were not very friendly. No wonder, then, she exerted herself to get on a better footing with England. Yet if we scrutinise this agreement more closely, we find that, just as in 1873, Russia surrendered next to nothing. The settlement of a frontier does not, surely, involve an undertaking not to transgress it on any consideration. Russia has acquired within the last few years such an extent of territory in Asia that she requires rest to organise her new possessions, and to connect them with her bases. In this direction she is displaying great activity, and has but lately completed the Trans-Caspian railway. Lastly, Afghanistan possesses internally so little consistency, that Russia has only to wish it, to find a pretext for interference in Afghán affairs. As a case in point we instance the insurrection of the Ghilzais in 1886, and the rising organised by Ishak Khan at Balkh and Maimana in 1888. Several discontented, high-placed Afgháns are now living in Bokhárá, and Russia can instigate an insurrection in Afghanistan as often as she pleases.

Should Shignan, Balkh, Maimana, or any other Khanate north of the Hindu Kush revolt, and submit to the White Tzar, Russia can occupy any one of them, before the British can hasten to the aid of the Amir, and she is as little likely to relax her hold on any territory thus acquired as she did on Khiva or Merv in their day. As an eye-witness Lieutenant Yate affirms that the loss of Panjdeh roused great animosity against England in Afghanistan. It is therefore quite possible that on any further loss of territory Russia may win over the Amir to her cause. Did not the British in 1879, after the assault of the Cabul citadel, obtain possession of the copy of a treaty between Sher Ali Khan and General Kaufmann?

"It is in the logic of facts," General Sobolev, Chief of the Asiatic Department of the Russian Staff, remarks, "that the Hindu Kush, the natural boundary of India, should shortly form the frontier of Russia, and that the province of Herát should fall into Russia's hands." At all events it is undeniable that England is powerless to prevent it.

Russia's position in regard to Persia is still more advantageous. Since the conquest of Turcomania the Russian frontier is conterminous with that of Persia for a distance of over 1,100 miles, and the army of the Caucasus is strong enough by itself to crush any opposition on the part of the Shah. The subjugation of the Turcomans, who were reputed to be the best horsemen and the bravest warriors in all Asia, enhanced, as the distinguished Hungarian Orientalist Arminius Vambéry says, Russia's prestige in the eyes of all Asiatics. This was associated with a feeling of gratitude for deliverance from the raids of the Turcomans, who advanced in small bands to a distance of 100 to

150 miles, causing great consternation not only in Persia, but also in Bokhárá, Khiva, and even up to the very ramparts of Maimana. These incursions were felt most acutely along the northern frontier of Persia, hence Vambéry in his book "The Coming Struggle for India" remarks: "Along the whole route through Khorasan, beginning from Shahrud, to Meshed and Sarakhs, but more particularly in the districts adjoining the newly-acquired Russian territory, namely, in Kabushan, Bujnurd, and Deregez, people are now most anxious to exhibit their sympathies with the Northern conqueror. Russian dresses are becoming the fashion of the day, Russian drinks get more and more into favour, every man of note strives to learn the Russian language, and there is no exaggeration in saying that Russia has already morally conquered the northern slopes of the Kopet mountains to such an extent that the physical conquest is only a question of time."

Lieutenant Yate, a member of the Afghán Boundary Commission, made a trip to Meshed in 1886, and bore out the statement that "Russophilism predominates in Khorasan."

Against such a state of affairs the diplomatic art of a Rawlinson or a Drummond Wolff can avail nothing. Persia cannot risk a breach, nay, not even strained relations, with Russia. She has to appease the Russian Government, which is angry at the concessions made to the British on the Karun river, by corresponding concessions to Russian economic interests. And that the Russian consul at Meshed will soon exercise a predominant influence in Khorasan, no one probably will question.

From the above survey of the Anglo-Russian diplomatic relations in regard to Asia in the nineteenth century it is evident that Great Britain is unable to arrest Russia's advance in Central Asia; and a careful study of the present situation leads us to the conclusion that in the future she will be equally powerless to check Russia's progress on the northern frontier of Persia and Afghanistan.

IV

STRATEGICAL RELATIONS OF THE TWO STATES

The strategical relations of two States are not immovably fixed. They vary in accordance with changes of frontier, of army organisation, internal politics, the entire political situation, and especially of alliances. They are, moreover, much affected by the prosperity or decline of whole provinces, the construction of railroads, the erection of fortifications, and so forth. If this be so even with neighbouring States, what a much greater change must the strategical relations of two widely separated States undergo, when their frontiers are brought nearer together by conquests.

The accuracy of this assertion may be easily demonstrated in regard to Russia and Great Britain in Asia.

At the beginning of the present century Russia's Asiatic frontiers were thousands of miles distant from the British possessions in India. Central Asia was then less known than the interior of Africa is at the present day. People had merely a dim idea of the "impassable" deserts, and the "inaccessible" mountains, which stretch between Siberia and the Indus. And although a great military genius took a lively interest in the idea of an invasion of India, and even discussed its practicability with the Tzar, yet at that time an invasion of India by way of Russia might be regarded as chimerical.

Even at the time of the Crimean war the British believed that the resistance of the Circassians, and the deserts of Central Asia, would suffice to protect India.

In the sixties too, after the conquest of the Caucasus by Russia, the expatriation of its heroic defenders, and the occupation of Tashkend, Lord Palmerston declared that "very many generations must yet come and go ere Russia succeeded in demolishing the Tartar barrier, and approaching the country between Bokhárá and India." In Russia, on the contrary, clearer views were entertained of the value of the Caucasus and the difficulties of a further advance in Central Asia. The strategical relations of these two European powers were already no longer the same as at the beginning of the century. After Shamil's capture, Prince Bariatynski, Governor of the Caucasus, submitted the plan of a campaign against India to the Tzar Alexander II. The plan was approved of, but it was thought that its execution must be deferred to a time when it would be possible for a corps marching from Siberia, *i.e.*, from the Issyk Kul lake, on Kashmir to compel the adversary to divide his forces, whilst a column proceeding from Orenburg towards Turkestan would be able to cover the advance of the main body marching on India from Asterabad. At that time a campaign against India from the Caucasus base was, indeed, a very difficult undertaking, but not by any means chimerical!

During the last twenty-five years Russia's extension has assumed proportions which were never anticipated. The Uzbek Khanates and the Turcoman tribes were subjugated in rapid succession; a railway now connects

Timour's ancient capital of Samarkand with the Tzar's Empire; and Russia is in possession of fertile oases which, being contiguous to the Afghán frontier and within a convenient distance of the Trans-Caspian Railway, are well adapted for concentrating large bodies of troops. England has thus lost, at all events for India, the advantage of unassailability which, thanks to her insular position, and the distance of her colonies from European States, she had hitherto enjoyed. She has become, as regards her most valuable possession, a continental country.

In England they are beginning to see the truth of this. The *Broad Arrow* of 7th January, 1884, writes: "If we wish to keep India, we must defend it, since we are about to become a continental State in regard to Russia. Sooner or later we shall be forced to fight a war with Russia on as gigantic a scale as modern European wars." This is not, however, the generally accepted view, even in military circles. In the issue of 17th March of the above important military organ we read in a review of J. Seymour Keay's pamphlet "The Great Imperial Danger": "We quite agree with the remarks which Sir Richard Temple made in the House of Commons last week." Sir Richard had proved that Great Britain was "by no means bound to engage Russia on the Central Asian frontiers of India, inasmuch as we are protected by the most colossal natural barrier and the strongest fortifications in the world, and our position within these limits is almost impregnable. Should a war break out between these two great nations, the choice of the scene of operations rests entirely with us, and the first shots will perhaps be fired on the shores of the Baltic, the Black Sea, or even the Sea of Japan."

Before discussing the question, how and with what chances of success a war may be waged between Great Britain and Russia, we must glance at the "fighting power" of each country.

For the last twenty years the continental powers have been vying with each other in placing their military resources on a formidable footing. According to the *Revue Générale de l'Etat-Major* of July, 1888, the aggregate military expenditure of the European states rose from 2,280,000,000 francs in 1869 to 3,550,000,000 in 1887; within the same period the peace strength of 2,195,000 men increased to 3,092,000, and the number of persons under obligation to military service was trebled, from 6,918,000 to 19,000,000; of which number 11,270,000 ranked as efficient. When the laws now in force have come into full operation, the number of men liable to military service in Europe will have increased to 29,750,000.

Russia's Land Forces.

Russia has kept pace with this movement, and nearly every year has seen an increase in her military resources. At one time the annual number of recruits has been augmented, at another, new regiments added to the establishment, or existing ones strengthened. Thus, for instance, of late years the number of squadrons in the cavalry regiments has been raised from four to six, part of the reserve battalions have been converted into reserve regiments, the rifle-battalions doubled, new native regiments raised in the Caucasus, and so on; in short, since the Russo-Turkish war the cadres of the regular troops have been augmented by 276 battalions, 90 squadrons, and 35 batteries. With every succeeding year, too, the Russian army has been made readier for active service, and the Russian Staff has exerted itself to attain as high a capacity as possible for rapid mobilisation. And although, owing to Russia's gigantic extension, the small carrying capacity of the railways, the mixed nationality of the soldiers forming the complement of the various regiments (75 per cent. of Russians, and 25 per cent. of Poles), and the concentration of troops on Russia's western frontier, her mobilisation may occupy a somewhat longer time than that of Austria, Germany, or France, yet it will in all probability be effected in a very different style to that of 1877. In 1888, 252,000 recruits were passed for the regular army, and 15,000 for the Cossacks. The active army, including Militia and similar formations (exclusive of the supplementary reserve, general levy, etc.) numbers 2,924,000. On a peace-footing the Russian army numbers 987 battalions, 330 squadrons, 238 "sotnias," and 398 batteries, and on a war-footing, 1,654 battalions, 442 squadrons, 710 "sotnias," and 535 batteries. The active forces stationed in Russia-in-Europe and the Caucasus are, with the exception of the 24th infantry-division, which is quartered in Finland, divided into larger bodies, and form 21 army corps. An army corps consists of 2 to 3 infantry-divisions, 2 to 3 brigades of artillery, and 1 cavalry division, and accordingly numbers 32 to 48 battalions, 4 cavalry regiments, 12 to 18 field batteries, and 2 batteries of horse-artillery. It is self-evident that such an increase of military resources has entailed a considerable expenditure; the army budget for 1888 amounted, for example, to 208,400,000 roubles (about 21 to 22 million pounds sterling).

England's Land Forces.

In England, on the contrary, each successive Ministry, whether Liberal or Conservative, has endeavoured to diminish military expenditure as far as possible, so as to create a favourable budget for its party. The result of this was that in 1884 the British army numbered 43,000 men less than in 1860. Since 1884 the British army has indeed been gradually increased by 20,000 men, yet it numbers at present 23,000 men less than in 1860, 16,000 less than in 1862, 8,000 less than in 1863, as Lord Wolseley stated in the House of Lords on 15th May, 1888. Of the 20,000 additional men since 1884, 10,000 are permanently employed in India.

The British army consists of the standing army, the militia, yeomanry, and volunteers. According to the Army Estimates for 1888 and 1889 the figures of the various categories were as follows:—

	Establishment.	Actual number, or effectives.
Regular Army (at home and in the Colonies)	139,801	138,575
Regular Army in India	71,691	73,666
Army Reserve, I. Class	52,000	50,555
„ „ II. „	3,200	4,100
Militia (including Cadres, Militia Reserve, and Channel Islands' Militia)	141,593	121,443
Yeomanry (including Staff)	14,255	11,424
Volunteers (including Staff)	257,834	228,038
Total	680,374	627,801

Even 680,000 men is not a considerable number when compared with the armies of the great European Powers, which are counted by millions, and yet the actuals as compared with the estimates show a deficiency of 52,500 men, which reduces the British

Army to 627,801 men. Even these 627,801 men, however, cannot be compared with the Russian troops which we have enumerated, and which are thoroughly trained and provided with permanent cadres and all requisites for war! We will now consider in more detail the several categories of the British army, and will commence our review with the volunteers.

The volunteers came into existence in 1860 to protect the British Isles against a possible invasion. They number at the present time 212 battalions of infantry, 2 light horse volunteer corps, 565 batteries of artillery, 19 companies of engineers, 1 railway battalion, 13 torpedo companies, 1 ambulance corps, and 1 cycle corps. Their permanent cadres are extremely weak, numbering in the aggregate for all corps of all arms 286 adjutants and 1,552 non-commissioned officers as instructors, *i.e.*, 1 man in the cadres to every 135 volunteers. The volunteers join or 'leave the various corps at pleasure, are aged from 17 to 50 years, and are divided into two classes: the efficients, and the non-efficients (recruits). The officers' posts are much sought after; but as they entail great expense, they can only be filled by rich people, whose degree of efficiency varies very considerably. The training of the volunteers is very wanting in uniformity. Sir Charles Dilke says in his well-known articles on the "English Army," that there are to be found among the volunteers the youngest and the oldest people, the best and the worst marksmen, the most efficient and the most ignorant officers.

The volunteers drill once a week. Every year some thousands of volunteers take part in the manœuvres of the regular army. In the present year 15,000 men, or $\frac{1}{17}$th of the entire volunteer force, are to join in these manœuvres. On such occasions it has been abundantly proved that their management leaves in every respect much to be desired. Not only have they no war-equipment, commissariat, transport, or sanitary organisation,[1] but they also lack field artillery, their ordnance consisting merely of guns of position, fortress and coast defence guns. During 1889 the volunteers were, indeed, to be supplied with 250 field-guns; but can a special weapon of so complicated a nature be worked efficiently with such weak cadres, and without horses? Judging, then, from their state of efficiency and readiness for active service, the volunteers can only render limited service in the event of an invasion of England. They can be employed in garrison fortresses, for coast defence and local garrison duties, and thereby set free divisions of the regular army. They are not, however, equal to the regulars, and can only be compared to a national guard.

The yeomanry consists of persons of means, who keep their own horses, or are at least in a position to hire horses. The Yeomen are mostly good riders, and good marksmen, and assemble annually for 14 days' drill. In 1887 only 9,479 out of 14,405 yeomen put in an appearance. They form 39 regiments, the strength of a regiment being from 200 to 460 men. Their cadres are almost as weak as those of the volunteers, and contain altogether 39 officers and 242 non-commissioned officers, i.e., 1 man in the cadres to every 51 yeomen.[2] Their officers are selected from amongst

[1] Since this was written some progress has been made towards supplying these deficiencies.—ED.

[2] The author here and on p. 141 gives as the cadres of the yeomanry and volunteers only the adjutants and staff-sergeants, but in strictness all the officers and non-commissioned officers of the volunteers and yeomanry should be added.—ED.

the wealthiest and most influential county families. In point of efficiency the yeomanry may be regarded as mere *irregular* cavalry.

The militia is called by Englishmen "the ancient constitutional safeguard of the country." By a law, which still exists, but is never enforced, the militia may, in case of absolute necessity, be recruited by conscription. In reality its ranks are filled by *enlisting* recruits, who engage for a term of six years, the limit of age being 18 to 35 years. Time-expired soldiers can enlist up to their 45th year of age. Its officers are appointed by the Secretary of State for War from among wealthy and influential families on the nomination of the Lord Lieutenant of the County, and have only to pass an examination in the year following their appointment. Many of them rise to the rank of brigadier without having served at all in the regular army. The soldiers are put through a six months' course of training, after which an annual drill of four weeks' duration is obligatory.

There are 134 battalions of infantry, of from 4 to 12 companies, 196 fort and coast batteries, 2 battalions of engineers, and 9 torpedo companies. The cadres of all the militia regiments of all arms number in the aggregate 5,134 men, *i.e.*, 1 man in the cadre to every 24 militia men.

It is the duty of the militia primarily to repel hostile invasions of the mother-country; further, to support the regular army; to act as a substitute for the latter on foreign service of a less arduous nature, and to supplement the same to a certain extent. Thus, for instance, during the Crimean war, militia regiments did duty in several of the Colonies, and the garrisons of regulars thus set free were employed before Sebastopol.

The militia reserve, which consists of trained soldiers who have taken part in at least two annual military exercises, and numbers 30,000 men, is intended to complete the regular army. Besides this, however, whenever there is war, numbers of militiamen enter the regular army.

Now it is doubtful whether the militia is sufficiently strong to satisfy all these demands upon it, and to form a reliable support of the army. The *Broad Arrow* estimates the strength of the militia as follows: The militia numbers according to the register 121,000 men. From the latest army estimates, however, it appears that in 1887 only 91,489 men took part in the military exercises, and we may assume that even in an emergency no more than this number of militiamen would join the colours. From these 91,489 men we must deduct 30,000 belonging to the militia reserve-and intended to complete the regular army, and 31,000 who have not yet attained the age of twenty years. There remain consequently only 30,000 men available for immediate disposal. At the most liberal computation, however, 50,000 is the utmost that can be relied on, and even that number can scarcely be considered sufficient. No such provision is made for the equipment and other requirements of the militia as will render them ready for immediate service. We may form an approximate idea of their military qualifications, if we picture to ourselves troops composed of partially-trained reserves commanded by officers of the reserve who have no army experience, never having served as officers with the colours.

The English regular army, like the militia, is recruited by enlistment. The recruits engage for long or short service with the colours, but the total service amounts in any case to twelve years. The number of recruits does not vary essentially, and in 1886 39,409 recruits entered the army. Compared with the Russian contingent of 252,000 men, the English contingent is remarkably small. This disproportion is rendered still greater by the circumstance that in Russia the period of service in the army, the reserve, and the militia is altogether twenty-three years, whereas in England the whole period is only twelve years. In Russia, too, as indeed on the continent in general, only young men fit for active service are accepted, whereas in England many of the recruits are too young, and deficient in stamina. Thus, for instance, in 1886 1,188 recruits were under eighteen years of age, 14,617 from eighteen to nineteen years, and 9,222 from nineteen to twenty years. Consequently 25,027 recruits would only attain their twentieth year—the prescribed age for foreign service—in one or two years' time.

The English regular army comprises, according to the Army Estimates for 1888–89, 148 battalions and 30 companies of infantry, 60 companies of engineers, 31 cavalry regiments, and 229 batteries (22 of horse and 86 of field artillery, and 121 batteries of siege ordnance). At the close of 1888 it numbered 211,020 men, who were distributed as follows: 107,306 on the Home Establishment, 4,738 in Egypt, 694 *en route* from Gibraltar to Egypt, 25,848 in the Colonies, and 72,345 in India.

On that portion of the regular army located in Great Britain, or the Home Army, devolves the task of keeping up to full strength all the troops in Egypt, the Colonies, and India; of training recruits for the whole army; of defending the country, if necessary, against invasion, and of furnishing on the shortest notice an army for service abroad. For the fulfilment of all the above requirements, the War Office has 107,306 men serving with the colours, 54,655 reserves, and 30,000 militia reserves, *i.e.*, a total of 191,961 men at its disposal in Great Britain. From this number must be deducted : 35,000 to 40,000 untrained recruits, or such as have not yet attained their twentieth year ; the men indispensably necessary as the cadres for the instruction of recruits, and to supply the gaps arising in the regiments in the field, and the necessary garrisons, especially those in Ireland. These several categories of non-available soldiers reduce the available forces considerably, and accordingly the War Office could only undertake, in case of need, to furnish 2 army corps, and 1 cavalry division. These 2 army corps are of course only available for service abroad when there is no possibility of an invasion, which will generally be the case.

The British cavalry division is to consist of 6 cavalry regiments, and 2 batteries of horse artillery, and each army corps of 25 battalions of infantry and 84 guns. A British army corps is consequently weaker than a *corps d'armée* of any first-class Continental Power.

The mobilisation would also probably occupy a somewhat longer time in England than on the continent. We read indeed in the Memorandum which the late Secretary of State for War, Mr. E. Stanhope, laid on the table of the House of Commons in February, 1888, in elucidation of the Army Estimates, that all the formations necessary for constituting and completing the organisation of 2 army corps and 1 cavalry division are already in existence, and that all the stores and material for the first army corps and the cavalry division are in readiness, whilst those for the remaining army corps can be provided on the shortest notice. Nobody believes, however, in England that the mobilisation will proceed smoothly and rapidly; and not only Sir Charles Dilke, but the *Broad Arrow*, and even Colonel Maurice, Professor at the Royal Staff College, entertain grave doubts as to its successful accomplishment. To start with, no provision is made for horses. On the continent horses are requisitioned. But in England all attempts made hitherto to secure in time of peace a certain number of horses for the possible contingency of a war breaking out have failed. Further, Colonel Maurice says: "We have a sufficient number of infantry, cavalry, and artillery brigades to organise our army corps, but we are deficient in the following: the train, the sanitary corps, the field-bridge pontoons equipage, the field telegraph parks, the field engineer parks, the field bakeries, the munition columns, and the field hospital corps."

The paucity of parade-grounds, shooting-ranges, and other places for exercising, has a deleterious effect on the education of both soldiers and officers. Merely theoretical examinations are held, and there is an utter lack in England, as Sir Charles Dilke says, of that practical instruction in the field which every German officer receives. Lord Wolseley admits that several British officers on the active list are, from want of practice, incapable of leading their commands conformably to the requirements of modern warfare, and it is only too well-known that after Sir Herbert Stewart's small column on the Nile had lost its two or three trained officers, Sir Redvers Buller had to be sent out to take over the command. A Royal Commission not long ago admitted that the officers possessed no knowledge of their profession, and that they must be instructed, cost what it might. In 1888 the Duke of Cambridge, Commander-in-Chief of the British Army, expressed great dissatisfaction with the training of the officers, and admitted that they were very clumsy in working out the most elementary tactical problems, as well as in outpost duty and reconnaissance. English officers have, moreover, much less to do with their regiments than is the case with officers on the continent. As, however, in spite of high pay, and prospects of rapid promotion, there is a great dearth of officers even for the peace-establishment, it is a difficult matter to raise the standard of requirements.

At all events one is entitled to expect that England, who is wealthy and technically so far advanced, should equip her army with the best ordnance and rifles in the world. But it is not so. For several years past no muzzle-loading guns have been seen in the field-batteries of any great continental power, and yet such are still in use with part of the British field artillery. In France, Germany, and Austria the arming of the infantry with magazine rifles will soon be completed. In England, however, a magazine rifle is but now being tested, and the British infantry is still armed with Snider and Henry Martini rifles.[1] On 28th January, 1889, the Secretary of State for War, Mr. Stanhope, in an address delivered at Brigg, said that the British army required better guns, and magazine rifles. On the Continent, where so much importance is attached to an advanced state of readiness for war, provisional arrangements whereby whole regiments are disorganised are carefully avoided, and military writers instance as a

[1] This has now (1893) ceased to be true of the regular infantry, except as regards a portion of the forces in India.—ED.

warning the state of the French army in 1867. It is recognised that an expeditionary corps should consist of entire regiments brought up to war strength, and provided with all accessories without drawing upon other regiments. In England, on the other hand, instead of calling out the reserves for the battalions mobilised during the Afghán and Cape wars, the necessary complement of soldiers was taken from eighteen other battalions, which in consequence remained below their normal strength. When it was found that the two army corps intended for foreign service had no munition corps, fourteen batteries were converted into as many ammunition columns. The British army was already indifferently provided with field artillery. In consequence of this reduction, when the two army corps are mobilised, the Home Army—regulars, militia, and volunteers—will be without field artillery.

From the above particulars it is evident that the British army is inferior to the armies of the first-class European Powers, not only in numbers, but also in readiness for war, efficiency, and armament.

THE BRITISH AND RUSSIAN NAVAL FORCES.

In regard to naval forces, the position of the two countries is reversed. Great Britain is the first maritime power in the world, whereas Russia ranks merely as a second-class maritime power. The British fleet numbers over 700 ships with 86,000 men, whilst the Russian fleet comprises 360 ships with 29,000 men. These figures do not, however, accurately represent the relative strength of the fleets of the two States. There are various classes of ships: battle-ships, cruisers, torpedo-boats, etc., and even ships of the same category differ essentially from one another in tonnage, velocity, the degree of technical perfection, and armament. We will now compare some of the classes of ships of both powers, according to Lord Brassey's specification. We have supplemented this specification by data taken from Durassier's admirable "Aide Memoire de l'Officier de Marine." To begin with the battle-ships. Lord Brassey divides these, in view of the great progress made in the art of building men-of-war of late years, into two categories, viz., into battle-ships which were launched prior to 1879, and those built subsequently.

Great Britain has seventeen serviceable iron-clad battle-ships built prior to 1879, aggregating 143,210 tons displacement, whilst Russia possesses only two battle-ships of an older type with 13,840 tons displacement.

Great Britain has 16 battle-ships built since 1879, with 155,280 tons displacement, whilst Russia's navy-list exhibits six similar battle-ships, with 13,840 tons displacement.

Great Britain possesses 18 armoured cruisers with 137,050 tons displacement; Russia seven similar cruisers with 40,312 tons displacement.

Great Britain possesses 65 unarmoured cruisers; Russia only 15. These ships, Lord Brassey says, should be classified according to their speed. Now Russia has only 1 cruiser with a speed of 19 knots, 2 with a speed of 16 knots, 2 with a speed of 15 knots, and 10 with a speed of 12 to 13 knots. Great Britain, on the other hand, possesses 29 cruisers which make over 20 knots, 3 over 19, 2 over 18, and 15 from 17 to 18 knots an hour; and in the course of 1889, two steel cruisers with a speed of 22 knots, and a displacement of 9,000 and 9,600 tons respectively, were to be launched.

From the above data it is clear that the British fleet is far superior to the Russian. The state of the British fleet gives rise nevertheless to serious misgivings; for the British maintain, and rightly so, that their fleet must be superior to the combined fleets of any two, or even more, continental powers. Great Britain must be undisputed mistress of the seas in order to protect her world-wide commerce from destruction, her people from famine,[1] and her industries from decline; to retain her transmarine territories and colonies, and to avert the forfeiture of her rank as a first-class power. The French fleet, however, is now developing so rapidly that, in conjunction with the Russian, it is almost a match for the British. For our purpose it suffices to prove that the British navy considerably surpasses that of Russia alone.

As we are now familiar with the resources (naval and military) of the two countries, we can proceed to examine their strategical relations.

Before entering upon this question, we think it advisable to explain to such of our readers as are unacquainted with military science, what is meant by the term "strategical relations." It means, how and with what prospect of success a war can be waged between two or more States. War is the *ultima ratio* of the sovereign State; the means by which it enforces its will in spite of the opposition of another State, or compels the latter to relinquish undertakings which are opposed to its interests. Hence war is an

---

[1] Great Britain obtains two-thirds of her food supply, an the greater portion of her raw materials, from other countries.

act of force, and the object of war can only be attained by compelling the state against which war is declared to surrender its will and submit to the will of the other state. The assailant often attains his object by determined action before blows are exchanged; frequently a war is of long duration, and is finally settled by compromise; lastly, the resistance of one of the belligerents may be crushed, and the vanquished have to submit to the victor's will. This is the issue! The consideration of the strategical relations of two states is therefore identical with the consideration of how one state can crush the resistance of another state, or so seriously injure it that it is compelled to surrender its own will, and submit to the will of the conqueror.

With continental states whose frontiers are conterminous, the seat of war, *i.e.*, the area within which the war is brought to an issue, is indicated to a certain extent in advance. And though one of the precepts of strategy is: "The main object is the enemy, and everything must be subordinated to the endeavour to annihilate the opponent," yet it is indubitable that the assailant by a proper choice of the object of attack can force the enemy to oppose him and fight a decisive battle. Thus, for instance, we know that in a war between France and Germany the collision of the two powers must occur on their common frontier between Belgian and Swiss territory; that the line of greatest attraction[1] must connect Paris with Berlin, and that the fate of the campaign must be decided on the line between the above two points. Should one of the two

---

[1] By line of greatest attraction ("schwerlinie") is meant the imaginary line which in any theatre of war forms the shortest connection between the most important districts of the two belligerent states.—ED.

STRATEGICAL RELATIONS OF THE STATES 153

belligerents not be in a position to accept battle immediately, the assailant, taking every advantage of the interval, would occupy the most important points on the field of operations, so as to secure an advantageous position. At all events, the French general could no more give up Paris than the German Berlin, without fighting a decisive battle. Either of them would be compelled to risk the result, even though the battle could not fail to be a desperate one. Should the war be a prolonged one without decisive results, and the two belligerents be compelled to conclude peace so as to avoid complete exhaustion, this too would be decided within the area designated.

The consideration of the strategical relations of Austria and Russia is obscured by the memory of the year 1812. The annihilation of the "grand army" which was led by one of the greatest generals of all ages, and had already taken Moscow, made a tremendous impression, and the view gained ground that Russia was almost invincible. Russia, it was thought, was designed for the defensive by her vast and thinly populated area, the sheltered position of her chief towns, and by climatic, political and social conditions. It was not until the beginning of the eighties that a flood of literature, in which Russia was discussed from a military standpoint, appeared in Germany: and in 1883 we, too, in a strategical study entitled "The Chief Object of the Coming Austro-Russian War," ventilated the question how Russia could be defeated and her resistance crushed. Since then there has been a growing opinion in military circles that the resources of modern warfare admit of the offensive being largely adopted. A repetition of the so-called Scythian mode of warfare of 1812 is not conceivable, inasmuch as it would be attended by great danger to Russia, promises little prospect of success, and would entail unprecedented sacrifices on the country.

This mode of warfare is dangerous for Russia, because her border provinces have only been incorporated with the Russian Empire for a century—Congress Poland, indeed, only since 1815—and are not yet Russianised. Consequently if the Russian armies retired into the interior of the Empire, the invading army would become possessed of territory, formerly Polish, which might be definitively lost to Russia, and the population of which might by raising the Polish question be won over to the assailant's cause, and even look upon him as a deliverer. The possession of this territory would add to the assailant's strength, instead of weakening it, as is usually the case when extensive lands inhabited by an inimically disposed population have to be conquered and retained by force of arms.

The Scythian mode of warfare should prove unsuccessful for the further reason that Russia's circumstances have altered considerably since 1812. If the advance into Russia be conducted systematically, point by point, the railways afford a safe means of providing the army of operation with all requisites. If, then, the march into the heart of Russia be only ventured upon when the country as far as the Dnieper is conquered and organised, and the line Kiev-Smolensk secured in all directions as the base of operations, the Russians cannot, as in 1812, evacuate and destroy their dwellings, as such a procedure if employed against well-found and provisioned armies can only result in disadvantage to the defenders, and the consequences would be that the Russian army, and not the invading army, would suffer from scarcity and privation.

Lastly, it requires no circumstantial evidence to prove that this mode of warfare would entail unprecedented sacrifices on the country.

It is a known fact that in 1812 there was no thought at the Tzar's head-quarters of an organised retreat involving a surrender of large tracts of country, but it was entered upon as it were instinctively, in order to elude the adversary's overwhelming superiority. Russia has at present just as little intention of parting with extensive territory as of repeating the methods adopted in the campaign of 1812 which terminated so brilliantly. A mere glance at the Polish seat of war, with its extensive fortifications, numerous strategic railways, and the distribution of the Russian forces, suffices to show that the first great battles will take place on Polish territory, and, as far as can be foreseen, not far from the frontier. It may be assumed with equal certainty that in a war between Austria and Russia the fate of the campaign will be decided somewhere between Vienna, Buda-Pesth and Moscow. Should Germany also participate in this war the space between Berlin and Moscow must then be included in our calculations.

The Anglo-Russian strategical relations are much more complicated, because the frontiers of these powers do not touch, and the question where they will come into collision cannot be answered in advance, as is the case with neighbouring states. This question has, moreover, been little discussed. At the present there are published treatises on the strategical relations of any two neighbouring European states, and this theme is discussed in every military geography. But the Anglo-Russian strategical relations have, as far as we know, never been the subject of special consideration the results of which were published. Consequently opinions on this point are not yet clear, as is very evident from the statements of the leading British politicians and military authorities on this subject. Lastly, the view is prevalent in British military circles that these questions should not be openly discussed. "It would be a great mistake," Colonel Maurice says in his work "The Balance of Military Power in Europe," to discuss publicly, at what points England will attack her Russian opponent.

". . . . Ignorance of the direction of our attack forms one of the most essential factors of our specific power." Finally, he remarks on page 62 : " If we were of the opinion that Vladivostok is Russia's sole weak point, we should look upon Sir Charles Dilke, who betrayed our intention to attack it, as a traitor to his country."

We readily admit that at times to take the enemy by surprise is one of the most essential conditions for the success of military operations, and fully comprehend the disinclination to publish the plans of operations elaborated in the executive offices of the Staffs. But even on the Continent, where the principal seats of war and lines of advance are defined beforehand, officers on the Staff who are initiated to a certain extent into the intentions of the highest military authorities do not scruple to discuss these subjects openly. This has its decided advantages, since the independent writer goes to work differently from the mere official. The latter has, indeed, as a rule, better information, but must conform to the wishes and ideas of his Chief. In this way a tradition may be established in an Office, and even continued at a time when the original circumstances have undergone essential alterations.

An author, on the other hand, can give his ideas free

play, and if he succeeds in advancing fresh points of view, and directing general attention to his publication, he invites inquiry and discussion which help to clear men's views, and even exercise an influence on undisclosed official labours. For this reason we believe that Colonel Maurice and his colleagues might discuss with a calm conscience Great Britain's strategical relations with the other European powers. It is even much more important for Great Britain than for the other great powers that public opinion should be accurately informed on those subjects which are so closely connected with foreign policy, inasmuch as with most continental states the settlement of a foreign policy falls within the province of the monarch, whereas in Great Britain a policy can only be pursued when public opinion has been enlisted in its favour. Moreover, continental governments are much better informed on military matters than the British Government, in which even the Secretary of State for War is not a military man, and at the head of which a Queen presides. We believe, then, that we are in nowise injuring British interests in discussing the Anglo-Russian strategical relations, especially as the Russian Staff has doubtless already minutely studied the question. Apart from Central Asia, the strategical relations of which we shall subsequently discuss, and with regard to which Great Britain, through her possession of India has become a continental power, England and Russia can only attack and engage one another by sea. We will therefore examine—

1. What Russia has to fear from England; and,
2. What England has to fear from Russia, assuming it to be the intention of each of the two states to attain the object of war, *i.e.*, to crush the resistance of the

adversary, and to compel him to surrender his will, and to submit to the will of the conqueror.

Great Britain commands the sea and can cripple Russia's sea commerce, close Russia's ports, and transport her own troops to any point on the Russian coast that she pleases. Let us consider what danger accrues to Russia therefrom.

Russia's merchant fleet numbers barely 3,500 vessels; hence her sea-commerce is relatively inconsiderable, and its ports of delivery may be transferred without great loss from the Baltic and Black Seas, say to Germany or Austria, for transmission overland. A blockade of Russia's coasts cannot, then, on the whole prove very injurious to her trade.

It would be of still less consequence to Russia were her fleets shut up in the Black Sea, the Baltic, or the Sea of Japan, as she has no extensive colonial or commercial interests to protect. At the same time it must not be forgotten that a blockade can only be carried out with much trouble and a great display of force, and that the watching fleet must be considerably stronger than that which is shut up. This measure would consequently tax England's strength severely.

Great Britain can, lastly, bombard any point she chooses on the Russian coast, transport troops thither, and possibly land them. It is, however, questionable whether she would gain anything by such a proceeding.

The shores of the Arctic Ocean, the Behring Sea, and the Sea of Okhotsk are so barren that an attack upon them would serve no purpose. We may consequently leave them out of the question.

On the Neva, forty kilometres from the Baltic, lies St. Petersburg, the capital of Russia. The fortress of Kronstadt, built upon an island of granite and a succession of other fortifications which are kept constantly up to modern requirements, bar the entrance to the Neva. In 1854 these fortifications held the combined Anglo-French fleet in check, and the boldest of British admirals, Sir Charles Napier, did not venture to attack them. They are still almost impregnable. St. Petersburg is, indeed, an open city from the land side. But in and around St. Petersburg a great number of troops are quartered, which on an emergency could be reinforced by means of the network of railways to such an extent that the two British army corps and the cavalry division, available for service abroad, could scarcely venture to attack St. Petersburg from the land side. The other towns and ports on the Baltic coast are only third-rate, and the bombardment of them would, indeed, harass Russia, but in no case force her to submit. A landing effected on the Baltic coast could at best be with the object of occupying this or that point for a short time, viz., until Russian troops arrived in force; since with the troops which England has available for disembarkation an expedition into the interior of Russia is out of the question.

Neither can England undertake an expedition into the interior of Russia from the Black Sea. A repetition of the Crimean war would be an impossibility at the present day, even for the coalition of that time, much less for Great Britain single-handed. An insurrection in the Caucasus is no longer possible since its final conquest by Russia, and the emigration to Turkey of the mountaineers who so heroically defended it. And as all the most important points are either fortified or protected by strong garrisons, England could merely occupy less important points for a short time, *i.e.*, till the intervention of an adequate Russian force, and bombard a few towns on the sea-coast. Sebastopol, the most important port of Russia, is so strongly fortified that it appears to be secure even from bombardment, and can be merely blockaded. The same may be said of Nikolaievsk and its marine establishments. There remain, then, Odessa, the principal commercial town of Russia, the rising port of Batoum, which has been recently fortified, and towns of minor importance. Even a bombardment of Odessa would scarcely lead to any decisive result. How much less, then, an attack on the other seaport towns mentioned.

Still less would be gained by an attack on Vladivostock and the Amur district. This territory was only acquired a short time since—the Amur district in 1851, and Primorsk, in which Vladivostok is situate, in 1860. Both are poor and sparsely populated. Amur has 62,640 inhabitants, spread over an area of about 269,700 square miles, and Primorsk 101,750 inhabitants, on an area of about 1,137,900 square miles. The climate is comparatively severe. The mean temperature for the year in Nikolaievsk is $-2°$ R.; the mean summer temperature being $+12°$ R., and the mean winter temperature $-12°$ R. The mean annual temperature in Vladivostok is $+4°$ R.; the mean summer temperature $+16°$ R., and the mean winter temperature $-7·6°$ R. Trade has scarcely made a start. According to official data there were at the close of 1885 fifteen vessels in Nikolaievsk, and six in Vladivostok, making a total of twenty-one vessels. As the entire Russian merchant fleet numbered in that year 2,992 vessels, the proportion in the Pacific Ocean was less than 1 per cent., and at Vladivostok only 0·2 per cent. Colonel Veniukov is consequently fully justified in remarking in his work "The Russo-Asiatic Border-lands," that the agricultural importance of these lands belongs to the future. A temporary occupation of Vladivostok—for anything else is out of the question—might possibly retard the development of these border-lands; but even if Russia lost the whole of Siberia, she would still remain a first-class power; how much more so, then, if she temporarily lost a land situate 6,000 to 7,000 miles from her central bases, and connected with Russia only by a single water-way, the Amur river. The Amur is over 1,200 miles distant from Irkutsk, and over 3,100 miles from Tiumen, the nearest railway station, and this distance must be traversed for the greater part on foot, or on wheels. On a peace-footing there are in the fifteenth military district, which comprises the districts of Amur and Primorsk, fourteen battalions, two companies, and four batteries with thirty-two guns, of regular troops, and two battalions, two companies, eight "sotnias," and one battery of Cossacks. Owing to the poverty of the country, and the consequent difficulty of transporting and provisioning large bodies of troops, Russia will hardly employ a larger number of troops than those mentioned in this district, and even their annihilation could in no case seriously affect Russia's power.

Hence it is remarkable that a politician of the importance of Sir Charles Dilke should seriously maintain that Russia could be bled quite as severely by a British attack on Vladivostok as she was at the siege of Sebastopol.[1]

An accurate investigation of the circumstances of the case leads us to the conclusion that owing to the

[1] Sir C. Dilke's argument was that Russia would struggle for success on the Pacific coast, and for that reason could be bled there.—ED.

relatively small extent of Russia's coast compared with her area, the barrenness of the greater part of it, the inconsiderable development of her sea-commerce, and the paucity of important seaport towns, an attack on Russia's coasts cannot produce nearly the same effect as an attack on the coasts of Great Britain, France, or Italy.

II.

As Great Britain is mistress of the sea, and Russia, elsewhere than in Central Asia, can only get at her by sea, it might be supposed that with the exception of the territory named Russia was powerless against Great Britain. This is not, however, the case. The weaker side is under no restriction not to take advantage of the shortcomings or the weak points of the stronger, where there is a chance of doing so successfully. It is hardly likely that either the Baltic fleet or that of the Black Sea would succeed in passing the Sound or the Bosphorus in the teeth of the British fleet. But will Great Britain be at all times able to prevent the Russian fleet stationed in the Sea of Japan from appearing in the Pacific?

According to the *Broad Arrow* of August, 1888, the Russian fleet in the Sea of Japan numbered 4 ironclads with 18 heavy and 41 light guns, and 12 cruisers and gun-boats with 6 heavy and 65 light guns ; whereas the British fleet in neighbouring Chinese waters comprised 3 ironclads with 18 heavy and 14 light guns, and 16 other ships with 7 heavy and 94 light guns. It is selfevident that this force is insufficient to blockade the Russian fleet, inasmuch as the blockading fleet must be much stronger than the blockaded. In the Sea of Japan especially the British fleet would have a very hard task, as Russia possesses several good harbours on the Primorsk coast, and the Sea of Japan forms part of the North Pacific Ocean, with which it is connected by five passages which are difficult to close. Moreover, the Gulf of Tartary narrows down to about four miles between Cape Lazarev and the town of Pogobi on Saghalien Island. By a judicious erection of fortifications, the Gulf of Tartary could be closed to the British fleet, and the Russian fleet would have the free choice of reaching the Pacific either by one of the four southern roads, or round the north of Saghalien Island under protection of the Gulf of Tartary.

We readily admit that the Russian fleet would hardly be able to maintain itself on the open sea for any length of time, or to attack Hong-Kong and the numerous Australian colonies of Great Britain. But the appearance of a Russian fleet on the high seas would create a panic on the Pacific wherever the British flag flies, and Great Britain would lose command of the sea, even if only for a short time. On this account we can quite understand that the increase in the Russian fleet in the Sea of Japan is regarded with a certain amount of disquietude in England.

On the British fleet, moreover, devolves the protection of the merchant marine. The latter numbers about 40,000 vessels with a tonnage of nine millions, and navigates all the seas of the world. We have already emphasised the importance to Great Britain of her sea-commerce. This commerce is, however, based on credit, needs security above all things, and can only prosper on a large scale when the merchant knows that the goods he purchases will arrive with certainty and in good time. Trade is consequently susceptible to the slightest disturbance, and a single hostile cruiser can do it great harm, as was proved by the *Alabama* during the war of secession.

This example was taken to heart by the Russians, and when the Anglo-Russian relations became more and more strained in 1878, a committee was formed which, in the belief that Great Britain could not long sustain a stoppage of her industrial establishments or a restriction of her sea trade, resolved to buy and equip vessels specially adapted for use as cruisers. The then heir-apparent and present Tzar, Alexander III., accepted the protectorate of this undertaking. In the beginning of June, 1878, the three first ships were fitted up at a total outlay of 1,600,000 roubles, and when the Berlin Congress had put an end to the prospect of war, the committee, which had received voluntary contributions amounting to 3,333,601 roubles, decided on building two new ships of war instead of acquiring ready-built ones. The Russian Government, moreover, purchased cruisers with State funds, as for instance the *Cimbria* and the *State of California*, the latter of which, manned by Russian sailors, cast anchor towards the end of April in Southwark harbour in the waters of Maine.

These proceedings created great consternation in England. Especially the destination (*i.e.*, America) of the *State of California* pointed to the possibility of Russia's finding means in the United States of successfully pursuing British merchantmen, and endangering the British Trans-Atlantic trade depôts, many of which are not at all, or very inadequately, protected.

Since that time every effort has been made in England to render the fleet capable of protecting the country's trade. Several new fast cruisers were built. The construction of fast steamers which would be adapted for use as cruisers in time of war was promoted by subsidies. In this way the British Government secured in 1888 six exceptionally fast ships at a cost of £26,000 sterling. Several coaling-stations were put into a state of defence, and on the 4th March, 1889, the British Government demanded an extraordinary credit of £21,000,000 sterling, to be devoted to the construction of seventy new war-ships, of which forty-two were to be cruisers. Finally, the question was zealously debated how the fleet could best protect trade. It was decided that the best method was that of blockading the enemy in a port. "When war with Russia seemed imminent in 1885," Lord Brassey remarked at a meeting on the 1st February, 1889, "the Admiralty, of which I then had the honour of being a member, sent out British cruisers to all ports where there were Russian ones, with orders to keep watch on the latter."

As, however, the naval manœuvres at Berehaven and Lough Swilly conclusively proved that fast ships are very difficult to keep a watch over, and easily evade the blockading fleet, this eventuality had also to be provided for.

For this purpose the highest authorities in England propose, in Parliamentary committees, at meetings, and on other occasions, that the most important trade-routes should be secured by groups of ships stationed at strategical points. With Great Britain's supremacy on the sea it may be assumed that if now and again a Russian cruiser should succeed in suddenly cropping up on an important trade-route, her activity would not long remain unpunished, and that Russia would not succeed in restricting the trade of Great Britain.

We have seen then that, except in Central Asia, a duel between Russia and Great Britain can lead to no result.

* * * * *

We now come to the consideration of the Anglo-Russian strategical relations in Central Asia.

In Chapter I. we described how slowly, laboriously, warily, advisedly, and consistently Russia established herself step by step in Central Asia ; how the vast and thinly populated tracts and arid deserts formed the chief obstacles to Russia's advance, whilst the population, numerically small, and moreover split up into an infinitude of Khanates, Sultanates, tribes and clans, offered but slight resistance. Further, we showed that a great portion of this population, bereft of its natural leaders, is either already Russianised, or on the high road to Russianisation, and that Russia has in no case anything to fear from it; lastly, we proved that Russia's possessions in Central Asia were valueless *per se*, and merely acquired value as a means to an end, viz., to further conquests.

From these facts the following conclusions may be deduced :—If Russia had to devote so much time and trouble to conquering Central Asia, which was inhabited and defended by the Kirghiz, Turcomans, Uzbeks, and other smaller tribes, how much harder would it be to wrest Central Asia from the Russians, seeing that the assailant can count on little or no support from its inhabitants. The British, it is true, will not admit this, and in Sir Henry Rawlinson's famous Memorandum the phrase occurs—"If Russia survive catastrophe in Asia!" Lieutenant Yate even asserts that "England's position in Asia is more secure than that of Russia." We think, however, our readers require no further proof that the hopes and assertions in question are based on self-deception.

The result of the Crimean war was in no small measure instrumental in begetting and spreading a

STRATEGICAL RELATIONS OF THE STATES

further error, even in British military circles ; namely, the opinion that Russia could be easily defeated and exhausted by an attack upon her extremities, in which she is in reality very weak. It was forgotten that at remote points, such as Vladivostok, or even in Central Asia, only comparatively inferior forces could be brought into action, and that as long as that portion of the Empire whence Russia derives her resources, and which forms the nucleus of her power, is unmolested, the Empire of the Tzar can continue the war without over-exerting itself, and without any fear of decisive results. Even in the Crimea a decisive result would not have been attained, had not Russia gradually transferred thither her entire resources. True, the capture of Sebastopol was a great triumph for the Allies ; but its momentary loss, and the annihilation of the Black Sea fleet would not have sufficed alone to place Russia *hors de combat.* Tzar Nicholas was consequently not by any means bound to accept battle in the Crimea on account of Sebastopol. He did so because the dangers of a campaign in Poland and the Caucasus were fully recognised at St. Petersburg. It was consequently decided to detain the Allies in the Crimea at any cost. Only the minor portion of the Russian army succumbed to the enemy's arms. The lion's share in the work of destruction fell to its own intendancy, and the enormous distances which the troops had to traverse on foot. Thus, for instance, the Grenadier Corps set out from Novgorod 60,000 men strong, and of these only 6,000 reached their destination. It is primarily to these circumstances that Russia's exhaustion must be attributed. With Russia's present railway system this cannot occur again.

And yet this is all misunderstood in England. In

that important military gazette, the *Broad Arrow*, we read in an article on a Russian campaign against India, published on the 7th January, 1888 : " The Russian soldiers will be as hard-pressed by our soldiers on the banks of the Oxus as they were on the banks of the Alma." Assuming that this were to happen, let us consider what would be gained by a victory on the Oxus.

Central Asia is the classic home of the Scythian mode of warfare. Its area is much more extensive, and more barren than Russia-in-Europe ; it possesses, moreover, no valuable geographical objects, the loss of which would, like that of Moscow, cause a severe pang ; and, lastly, Russia does not by any means derive her resources from Central Asia. Central Asia, albeit in every respect passive, was conquered merely for the prospects its acquisition opened up in regard to India. Its temporary loss would not affect Russia's power. Central Asia is essentially the field for a mode of warfare such as that adopted in 1812. The Russian army would have the advantage of being able to retreat before a victorious British army, until the latter, weakened by the march, and by garrisoning and securing the territory occupied, was at length incapacitated from continuing offensive tactics. The farther the British army moves from its base, the greater the risk it runs of being cut off by the Russian troops marching rapidly from the Caucasus and Semipalatinsk ; and in this case the fate of the British will be similar to that which befell the French on the Beresina.

With such a vast expanse of territory as that of Central Asia, a systematic, strategic advance is not at all conceivable with the forces which would in all likelihood be available.

A victory on the Oxus, or on the northern frontier of

Afghanistan could not be utilised, even if the victor were content with modest aims, on account of the lack of important geographical objects. Merv only acquired a value for Russia as forming a stepping-stone for further advance.

Samarkand, which is about 180 miles distant from the Oxus, would be hard to take, and still harder to retain. The capture of one or another point would not influence the result of the war, because the whole of Central Asia represents but little value, and each single point must consequently be rated at so much less.

Hence it is apparent that Russia cannot be attacked by Great Britain in Central Asia, and that the British are from the very commencement restricted to the weaker form of warfare, viz., defensive tactics.

* * * * *

We have still to consider what Russia can undertake in Central Asia, and with what prospects of success.

In all probability Russia will remain true to the method she has hitherto adopted, and continue to advance systematically, step by step. Any one who has observed the course of events in Afghanistan of late years, can imagine how this will go on. As we are aware, the Amir Abdurrahman had first to contend with an insurrection of the Ghilzais which broke out in 1886, and with another insurrection at Balkh and Maimana in 1888, which was led by Ishak Khan, grandson of Dost Mahomet, and a hireling of Russia. Should Russia, then, wish to take a further step in Central Asia, she could instigate an insurrection in Balkh, Maimana, Kunduz, Badakshan, or even Herát, secretly support it, and finally accept the protectorate offered her over this or that Khanate, to secure it against the Amir's cruelties. She might also, out of apparent regard for England, decline the proffered protectorate, and confine herself to creating a state of anarchy in Afghanistan. In any case, the *status quo* in Central Asia will not be maintained for long. " The inevitable logic of facts," as General Sobolev says in the *Russkaia Starina* of May, 1888, "indicates that the time is approaching when the Hindu Kush, the natural boundary of India, will form the frontier of Russia in Asia, and when Herát will probably also be incorporated with the Russian Empire. In that case Great Britain will be obliged to occupy Cabul and Candahar. This is unavoidable." We hardly think so, as the British wish to defend India on India's frontier. On the other hand, it must not be forgotten that Great Britain is bound by treaty obligations to support the Afghans against a foreign enemy. As the British are powerless to arrest Russia's progress on the northern frontier of Afghanistan, or to prevent her occupying the country north of the Hindu Kush, it is clear, that after any such success on the part of Russia the Amir must cease to be a reliable friend of Great Britain. The line designated by General Sobolev corresponds with the third parallel referred to by Sir Henry Rawlinson in his famous Memorandum.

Not to anticipate the future, we will avoid discussing the strength of this line, and the prospects in store for an army using it as its base for an advance upon India, and confine ourselves to a consideration of the chances of invading India from the present base, —the Anglo-Russian frontier.

With an accurate perception that India cannot escape the Empire of the Tzar, Russia employs her chief resources in Europe, where she has to overcome considerable opposition, whilst in Asia she pursues her aims with inferior forces only. Accordingly Russia could only embark upon a campaign against India if she decided upon remaining inactive for a time in Europe, or if, being implicated in a war with Great Britain, she wished at any price to deal a decisive blow at the latter.

Having said so much, we will consider :—1. How strong should the Russian invading army be? 2. Is Russia able to concentrate sufficient forces on the Russo-Afghan frontier? 3. What distances and natural obstacles have the Russians to contend with in order to reach the Indus? 4. What forces have the British available for the defence of India? 5. What can Russia aspire to in a campaign against India?

1. It is not easy to give a positive answer to this question. As, however, General Sobolev, in the article already alluded to, "England and Russia in the Far East," says that Russia with her inexhaustible resources can without any exertion place an army of 200,000 regular troops and 100,000 irregular Asiatic cavalry in the field, we will abide by that number. We do so the more readily, as General Sobolev is a very great authority in Russia on Asiatic questions, and Lieutenant Yate of the British Staff likewise mentions 200,000 men as the minimum strength requisite for an army operating against India. This number, then, appears to have been contemplated both by the Russian and the British Staffs, and on closer consideration we believe that it would suffice.

2. Now that Russia has crossed the Turcoman desert, acquired the fertile oases south of the latter, and completed the Trans-Caspian Railway, she is in a position to concentrate large masses of troops on the Afghán frontier. Her troops need not be pushed forward as

rapidly as would be necessary in Europe, since Russia is separated from the British possessions by Afghanistan. Consequently there will be no anxiety lest the concentration should be disturbed by the British. The troops in garrison in the Trans-Caspian district and Turkestan are strong enough to secure her against the Afghán forces.

To facilitate transport, the completion of the branch lines, Kashka-Sarakhs and Charjui-Kilif, as well as the establishment of a flotilla on the Amu Daria for the conveyance of troops and stores from the territory round the Sea of Aral and the Sir Daria, would be of the greatest importance. It is highly probable that these preparatory measures will soon be adopted.

Russia has, in the Trans-Caspian district, 24 battalions, 8 "sotnias," 6 batteries, 2 railway battalions, and 1 company of sappers ; and in Turkestan 22 battalions, 5 batteries, 1 horse battery, and 2 companies of sappers. When these troops are mobilised, Russia can draft about 30,000 men from them to the army of operation, especially as a number of troops always remain behind in the reserve depôts of an army in the field. These latter, therefore, in conjunction with the troops of the Trans-Caspian and Turkestan military districts that are left behind, will be sufficiently strong to prevent any desire to revolt.

In order to bring the army of operation up to 200,000 men, about 170,000 men would have to be sent forward from the Caucasus and Russia-in-Europe by the Trans-Caspian railway. The latter is already working as far as Samarkand, and the Russian Government takes considerable pains gradually to increase its efficiency. In August, 1888, its rolling stock consisted, according to the *Rivista Italiana*, of 88 engines and

1,410 wagons. Since then the rolling stock is said to have been increased by 2,000 wagons, and a proportionate number of engines. Hence we think that we shall be far behind the reality if we assume that the Trans-Caspian railway can transport daily 1,000 men with a corresponding amount of war material. This appears all the easier of accomplishment as a considerable portion of the troops would only have to be carried as far as Kashka (360 miles from Uzun Ada on the Caspian) and Merv (480 miles), and the remainder as far as the Amu Daria, whereas the Trans-Caspian railway is 840 miles in length.

We assume, then, that in six months at latest, but probably much sooner, Russia can accomplish the concentration of her army.

Simultaneously the enlistment and organisation of the irregular Asiatic cavalry would be diligently proceeded with.

3. We have no intention of planning a campaign against India for the Russian army. Still, we are obliged to discuss the base and most important lines of operation, so as to become acquainted with the distances and natural obstacles which the Russians must surmount before reaching the Indus.

In order to reach a remote object, it is necessary to advance with as extended a front as possible. In the case under consideration this is the more important as the Russian army can only come into collision with the enemy after a long and fatiguing march: the several lines of march converge, and the appearance of a Russian army at any point on the Indian frontier would have a great moral effect. The British will therefore be compelled to divide their forces according to the distribution of the Russian troops.

There are two main routes which lead from Central Asia through Afghanistan to the Indus. The one is by way of Herát, Girishk, Candahar, and Shikarpur; the other by Balkh, Cabul, Peshawar, and Attock. In the east of Afghanistan there are two other very difficult mountain passes into India, one of which leads from the Oxus by Faizabad and Chitral to Peshawar; the other along the course of the Upper Oxus as far as Sarhadd, thence across the Pamir plateau, through the Baroghil and Darkot Passes and viâ Yassin and Gilgit to Cashmere.

An ancient proverb calls Herát "The gate of India," and its eminent strategical importance has been frequently recognised. On the other hand, great stress has been laid upon the importance of Cabul, the capital of Afghanistan, which is only 180 miles distant from the British entrenched camp at Peshawar, and 216 miles from Attock on the Indus. We will not join in the discussion as to whether Herát or Cabul is strategically of greater importance, as we are of opinion that any army 200,000 men strong, which is, besides, at a great distance from the enemy, should not march by a single route. We even think that the two mountain passes should be utilised as well, and that the Russian army might be distributed somewhat as follows: 90,000 men to each of the two routes leading respectively to Herát and Cabul, and 10,000 to each of the Passes. The irregular Asiatic cavalry would probably be apportioned to the Russian columns with due regard to the districts where they were enlisted.

Accordingly the army marching by the Herát route would concentrate probably at Sarakhs, Merv, and Panjdeh; that on the Cabul route in the valley of the Amu Daria, between Khwaja Salar and Hazrat Imam, and the two other columns perhaps at the debouchure of the Kokcha into the Amu Daria, and at Kila Kum. A more intimate knowledge of Central Asia teaches us that the first column could establish its base in rich and favoured districts, and the remaining three in the fertile valley of the Amu Daria.

Those who wish to obtain an accurate military-geographical picture of Central Asia we refer to "Ultima Thule," by Major-General Alois Ritter von Haymerle, and to the professional literature on the subject. We will confine ourselves to as short a description as possible of the four routes mentioned above, commencing with the easternmost one.

The road from Kala Kum to Gilgit is very inconvenient throughout, but the critical part is the Barogil Pass, which rises to the height of 12,000 feet between Sarhadd and Yassin. This road forms the sole continuous line of communication across the Pamir plateau, and enables the Russians to foment disturbances in Kashmir, where British authority is by no means firmly established. This road is about 360 miles long. From Sarhadd, however, where it leaves the valley of the Amu Daria, the distance from the Indian frontier is not 120 miles. According to General Sobolev's " Invasions of India," in the ninth century Uguz Khan is said to have marched at the head of an army consisting exclusively of cavalry from Kashmir *viâ* Gilgit, Yassin, and the Darkot and Barogil Passes to Badakshan.

The Chitral route is of about equal length, and less troublesome than the foregoing, but is nevertheless a difficult mountain road. It leads from the junction of the Kokcha with the Amu Daria by way of Rustak, Faizabad, Zebak, crossing the Hindu Kush by the Dora

Pass, or the more northerly situate Nuksan Pass, and reaches Chitral in the valley of the river Chitral, otherwise called the Kunar. Thence the route proceeds either through the valley of the Kunar to Jelalabad on the Cabul river, or *viâ* Dir and the Laram Kotal into the valley of the Swat, and so on to the Anglo-Indian station of Peshawar, or, lastly, from the valley of the Swat through one of many passes into the valley of the Buner, reaching the Indus about 60 miles above Attock.

The advance of a Russian column by this route would considerably add to the effect which the approach of that marching across the Pamir plateau towards Kashmir might be expected to create, and the uncertainty whether it would debouch at Jelalabad, Peshawar, or on the Indus, would be likely to mislead the defence to some extent. The history of past wars indicates, too, the strategical importance of Kafiristan. Alexander the Great undertook his expedition against India from Baktria. The main body of his army marched along the valley of the Cabul river, whilst he himself led the left wing northwards into the valleys of the Swat and Buner, and reached the Indus by that difficult mountain pass. Similarly Timur himself led the left wing of his invading army over the Khawak Pass, and subjugated the country of the Siahposhes. The greatest generals, then, sent forward a part of their forces through the mountainous region east of Cabul, and thereby testified thus early to its military-geographical importance. The two most important routes, however, from Central Asia to India lead through Cabul and Herát.

The road from the Amu Daria to the Indus by Balkh, Cabul, Peshawar, and Attock is about 540 miles in length. All the routes leading southwards from the Oxus between Kilif and Hazrat Imam, as well as those leading westward from the Indus between Attock and Dera Ismail Khan converge towards Cabul, the value of which city is still further enhanced by the fact of its being the capital of Afghanistan. Almost parallel with the Oxus in Northern Afghanistan, and, as the crow flies, only from thirty to fifty miles distant from that river, there is a road which connects Andkhui, Shibrkhan, Balkh, Khulm, Kunduz, and Faizabad, the capitals of formerly independent Khanates. From each of these towns there is a road leading to Cabul by a more or less difficult pass over the Hindu Kush.

The Hindu Kush is a prodigious range of mountains extending westward from the Pamir plateau, the ridges of which have an average elevation of from 10,000 to 13,000 feet, its peaks even reaching an altitude of over 19,500 feet. According to General Haymerle, there are more than twenty passes over the Hindu Kush, which are impassable for five months in the year owing to enormous masses of snow, and during the season of thaw are much endangered by avalanches. Of these twenty passes, however, only a few, General Haymerle observes, can be turned to account for military purposes. Zahír-ud-dín Muhammad, generally known by the name of Baber, founder of the dynasty of the Great Mogul, says in his famous Memoirs, that the Hindu Kush can be crossed in seven places. The question of the practicability of a mountain is, however, to a certain extent a matter of opinion, and a good mountain climber will judge many things differently from the ordinary traveller. The successful passage of large armies consequently throws more light upon the military practicability of a mountain than any description. And as the Hindu Kush has been frequently crossed by armies, we will profit by the lessons of military history. Our facts are based on the data given in General Sobolev's exceedingly interesting work "Invasions of India."

In the year 329 B.C., Alexander the Great crossed the Hindu Kush, the passage of which from south to north occupied fully seventeen days; conquered Baktria, Sogdiana, Ferghana, etc., in a word the whole of Central Asia as far as the Caspian, and in the year 327 B.C. undertook his famous campaign against India. The passage of the Hindu Kush from north to south occupied only ten days, and the main body of his army reached Cabul without difficulty. With just as little delay Chingiz Khan's army which was counted by hundreds of thousands, and consisted chiefly of cavalry, crossed the Hindu Kush at the beginning of the thirteenth century of the Christian era. At the close of the fourteenth century, Timur's army passed over the Hindu Kush range by the Khawak, and the Tul Passes, the two portions uniting at Cabul. Finally, the previously mentioned Sultan Baber frequently crossed the Hindu Kush, on one occasion even undertaking the passage at the head of certain tribes which took their families and herds along with them. "The Hindu Kush, then," General Sobolev says, "is not the insuperable barrier which it is represented to be."

The shortest route from Cabul to the Indus traverses the valley of a tributary of the latter, the Cabul river. On this route lies the thirty-two miles long Khyber Pass (which may be avoided by taking one of six other more difficult passes), and at a distance of fourteen miles from the east outlet of the pass is the British fortified camp of Peshawar.

South of the Cabul river rises the Safed Koh, a short but wide range of mountains 15,260 feet in height. Its southern ramification is the Suliman range, which divides into two great branches. The eastern one stretches along the right bank of the Indus at a distance from the latter varying from eighteen to seventy-five miles. The other branch, called the West Suliman Mountains, extends at a distance from the eastern range which varies from sixty to ninety miles. The eastern range is 9,700 feet high in the centre; the western is absolutely higher as the intervening country between the two ranges forms an elevated plateau.

According to some accounts there are fifty, and according to others twenty, passes over the Suliman Mountains. We will not, however, enter into a description of the better of these passes, but simply draw our conclusions as to the military practicability of the Kabul valley and the Suliman Mountains from the passages that have been accomplished by large armies.

At the commencement of the eleventh century Mahmud, ruler of Ghazni, led his hordes twelve times to India. On most of these occasions he proceeded through the valley of the Gumul, crossed the Gwáyí Lári Pass, and reached India about Dera Ismail Khan.

Mahomed Ghuri, ruler of Ghazni at the close of the twelfth century, undertook nine campaigns against India. He used by turn the Khyber, Gwáyí Lári, and Bolan Passes.

Shortly after Chingiz Khan with his numerous army crossed the Sulimans by the Gwáyí Lári Pass.

In 1397 Timur advanced on India with an extended front. His grandson Pir Muhammad led the right wing of the army from Candahar *viâ* Pishin and the Tal and Chotiali Passes to Dera Ghazi Khan, and sent off a column through the Gumul valley and the Gwáyí Lári Pass. Timur himself marched by way of the Shuturgardan and Peiwar Passes into the valley of the Kurram, whilst his left wing took the route through the Cabul valley and Khyber Pass.[1]

In 1525 Sultan Baber undertook his Indian campaign from Cabul, and marched through the Cabul valley and Khyber Pass. Nadir Shah proceeded in 1740 from Candahar to Ghazni and Cabul, and reached the Indus likewise in the valley of the Cabul river. Lastly, in 1839 and 1878, the British advanced on Cabul through the valley of the Cabul, and on both occasions went through the Khyber Pass. On this route the Khurd-Cabul Pass may still be mentioned, in which the British army met such a terrible fate in 1841.

From the above historical data we see that neither the Hindu Kush nor the Suliman Mountains have ever prevented large armies from invading India. Both exhibit a respectable number of passes adapted to military requirements, which cannot but still further increase the inherent superiority of the assailant. Lastly, the maintenance of troops in the mountains of Afghanistan which afford pasturage for numerous flocks of sheep, presents, according to General Sobolev, no great difficulties.

The road from Sarakhs to Shikarpur by way of Herat is about 960 miles long, and although Russia's frontier extends ninety miles south of Sarakhs, yet there still remains a distance of over 840 miles from the Russian frontier to the Indus *viâ* Herat, Candahar, and Shikarpur. This, then, is the longest, but also by far the best, of the four routes we are

[1] The accuracy of Timur's route as given above is questioned by Major Raverty.—ED.

describing. It traverses almost throughout its entire length fertile, well-watered regions, and presents no difficulties of any consequence either for the march or the maintenance of the troops.

On this route the most noteworthy objects are: Herat, which an Oriental proverb terms "The Pearl of the Universe," and the plain of which is regarded as the granary of the whole surrounding country; the Helmand river which flows at right angles to the road from Herat to Candahar, and forms a good *point d'appui;* Candahar, which ranks second in importance among the towns of Afghanistan; and, lastly, the strongly fortified British camp at Quetta.

From Quetta to Shikarpur there are two good roads: one through the Bolan Pass, the other through the Mula Pass. A railway runs parallel with the road which leads through the Bolan Pass; and the Sarawan mountains, as the country through which these lines pass is called, are by no means impassable.

In spite of the advantages of this route it has been seldom used by armies invading India. Not only did the conquerors hailing from Central Asia proceed by the Cabul route to the middle course of the Indus between Attock and Dera Ismail Khan, but Alexander the Great, and Nadir Shah too, both of whom came from Persia and conquered Candahar, betook themselves to the north-east, and reached the Indus either by the valley of the Cabul, or that of the Gumul, rivers. Pir Muhammad, Timur's grandson, turned his steps from Candahar to Dera Ghazi Khan.

4. We will now consider what forces the British have available for the defence of the north-west frontier of India.

The present organisation of the Anglo-Indian forces

dates from the year 1857. After the suppression of the Indian Mutiny the British Government decided on a thorough reform of the Indian Army system. The Anglo-Indian army is, indeed, still composed as before of European and native troops; but the British regiments of the East India Company were converted into Royal regiments, and it was decided to relieve them at regular intervals by home regiments. The European troops stationed in India were organised on a uniform basis, and since then have formed a uniform army; whereas up to 1857 each of the three Presidencies of Bengal, Bombay, and Madras, had its own separate army. Lastly, it was decided that the European troops should constitute one-third of the Indian military forces. Accordingly the number of native troops was reduced. Moreover, in the composition of the latter troops care was taken to prevent their being of the same nationality or religion, or possessing common political interests. Before the mutiny the native troops were recruited from the higher castes. Since then it was specified from what nationalities and castes the recruits were to be enlisted. The castes fixed upon for this purpose were the lower and less numerous ones which mostly had little fellow-feeling with the mass of the population, were content with the existing *régime*, and had no desire for a revival of the previous order of things. So as not to create a uniform native army, each of the three presidencies retained its own native army. This has, however, considerable disadvantages, and for the last ten years the Indian Government has urged the amalgamation of the native army. The Viceroys, Lord Lytton, Lord Ripon, and Lord Dufferin, as well as the Commanders-in-Chief of the Indian Army, Sir Donald Stewart and Sir Frederick (now Lord) Roberts, have repeatedly expressed themselves in favour of such a measure; yet it has not hitherto been sanctioned by the Home Government. Each army recruits itself from accurately defined districts, and the various nationalities and castes are mingled together by three methods. Either a whole regiment consists of a nationality differing from or inimically disposed to the mass of the population, as, for instance, the Gurkhas (emigrants from Nepal), Afghans, Baluchis, Sikhs; such regiments are termed class regiments; or, secondly, each company or squadron is composed of men of a different nationality or caste. Lastly, soldiers of the most diverse nationalities and castes are mixed together. Such regiments are termed "mixed regiments."

The first two methods are adopted in the Bengal, the last-named in the Bombay and Madras armies.

The value of individual portions of the native army varies very considerably, according to their composition. Sir Charles Dilke says that he took great pains to obtain the opinions of Sir Frederick, now Lord Roberts, and other officers of the Anglo-Indian Army. They are all of the opinion that there are very good and very bad troops in the Indian Army. Thus, for instance, the Madras Army is said to be inferior, whilst the Gurkhas, Pathans, Sikhs, the Panjab Infantry, and all the regiments of Bengal Cavalry are very good. On the whole scarcely half of the native troops possess the necessary qualifications for engaging a European adversary.

One-third of the officers of the native regiments are British, and two-thirds native. The British officers serving in each of the three armies of Bombay, Madras, and Bengal are selected from the best material of the British army and form a Staff Corps. To obtain a permanent appointment on the Staff Corps, they must have been well reported on, have served a probationary year with a native regiment, passed a special examination, and have a knowledge of at least one of the languages spoken in India. The native officers are recruited from the most capable among the non-commissioned officers, who have gone through the regimental school, and from rich natives who keep a certain number of soldiers at their own expense.

The British occupy all the higher commands, whilst natives can only command a company or a half squadron. Certain posts are exclusively filled by British, and others by native officers. Consequently there are really two corps of officers. The one which is uniform, is composed of the best representatives of the British army; the other of indifferently instructed subalterns who are nevertheless accurately acquainted with the regimental routine, and of the sons of families that have but a slight knowledge of their profession.

A peculiarity of the Anglo-Indian army are the so-called "camp followers," who are employed for various duties in camp, and on the march. By this means the troops are spared, and can remain on duty, whilst Indian custom is complied with. But at all events these camp-followers add to the difficulty of maintaining an army, and detract from its mobility. In former times they were from three to five times as numerous as the combatants, but even in the plan of mobilisation of 1885 the number of camp followers allowed to an army of 56,000 men was 58,000, and Lieutenant Yate of the British General Staff even maintains in his work, "The Afghan Boundary Commission," that one follower per man is much too little.

Since 1860 the British army in India has been continually reduced—indeed, in 1885, from 83,161 to 59,107 men. This necessitated a corresponding reduction in the native troops, which finally numbered only 112,072 men.

On the 14th August, 1885, the Indian Government proposed an increase in the Anglo-Indian army. It was adduced in support of this proposition, that "hitherto the duties of the Anglo-Indian army had been restricted to the maintenance of order and quiet in the interior, and the provision of small expeditionary forces against enemies whose military resources were inconsiderable. Owing to Russia's latest advance the military task devolving upon the Indian Government had undergone a complete change. A great European power is now established in close proximity to our frontier, with whom we may at any time come into collision ; for this task our forces are inadequate." On the 29th October, 1885, the propositions of the Indian Government were sanctioned. In accordance therewith the strength of the British troops was increased by 196 officers and 10,567 men. The strength of the native troops was also raised, that of the cavalry by 56 British officers and 4,572 native officers and men; of the infantry by 63 British officers and 11,968 natives, and until the formation of a reserve by a further 6,432 men. Further, it was decided to create a reserve, to be composed of men selected with the greatest care from the native army, who had served at least three, and at most twelve years with the colours. These men were promised monthly pay on their undertaking to join their regiments for two months' exercise every alternate year until the expiration of their 21st year of service, and to go on active service in the event of war. From the 21st to 32nd year of service they were to be transferred to the second-class reserve, whose duties were merely local. On completing their 32nd year of service they were entitled to a pension without any further obligation. The first-class reserve was fixed at 23,232 men, *i.e.*, 218 men per battalion in the Bengal army, and 160 in the Bombay and Madras armies. But no later than 25th October, 1886, it was decided on financial grounds to organise a reserve for the Bengal army only in the proportion of 100 men per battalion, from such as had seen at least five years' active service. The strength of the second-class reserve is dependent upon the number of able-bodied men leaving the first-class reserve. Finally, up to 1885 the great majority of the native infantry regiments had consisted of one battalion only. It was decided to augment the strength of each regiment to three battalions. This presented the following advantages: As it was not intended to employ whole regiments on foreign service, and part of the troops had to be left behind to maintain order, the battalion remaining at the depôt of the regimental staff would be able to do duty as a supplementary cadre for the marching battalion, or both battalions. Thus, first of all, the marching battalions would be brought up to full strength by calling out the reserves, and by drafts of picked soldiers from the battalion left behind, which latter would also have to provide for their further completion. The object aimed at was that the battalions employed on foreign service should be taken as uniformly as possible from all regiments, and that the second battalion of a regiment should not be mobilised until all the Indian regiments had already furnished one battalion for the army of operation. Then the second battalion was to be taken, first of all from the regiments of the Bengal army. A further advantage which would accrue from 3 battalion regiments would be that whilst hitherto the 7 British officers of each battalion had formed a cadre of their own and were promoted among themselves, henceforth the cadre of an infantry regiment numbered 21 British officers.

The experience of the Afghan war of 1878–1879 proved how slowly and with what difficulty an army can be mobilised in India. The military expert can easily account for this by the want of larger combinations, trains, and all the other accessories without which an army is hardly ready to march. When, therefore, in 1885 the Anglo-Russian relations were becoming more and more strained, it was decided to take preparatory measures for the mobilisation of an army on the north-west frontier of India. This army was to comprise 2 army corps, and a reserve division.

	British.	Native.	Total.
The 1st Corps consisting of	13,000	16,000	29,000
,, 2nd ,, ,,	12,000	15,000	27,000
Total	25,000	31,000	56,000
The reserve division of	6,000	7,500	13,500

In time of war the Indian Government also has the volunteers at its disposal. The latter, which number 16,500, consist of British residents in India who have engaged to do garrison duty. They are, indeed, deficient in training, but yet capable of performing local duties, whereby detachments of regulars are set free.

The Indian Princes who occupy the position of British vassals have their own armies, which number altogether 325,000 men with 3,500 guns. The artillery is, however, for the most part quite useless, and the actual strength of the armies of the native princes scarcely reaches a third of the number mentioned.

These armies are composed of feudatories, and levies. The former are bad and undisciplined; the latter are much better. However, the British residents at the Courts of the Indian Princes take care that these armies should be neither too strong, nor too good. Certainly the best is the army of the Nizam of Hyderabad, which supplies the British with a contingent of 7,888 men.

According to the latest "Army Return" there were in India in 1888:

British troops	72,345 men.
The native army numbered	127,815 ,,
Total	200,160 men.

The first class reserve numbered only 6,000 men, and the second class reserve was quite insignificant.

On this army devolves the following duties:

1. The maintenance of order and quiet throughout the Empire.

2. The supervision of the armies of the Indian feudatory princes.

3. The supply of the corps of occupation in Burma, which in 1888 numbered 17 battalions of infantry, 4 regiments of cavalry, 6 batteries of artillery, and 3 companies of sappers.

4. The defence of the Indian frontiers against foreign foes.

If we deduct the forces required to fulfil the first three tasks, we arrive at the conclusion that the Anglo-Indian army will even now be scarcely able to place on the North-West frontier of India more than the two army corps and one reserve division contemplated in 1885. An army of 56,000 men in the first line, and a reserve of 13,500 men appears, then, to be the total Anglo-Indian force available for foreign service.

Let us now consider what tasks would devolve upon this army of 56,000 men.

Afghanistan first claims attention, Great Britain having entered into certain engagements with that country, as is evident from the "Correspondence on the Subject of the Increase of the Army in India," printed by order of the House of Commons on the 16th September, 1887, where in a confidential report by Sir T. D. Baker, K.C.B. Adjutant-General in India, dated the 3rd July, 1885, we find among other matter the phrase: "The renewed engagements which we have undertaken in regard to the integrity of Afghanistan." And in their covering despatch of the 14th August, 1885, to the Secretary of State for India, the Government of India wrote as follows:—"We have now in close proximity to our frontier a great European power with which we may at any time be brought into hostile contact." Now the Government of India must have an accurate knowledge of the frontiers of India, and the expression "in close proximity to our frontier" can only be explained by the existence of an undertaking to preserve the integrity of Afghanistan, and consequently to defend its northern frontier.[1] This does not, however, appear to be the intention of the British Government. On the 13th March, 1888, there was a debate on its Indian frontier policy in the House of Commons, and Lord Randolph Churchill (who had been

[1] This appears to us to be a rather far-fetched interpretation. It seems more reasonable to suppose that by "our frontier" the Government of India meant such places on our own borders as Gilgit and Hunza which adjoin the Oxus basin and the Russian territory. At the same time we are undoubtedly pledged to assist the Amir to repel unprovoked violation of his own frontier.—ED.

Secretary of State for India in 1885) declared that the real object of the military preparations which were then being made in India, was not to enable the Government of India to occupy Afghanistan, or to advance towards Central Asia, but merely to enable it to await the advent of a Russian army in India itself in greater strength and in better positions than heretofore. Several speakers approved of India being defended on its frontier, and Mr. Maclean alone affirmed that as Russia and Great Britain had jointly determined the northern boundary of Afghanistan, Great Britain consequently had a right, with the assent of the Amir, to defend this boundary. But even he only spoke of a "right," and not of a "duty." On the other hand, during the same debate stress was laid on the excellent relations of the British with the Afghans. "The Afghans," Sir Richard Temple remarked, "had now come to look upon us not as invaders, but as their protectors against possible enemies ; they had heard of all the awful stories connected with Russian conquests, they contrasted our action with that of the Russians, and they had learnt to respect our wisdom and to admire our forbearance." The Under Secretary of State for India, Sir John Gorst, stated that during the Ghilzai revolt not a shadow of hostility was shown to the English.

The total impression which we have derived from this debate is, that the British are not clear about Afghanistan. Either Afghanistan is to be relied upon and must in that case be defended ; or it may be left to itself, in which case it will soon be subjugated by Russia, and whether annexed, or left under an Amir in a position of vassalage, will equally be the ready tool of Russia. If, then, it is decided to defend India on India's frontier, it should be understood that Afghanistan will be on Russia's side, whether voluntarily or under obligation. This is unfortunately inevitable, inasmuch as Great Britain is unable to engáge Russia on the northern frontier of Afghanistan, and that country can only be defended on its northern frontier.

Let us now proceed to the defence of India against Russia.

India is bounded by China on the north-east, and can therefore only be attacked by Russia on its northwest frontier. The latter is, however, over 1,250 miles in extent, from Karachi at the mouth of the Indus to the northernmost point of Hazara. Of late years much has been done in India to strengthen the north-west frontier. Roads and railways have been constructed to facilitate a rapid concentration of troops. Forts and fortified outposts (block-houses) cover Peshawar and the Khyber Pass. Other passes and all railway bridges either are already, or very shortly will be, fortified. Lastly, extensive works in two lines secure the Amran Mountains, near Quetta. The object of all these works, as the Under Secretary of State for India, Sir John Gorst, remarked during the already-mentioned debate on the Indian frontier policy, was to remove as far as possible any temptation to anybody to invade British India. At all events what was principally aimed at was the position Quetta-Pishin. The Government of India, Lieutenant Yate observes, has been active in this direction only. Two railways and a military road from Dera Ghazi Khan lead thither. At Quetta supplies are stored for 25,000 men and 25,000 followers, and Quetta-Pishin is the destination of our two army corps which are to form the army of operation. The reason of this preference for Quetta-Pishin was stated in the debate of the 13th March, 1888, by General Sir

Edward Hamley, a recognised authority in England on military matters. "Events of the past," he said, "make it clear that Russia was prepared now, whenever her policy needed it, to put pressure upon England through our Indian frontier. . . . The chances were that if she should find occasion to threaten our frontier, she would begin by the invasion of Afghanistan, and when she had possessed herself of the three corner cities of Herat, Cabul, and Candahar, she would, in the space between them, proceed to create an advance base of operations by filling it with immense supplies of men and material for a campaign against India. This was the programme that our Indian officers had had to face, and he would, for a moment, place the House in their position. Half-way down the upper part of the Indus was a great mass of mountainous country, having a great depth of passes, 200 or 300 miles in length, and thus it formed a natural rampart; and so long as we watched the issue on the banks of the Indus we might be satisfied that the invader would only attempt an entrance at his own peril. But half-way down this natural rampart ceased, and the lower part of the Indus down to Kurrachee had for its right bank a great plain stretching away up to Candahar, presenting no serious obstacles to the march of an army. If we were to await Russia behind the Indus we should certainly, in the event he had been imagining, find her coming down this plain, and should she succeed in planting herself there she would be able to operate with enormous advantage. Moreover, our Indian officers were of opinion that nothing could be more dangerous than to sustain even the slightest reverse upon the frontiers of India." He had another authority to the same effect, and that was General Skobelev.

STRATEGICAL RELATIONS OF THE STATES

"Everybody," said Skobelev, "who has concerned himself with the question of a Russian invasion of India would declare that it is only necessary to penetrate a single point of the Indian frontier to bring about a general rising. Even the presence of an insignificant force on the frontier of India might lead to a general rising throughout the country and the collapse of the British Empire."

"It is therefore," General Hamley continued, "fortunate that our officers had a country suited to carrying their resources forward from the Indus. The railway ran up the banks of the Indus, meeting the railway coming from Calcutta and passing on, so that they would be able to concentrate the resources of Bengal and the resources from England by Kurrachee. From this point (Shikarpur) the railway ran on to Quetta, and they were now engaged in constructing an entrenched camp, which would enable them to defend themselves against an enemy of greater force than could be brought against them, and protect this important line of communication. *They might thus hope to give tranquillity to India for generations.*"

This speech displays a perfectly unwarranted optimism. Should Russia, as General Hamley supposes, establish herself in Herat, Candahar, and Cabul, she will use her own discretion in regard to her further advance. She can accordingly remain in this advanced base of operations until she has concentrated at Candahar a sufficiently strong force for an attack on Quetta, the garrison of which cannot exceed 50,000 men. We readily admit that Quetta, as long as it is not taken or blockaded, secures the Lower Indus. Only we estimate the resistance of Quetta at some months, or at most one or two years, but not at whole generations.

We shall probably not under-estimate the value of Quetta if we assume that it guards the Indus from the mouth of the latter to Dera Ghazi Khan. There then still remains, however, the northern part of the north-west frontier of India, about 480 miles in extent. General Hamley proposes to leave the defence of this portion of frontier primarily to the mountain range fronting it, merely keeping a watch on the outlets to the passes. His assurance is, however, by no means supported by facts, since we know from history how often large armies, composed mostly of cavalry, crossed both the Hindu Kush and the Suliman Mountains without any hesitation. According to General Hamley's supposition, the Russians will establish themselves in Candahar and Cabul prior to advancing on India. To reach Cabul, however, the Hindu Kush must either be crossed or turned. Deduct, then, the loftier and more arduous Hindu Kush range, and there remain as a bulwark the Suliman Mountains with their numerous passes. Does General Hamley really believe that the Suliman Mountains form a sufficient protection for India ? It is no light task, that of watching the exits from numerous defiles spread over such a wide extent ; and small detachments of light Russian troops with mountain equipment can also invade India by the Chitral and Gilgit route. A Russian contingent in Kashmir would, however, be particularly dangerous to the British, considering the internal state of that country. Hence we see that troops are also necessary to secure the northern portion of the Indian frontier. Now the question arises : Are the two Anglo-Indian army corps with their contingent of reserves strong enough to defend the north-west frontier of India ? At least one army corps must occupy Quetta and Pishin, if that position is to retain its value, and to cover an extensive area. The second army corps would have to keep a watch on the numerous defiles of the Suliman Mountains, and the roads from Chitral and Yassin. Even if England resolves to renounce all other expeditions whatever, and to send out her two European army corps intended for service abroad, so as to place as imposing a force as possible on the north-west frontier of India, even then the British will have no easy task.

The distribution of these troops will of course depend on that of the Russian army. If we assume, for instance, that two army corps are stationed at Quetta to assume the offensive, and the remaining two drawn up in echelons from Dera Ghazi Khan as far as Gilgit to watch the frontier, we know that the task of the British Commander-in-Chief is a very arduous and—as is generally the case with the defence of a long line exposed to inroads at numerous points—a very thankless one.

Certainly the defence of India would be much easier if the British could thoroughly rely on the loyalty of the natives. In that case it is not very likely that small detachments would venture on incursions into India; and such incursions, mercilessly avenged, would have no effect whatever. Then, only a strong invading army which had a prospect of defeating the Anglo-Indian forces in open battle, and crushing all opposition, could cross the frontier of India. With a population of 250 millions, it would at all events be no difficult matter to obtain a sufficient number of cadres, and trained soldiers, to render the task of the assailant well-nigh impossible.

The British Government, however, does not trust the natives. This is evident from the resolution that the number of European troops must equal one-third of the Anglo-Indian forces, that native officers should be excluded from the higher commands, and that the native troops should only be enlisted from certain castes and nationalities. The same mistrust of the natives is observable in the administration, and in the relations with the Indian princes.

Nevertheless it is undeniable that Great Britain is accomplishing a grand work of civilisation in India. She has secured order and tranquillity to a country hitherto wholly given up to the quarrels of petty potentates. She has given it impartial justice, a settled government, and good laws which afford free scope and assistance to all projects and undertakings. Public works on a large scale have added to the prosperity of the country. Numerous schools and universities render the benefits of education accessible to all classes of the population. Lastly, the love of liberty and the moral determination of Englishmen exercise a great influence on the natives; and the freedom they enjoy, a free press, free associations, etc., contribute largely to the education of the people. M. Cucheval-Clarigny who, as a Frenchman, is not disposed to recognise British merit in a country wrested from his countrymen, observes in the *Revue des Deux·Mondes* of the 15th June, 1885 [*L'avenir de la puissance Anglaise.—L'empire Indien.—Le conflict Anglo-Russe*] : " A sense of justice compels us to admit that Great Britain has not neglected in India any of the duties of a civilised government."

The British are taxed with exploiting the country in an unheard-of manner solely for their own benefit, with bringing their own manufactures only into the market, completely suppressing native industry, and even ruining agricultural production.

To this may be replied: If the British find a market in India for their home manufactures, the bulk of Indian manufactures, on the other hand, such as cotton, shawls, carpets, brocades, mats, articles in tortoise-shell, mother-of-pearl, coral, ivory, sandalwood, etc., go to Europe. As, moreover, Great Britain is not an adherent of the prohibitive system, other nations besides her can forward their wares to India. It is, however, intelligible that the British Government should support and aid British manufacturers and British merchants as much as possible. Moreover, "home" industries are avowedly incapable of competing with those of the factory, and must inevitably be more and more supplanted by the latter; and on this account several branches of Indian home industry have succumbed to the competition of the factory. Other branches of industry which have found a sale in Europe have, on the contrary, developed and prospered. Further, it is undeniable that the successful introduction of a new industry is up-hill work compared with that of an old trade backed by abundant capital; and this explains why Indian industry develops but slowly. It is a known fact that much is done in India to improve agriculture. We need only mention the extensive net-work of canals by which large tracts can be artificially irrigated in a climate where prolonged drought is of frequent occurrence. The increase in the export of ground-produce refutes the imputation of the decline of agriculture.

Finally, the charge of exploiting India may be met by a reference to India's economic condition.

The people of India are beginning to recognise the benefits of the British *régime*, and though the native press which enjoys unrestricted freedom is for the most part antagonistic, and represents every act of the Government in an unfavourable light, yet, on the other hand, declarations of loyalty and devotion are increasing in fervour and frequency. When the Russians defeated the Afghans on the Kushk river in 1885, and war was expected to break out, the Viceroy of India was deluged with offers of assistance from the native princes; and rich people of all races and classes gave the most convincing proofs of their loyalty, and held out prospects of abundant pecuniary supplies. These declarations of loyalty are all the more valuable, as in India people can give free expression to their opinions. "The educated natives of India know perfectly well," to quote the *Münchener Allgemeine Zeitung* of April, 1885, "what their lot would be under Russian officials. They know, too, that in spite of various grievances which they occasionally have to prefer against the British Parliament, there remains after all a free English press, and a supreme court of justice entitled the Imperial Parliament in London, to which an appeal may be made. How does the case stand in Russia in this respect? Security of life and property, personal liberty of the individual are, at all events, managed otherwise under the British sceptre than in the Russian Empire." And "Unsere Zeit" declares that "with the proclamation of the Empress national self-respect and a feeling of fellow-citizenship awoke."

India has, however, never formed a homogeneous State, and the natives of India have neither a common language, nor a common parentage, nor yet a common religion. Robert Cust states that 97 languages and 243 dialects belonging to five different groups are spoken in India. There, too, nearly all the races of mankind are represented. Its original inhabitants belong to a race akin to the negroes, and a remnant of this race is still to be found in the Deccan. The majority of the population, *i.e.*, the Hindus, Afghans, Tajiks, and Baluchis, belong to the Indo-European race. Besides these there are Dravidians, almost savage mountain tribes, Cinghalese, Semites, Malays; and the members of each race are subdivided into numerous tribes. Lastly, 188,000,000 of natives profess Brahminism; 50,000,000 Mohammedanism; 8,000,000 Buddhism; 1·8 millions Christianity, etc. The natives of India are, however, chiefly divided by caste; there are said to be 140,000 different castes, 209 of which have over 100,000 adherents. Such being the state of society, it is difficult to speak of Indian public opinion or sentiment.

Mr. H. J. S. Cotton who lived for a long time in India says in his exceedingly interesting work "New India" that "British rule contributes more than all the previous governments to the cultivation of national self-respect." As a proof he adduces the unanimous enthusiasm displayed by all natives, and the co-operation of all classes and religions, in doing honour to Lord Ripon on his departure from India; and the great national demonstration on the death of one of the leaders of the Brahminical movement, Keshub Chunder Sen. The masses, Mr. Cotton avers, betray an inclination to confide themselves to the guidance of their educated countrymen. Calcutta exercises a greater influence on Bengal than Paris on France. Madras and Bombay are equally influential in their respective spheres; and Indian students play a great part, as youth always assumes the leadership in times of agitation.

The exclusion of natives from all the higher appointments both in the Army and the Civil Service,[1] and the contemptuous treatment of natives by Europeans embitter the educated classes. There is an amount of discontent in India which, in the opinion of Lord Mayo, a former Viceroy, constitutes a political danger; and the ex-Viceroy, Lord Ripon, was wont to remark: "Now that we have educated the natives in our universities and given them the requisite knowledge, we must also satisfy their ambition."

Mr. Cotton attributes the loyal declarations of the educated classes to the fear lest the British Government should be supplanted by a worse one. The more sensible natives wish to retain the British Government till the time arrives when they will be able to assume the reins of government themselves. They all fear the Russians. The latter are more especially feared by the educated classes, who are well aware that India under Russian rule would be deprived of the benefits of civilisation which she has acquired up to the present. At all events not all of the loyal declarations are trustworthy. Thus, for instance, many a prince fears that his army will be disbanded, and seeks to avert it by this means. But both the princes and the majority of the people will not hear of the entry of the Russians.

In the present state of India, when there is merely a nascent public opinion, and a certain amount of agitation exists, numerous elements will nevertheless be found that are accessible to any instigation, and the Russians, according to their traditional practice, will turn this to the best account. Already in the sixties they entered into communication with the Maharajah

---

[1] This erroneous statement is in curious contrast to the general accuracy of the author; but we have deemed it better to let it stand.—ED.

of Kashmir; and in 1887 the ex-Maharajah Dhuleep Singh stayed at Moscow. The nearer the Russians approach India, the more numerous and active their agents will become, and the larger the funds that will be at the disposal of the latter. Great stress is laid in Russia on the fact that in all previous invasions the assailant has found support in India itself, and the British are fully alive to this danger. "We hear and read a great deal," Lord R. Churchill says, "about the loyalty of the peoples and princes of India, and I believe that at present they are loyal to us; their loyalty is, however, a conditional one which will last as long as they have confidence in our ability and honest intention to fulfil the engagements which we have entered into to protect them from internal conflicts and external attacks." "It would be a thorough misconception of human nature," says the author of "The English in India," "to suppose that if there were a prospect of fighting for their independence, the natives of India would not make the attempt. Without wishing to predict what attitude the people of India will assume in a future Anglo-Russian war, we maintain with General Sobolev that the stronger Russia becomes in Central Asia, the weaker will British rule in India be."

5. We have finally to consider what Russia can aspire to in a campaign against India.

To obviate any misconception we emphasise the fact that we propose merely to discuss the case of a *campaign* against India, *i.e.*, the case in which Russia determines to deal a decisive blow at England with considerable forces. For the traditional, slow, systematic advance in Central Asia her forces in the Trans-Caspian district and Turkestan suffice, and will not need any considerable reinforcement for some time to come.

The means necessary to the attainment of an object must be in due proportion to the object to be attained. Hence should Russia decide on temporarily decreasing her forces in Europe, and concentrating a large army on the northern frontier of Afghanistan, she could scarcely rest satisfied with the capture of Balkh or Herat. That could be accomplished with a far inferior force. If she employ larger means Russia must assuredly be pursuing larger aims.

The concentration of a large army on the northern frontier of Afghanistan would create a tremendous commotion throughout the whole of Asia, and with each day's advance this connection would increase. The Afghan army is quite incompetent to cope with a large Russian army, and the latter could in all probability reach Candahar, Cabul, and in the East, Chitral and Sarhadd, perhaps also Yassin, without having to fight any serious battles. Cabul is 180 miles from Peshawar, and Candahar 136 miles from Quetta, and the British are scarcely in a position to accept battle so far from their frontier, or to occupy these points in sufficient force. On the other hand, Cabul is over 360 miles, and Candahar over 600 miles, from the probable bases of the Russians. The line Cabul-Candahar would probably form an objective point for the Russians, on reaching which the Russian Government would have to consider the losses hitherto sustained, the state of feeling in India, and other factors, so as to decide whether it should continue the war, or rest satisfied with what it had so far attained.

As assailant, Russia *vis-à-vis* to England in Central

Asia, possesses both the military and political initiative, the value of which is enhanced by the fact that in the present state of affairs in Central Asia England cannot successfully assume the offensive. This cannot be rated too highly, and it is on this ground that we maintain that the strategical relations of England and Russia in Central Asia are disadvantageous for England.

V

ENGLAND'S VALUE TO THE CENTRAL EUROPEAN COALITION.—FINAL CONCLUSIONS.

AFTER a minute investigation of the political and strategical relations of Russia and England we come to the conclusion that England can neither arrest the advance of Russia in Central Asia, nor go to war single-handed—without allies—with Russia with any prospect of success. We will now determine the increase in strength which would accrue to the Central European coalition by England's accession, so as to obtain an accurate idea of the value of England for the coalition.

By England's accession to the coalition the latter secures command of the sea, and the considerable influence which Great Britain possesses over the smaller European States, which would have the following advantages:—

1. As long as the coast of Italy is exposed to the danger of a landing, Italy's forces are tied. With the command of the Mediterranean, on the other hand, all chance of a landing is obviated, and Italy can place an army of 300,000 men at the disposal of the coalition.

2. The command of the German Ocean and the Baltic relieves Germany of the care of defending her

coast, whereby a further 100,000 men would be available for operations.

3. By the command of the Baltic, moreover, St. Petersburg will be menaced. Russia would have to secure it against a landing, which would render her armies on the decisive scene of operations proportionately weaker.

4. The command of the Black Sea carries with it equally great advantages. As long as Russia commands the Black Sea, her fleet can attack both Varna and Constantinople from the sea side, can support operations (if any) on the Lower Danube and in Bulgaria, and transport her troops from the Caucasus and the South of Russia to any point on the coast that she pleases. On the accession of England to the coalition, the Anglo-Austrian fleet would command the Black Sea, Russia's operations on the Lower Danube and in Bulgaria would be very much hampered, and a portion of her troops would be detained in the Caucasus, and on the coast of the Black Sea.

5. Although Great Britain's land-forces are inconsiderable in comparison with the armies of the great European Powers, yet her two army corps and one cavalry division, destined for service abroad, must be mentioned.

6. Great Britain's influence with the smaller States would be brought to bear on Roumania, Bulgaria, and Turkey, to induce them to join the coalition, and also to impose neutrality on Denmark.

7. Lastly, Russia and France have not concluded an alliance. Russia, indeed, hopes to be able with the aid of France to carry out her ambitious projects, and France thinks she will regain Alsace-Lorraine during a Russo-German war. It is, however, by no means

impossible that the Central European coalition may take part in a war between Austria and Russia, and that the accession of Great Britain to the coalition may induce France to remain a passive spectator of the war. From our standpoint this would be highly desirable, as we look upon this war as a combat between two civilisations, and rank France among the most brilliant representatives of West European civilisation. If France took part in the war, it would be a more difficult and sanguinary one; the contest for supremacy would come out more prominently, and its civilising character recede into the background.

These are the principal advantages which would be gained by Great Britain's accession to the Central European coalition. The British will, probably, not reproach us with having under-estimated their power. And yet we do not believe that the expectations of Colonel Maurice are likely to be realised, namely, that Great Britain should make such arrangements with the coalition that "neither Russia nor France could attack her in Herat or anywhere else" without having to do with the whole coalition.

A sovereign State must itself take action on behalf of its own interests, and a coalition is formed for the joint protection of the common interests of two or more States. Thus, for instance, the controversy pending between Great Britain and France regarding the New Hebrides was of no consequence whatever to Austria, Germany and Italy, and on that account could not possibly become a *casus fœderis*. Herat, and even the whole of Afghanistan are equally indifferent to the States mentioned. Hartmann, who is said frequently to express the ideas of Prince Bismarck on foreign questions, wrote in 1887 in the *Gegenwart* in an article entitled "Russia in Europe": "If Russia seeks future conquests in Asia, she will not be hindered from doing so by any European power." It is, however, impossible for Great Britain to join a *peace-coalition* which cannot take notice of all the British interests. This is also the standpoint of the British Government. On the 19th August, 1889, Sir James Fergusson spoke as follows in the House of Commons: As our interests throughout the world are various and far-reaching, indeed so world-wide that a disturbance of the peace in whatever quarter of the world must seriously affect them, it is all the more necessary that the British Government should be at liberty in any eventuality to take such steps as the interests of the country might demand. England therefore reserved to herself full liberty of action, and was bound by no engagements." The visit of the Kaiser Wilhelm II. to England, however, brought about a *rapprochement* between the Courts of St. James's and Berlin, and an exchange of opinions (Sir James Fergusson confirms this) took place. Considering the community of interests and the mutual recognition of the necessity for action, this may take the place of engagements, should a crisis occur, and we are convinced that Great Britain will not fail to join the coalition, if the latter decides on going to war with Russia.

We think we may take this for granted because Great Britain, if she takes part in such a war, would have the opportunity of securing her interests, even those which in recognition of her weakness she was about to renounce. The following among others are regarded in England as British interests :—

The preservation of Belgium's neutrality;
The exclusion of Russia from the Balkan Peninsula,

especially from Constantinople, and the Mediterranean ;

The security of Turkey-in-Asia, and of the Suez Canal, Persia, and Afghanistan ;

Lastly, and above all, the security of India.

It is true that the only dangers which threaten alike the States of Central Europe and England, and the security of the Balkan Peninsula, are those which accrue from Russia's impulse towards expansion. Yet Great Britain's Asiatic interests are also by no means at variance with the interests of the Central European States. The latter cannot therefore object to Great Britain's securing her Asiatic interests, provided she fights at her own risk for her own particular objects. The British ought at all events to be aware that they will no more succeed in inducing Germany, Austria, or Italy to take action in a direction which promises them no particular advantages than they succeeded in 1854 in persuading France to carry the war into the Caucasus. The difference is mainly this, that if Great Britain had to go to war single-handed with Russia, she would have to engage the whole Russian power; whereas, if she takes part in a war as ally of the Central European coalition, Russia would then be forced to carry on the decisive contest with her chief resources on her western frontier, and could consequently only confront the British with a small portion of her troops.

We will now examine how far Great Britain as an ally of the coalition can secure her interests which we have already enumerated by war.

The neutrality of Belgium was guaranteed by the great Powers in the treaty of 1839, and since then its maintenance has been regarded in England as a British interest of the highest importance. Up to so recent a date as 1870 the view was prevalent in the Island-Empire that it was absolutely necessary to protect Belgium from annexation either by France or Germany; and even now, Sir Charles Dilke says, a statesman might be named who would plunge England into war for the sake of Belgium's neutrality, if he were at the helm at the time when this question had to be decided. Although at the present day interest in Belgium has considerably decreased, yet at a time when the possibility of a landing occupies so much attention, it cannot be a matter of indifference to the British, if the coasts of Belgium fall into the hands of France or Germany, which would most certainly happen if the neutrality of that country were no longer respected, and Belgium were used as a battle-field by those powers. On this account we believe that any British statesman would be glad if he could maintain the independence of Belgium. Now, in the event of a Franco-German war, the passage through Belgium only offers considerable advantages for Germany. Hence it is not to be supposed that France would violate Belgium's neutrality. Germany for her part may, in consideration of the great advantages that would accrue to the Central European coalition from Great Britain's accession, as a favour to the British, abstain from marching through Belgium. This sacrifice would be the easier for Germany, as latterly great progress has been made with the fortification of Liège, Namur, and the line of the Maas, and the more complete Belgium's state of defence is, the less will be the temptation to violate her neutrality.

Russia's aspirations in the Balkan Peninsula menace primarily Austria, who cannot suffer herself to be enclosed by Russia. If, then, the coalition carries the war to a victorious conclusion—and the participation of

Great Britain will doubtless increase the prospect of success—Russia will lose all influence in the Balkan Peninsula for long years to come, and the road to Constantinople and the Mediterranean will be closed to her.

Let us now proceed to consider the special interests of Great Britain in Asia.

Russia's advance in Western Asia, in Turkey-in-Asia, as well as in Persia and Afghanistan, is opposed to British interests. By the conquest of Turkey-in-Asia Russia would—*viâ* Asia—reach Constantinople, the Mediterranean, and the Suez Canal. Thereby Great Britain would lose a possibly very useful ally, and in the event of a "struggle for India," would have to revert to the long voyage round the Cape.

Lastly, in Turkey-in-Asia Great Britain has important trade-interests, and a good market for her merchandise. All this would be lost by a Russian conquest of Turkey-in-Asia, as Russia, like France, introduces protective tariffs into all her possessions. With an accurate recognition of these important interests Great Britain adopted one of her favourite measures, and in 1878 concluded a convention with Turkey, by which she became surety to the Sultan for his Asiatic possessions.

We say "favourite measures," because Great Britain has everywhere concluded such conventions with second-rate powers, where important British interests were at stake. Apart from Belgium, whose neutrality she guaranteed in conjunction with the other powers, Great Britain became surety to the Shah of Persia and the Amir of Afghanistan for their possessions.

The British do not, however, take such guarantees too seriously. In spite of the British guarantee, the Shah of Persia several times has had to cede provinces to Russia, and British public opinion, in recognition of Great Britain's weakness, reconciles itself to the idea of renouncing the defence of Belgium, Turkey-in-Asia, Persia, and even Afghanistan, although no special argument is needed to prove that Russia's advance in Persia, and particularly in Afghanistan, endangers in the highest degree Great Britain's position in India.

If we leave the Russo-Chinese frontier out of account, Russia's southern frontier in Asia from Batoum as far as Chinese Eastern Turkestan has a length of about 2,100 miles. Throughout this entire length Russia borders either on States whose spirit she has already broken in victorious campaigns, such as Turkey and Persia, or which are so weak that they cannot think of measuring their strength with the White Czar, such as Afghanistan. On the east of Afghanistan there are Khanates over which the Amir exercises a merely nominal supremacy; lastly, on the Pamir plateau, and around it, we find political organisations which scarcely merit the name of State.

Hence Russia commands the situation in Asia; and carries out her intentions systematically, without allowing herself to be misled either by the excessive zeal of her agents or by petitions for her protectorate, and requests for enrolment as Russian subjects by neighbouring independent or insurgent tribes. She carefully retains her initiative, systematically prepares the ground in advance, and makes each move at the time, and in the direction, which, in the exercise of her own discretion, she deems fitting. With such opponents, and under such conditions, Russia's final success is beyond all doubt, and Great Britain, with her small military resources thousands of miles away from Russia's southern Asiatic frontier, may cry her well-known "hands off" without disturbing Russia in her forward march. The defence of countries so extensive and so distant from Great Britain against Russia's encroachments would be an impossible task, even if the British army were as strong as the armies of the great European Powers.

Luckily for Great Britain, all the British interests in Asia that are menaced by Russia may be collectively defended in the Caucasus. From her Caucasus base Russia menaces Turkey-in-Asia, and Persia; thence she conquered Turcomania; lastly, by way of the Caucasus, the Caspian Sea, and the Trans-Caspian railway she gets to Afghanistan. The Caucasus, then, forms the key of the situation, and if it were wrested from Russia, then Turkey-in-Asia, Persia, Afghanistan, and with it India, might be considered safe for a long time to come.

A glance at the map shows us that Russia can only advance on Turkey-in-Asia and Persia from her Caucasus base, and if she lost the latter, the two countries named would be secure from Russia until she had recaptured the Caucasus. The question now arises, whether Russia, who carried the Trans-Caspian railway through the Turcomanian desert, would be able to find another route to Afghanistan?

The Sea of Aral is only 180 miles from the Caspian in the shortest direction, and on this intervening space there are a number of other inland seas. If Russia, then, sought a starting-point for a new line of communication with Central Asia on the shores of the Caspian, the new railway would have to run from a point in the Bay of Mertvi to the Sea of Aral, and make a circuit of its barren shore in a curve measuring about 300 miles, in order to reach the valley of the

ENGLAND'S VALUE TO THE COALITION 213

Amu Daria. On this railway Astrakhan might take the place of Baku on the Trans-Caspian line. We think, however, that the power which might wrest the Caucasus from Russia, would necessarily have an absolute command of the Caspian. Russia would in that case be compelled to make Orenburg the starting-point for a railway to Central Asia. The length of such a line as far as the Sir Daria would be the same as that starting from the Bay of Mertvi, or 480 miles, and, as the crow flies, 1,020 miles to Samarkand, but in reality 1,200 miles. This railway would have to traverse a line of country where the Asiatic climate is experienced in its utmost severity, intersected by the most desolate deserts of Central Asia, and would be exposed in winter to terrific snow-drifts, in summer to sand-storms. It is questionable whether Russia would be able to transport a sufficient force for a campaign against India to the Afghan frontier by this route and to furnish the same with all requisites. Moreover, the extended base and the possibility of encompassing Afghanistan from the Heri Rud to beyond Badakshan constitutes one of Russia's chief advantages. If Russia were to lose the Caucasus, Herat would be beyond her reach, and in order to reach India, Russia would be compelled to advance across the Hindu Kush; under such circumstances the defence of India would be much easier of accomplishment.

We think we have given a sufficiently clear description of the advantages which would accrue to Great Britain from the conquest of the Caucasus. We now come to the question: Is England able to wrest the Caucasus from Russia?

This question, if it be a case of a war between Great Britain and Russia alone, or even with a coalition consisting of Great Britain, Turkey, Persia, and Afghanistan, must be answered with a decided *No*. As long as Russia can defend the Caucasus with her entire resources, Great Britain, whether single-handed, or in conjunction with Turkey—Persia and Aghanistan can scarcely be taken into account for offensive warfare—is unable to land a sufficiently strong force in Armenia to attack the Caucasus.

Even in the event of Great Britain joining the Central European coalition, and Turkey remaining neutral, Great Britain cannot attack the Caucasus. Great Britain, even with the addition of her Indian troops, cannot muster an army of more than 100,000 men, and that not all at once, but only by degrees. The Russian forces in the Caucasus are fully competent to cope with such an army.

A successful attack on the Caucasus would only be conceivable if Great Britain went to war with Russia as an ally of the Central European Coalition, and succeeded in inducing Turkey to join the coalition. Turkey has an equal interest with Great Britain in such an attack. Turkey is above all an Asiatic State. Her directly controlled possessions in Europe number 45 millions of inhabitants; those in Asia over sixteen millions. Turkey is separated from Russia-in-Europe by Roumania and Bulgaria, and were the Central European Coalition to carry the war to a successful conclusion Turkey-in-Europe would be secured from Russia. The latter would, however, be all the more dangerous in Asia, should she transfer her activity thither, and on this ground both Great Britain and Turkey are compelled to interpose a barrier to Russia's expansion in Asia.

The European Central Powers would probably agree

to the exclusive employment of the Turkish armies in Asia, as it would be unadvisable on the score of conveniency to allow the Turks to march through Bulgaria and Roumania, and fight alongside of the troops of their former subjects.

Let us now glance at the military resources of Turkey. The Turkish regular army has a peace-strength of 12,000 officers, 170,000 men, and 30,000 horses, with 1,188 field and mountain guns, and numbers 272 battalions, 195 squadrons, and 198 batteries. As reserves Turkey has 96 infantry regiments of Redifs of 4 battalions each, making a total of 384 battalions, for which there are permanent cadres in time of peace, and lastly, a general levy of 48 regiments of Moustafiz without permanent cadres.

A few years ago the Sultan with the consent of the German Government appointed prominent German officers, among others Freiherr v. d. Goltz, author of the well-known book "Das Volk in Waffen" ("The nation in arms") to reorganise and train the Turkish army. Their labours would probably not be fruitless.

Colonel Maurice asserts in his book "The Balance of Military Power in Europe," that Turkey can even now muster an army of 300,000 men in Europe, and, if she called out all her Asiatic reserves, she could place 700,000 men in the field. We will not inquire whether the gallant Colonel's statements are not too optimistic, since it suffices for our purpose to state (what no one probably will dispute) that Great Britain and Turkey together can place an army of 300,000 men in Armenia, and furnish such an army with all requisites. We restrict ourselves to 300,000 men, as we believe that at a time when Russia's chief resources are tied to her western frontier, and her troops in the Caucasus can only receive insignificant reinforcements, this force will suffice for the conduct of an offensive campaign against the Caucasus. And, if only on the ground that small armies are easier to complete, to handle, and to maintain, it is not advisable that the army at starting should be larger than necessary.

Neither the British nor the Turkish armies are as ready for mobilization as the armies of the European military powers, and a long time would doubtless elapse before the Anglo-Turkish army could be concentrated, and provided with everything necessary to the acquirement of the requisite mobility. Neither, however, is the Russian army of the Caucasus anything like so well prepared for mobilization as the Russian armies on the Austrian and German frontiers. We do not think, then, that Russia could gain any special advantage from the length of time occupied in mobilizing the Anglo-Turkish army. The decisive operations at the seat of war in Asia would merely commence a few weeks later than those in Europe.

Impressed by the long duration of the Caucasian war and the heroic defence of the Circassians, many shrink from the idea of a war in the Caucasus. It must not, however, be forgotten that it was not the whole of the Caucasus, but the Caucasian mountains, which resisted the Russians so pertinaciously. The remainder of the Caucasus was for the most part apathetic.

To enable our readers to form some idea of a Caucasian campaign, we will give a slight sketch of one. The Caucasus, which lies between the Black and the Caspian Seas, has an area of 184,000 square miles, and varies both in length and width from 300 to 450 miles. An Anglo-Turkish army concentrating in

Armenia would first have to beleaguer Kars and Batoum, and then to advance on Tiflis. Perhaps, too, the principal battle might be fought shortly after the commencement of hostilities, as the Russian army would neither suffer Kars nor Batoum to be invested, nor evacuate Tiflis without giving battle. Should the Russians be victorious, then the Anglo-Turkish army would be thrown back into Turkish Armenia, which would put a final stop to the Anglo-Turkish offensive tactics. If, however, the Anglo-Turkish army were victorious, it would then have to endeavour to reach Tiflis as soon as possible, and entrench itself in the section formed by the rivers Kura and Rion. The base would have to be transferred to the Kura and Rion in order to organize the advance on the Caucasian mountains.

But is it possible to wrest the Caucasus from the Russians? The Circassians repulsed all the attacks of the Russians for so many decades; and with all due deference to their courage, the superiority must yet be conceded to the Russians.

We readily admit this, but take leave to remark that every nation and every civilization has its own peculiar tactics. The Circassians carried on a guerilla warfare. Now guerilla warfare is specially adapted to the weaker party. Like the tactics of the Parthians, it is a species of defensive tactics, which suits certain districts and fixed conditions. To carry on guerilla warfare with success, an inaccessible, uncultivated country, inhabited by a warlike population animated by a fanatical patriotism is requisite.

Let us consider whether the conditions appropriate to guerilla warfare still exist at the present day in the Caucasian mountains.

The Caucasus now presents a very different aspect to what it did at the time when Shamil's hordes achieved their most brilliant successes. During the Caucasian war several roads were made, and forests felled; or, where the forests were more extensive, openings cut corresponding in width to the range of the artillery. Commensurately with the subjugation of the country, and its occupation by cordons of Cossacks, colonies were pushed forward up to the foot of the mountains. Finally, on the conquest of the Circassians, a number of them were removed from the mountains, and their Auls assigned to Cossack colonists. Since that time the Caucasus has continued to develop. Colonies were founded, roads constructed, forests felled,—in short, with each succeeding day the Caucasus is becoming less adapted for guerilla warfare.

But besides this the Caucasian mountains are no longer inhabited by a patriotic and fanatical population resolved to enter on a combat à outrance in defence of its liberty. We have seen from the statistics given in Chapter I. that the Russians in Trans-Caucasia number scarcely three per cent. of the total population. In Cis-Caucasia there are, according to the census of 1885, about 1·5 millions of Russians in a population of 2,591,411 inhabitants. The northern portion of the Caucasus beyond the Terek and the Kuban forms an extensive plateau, and for the sufficient reason that acquired territory must necessarily be defended, the allies need at most conquer the Caucasus as far as the Terek, and a line drawn from Ekaterinogradsk to the Black Sea in accordance with military considerations. The northern portion of the Caucasus is almost exclusively inhabited by Russians. If, then, we deduct from the population of Cis-Caucasia the Russian inhabitants north of the line we have designated, there remain in the southern portion of Cis-Caucasia scarcely 500,000 Russians against 400,000 Circassians. These Russians would doubtless be capable of holding the Circassians in check, but not of conducting a serious guerilla warfare. Then, too, neither the Russian, accustomed as he is to blind obedience, nor the more enterprising Cossack as son of the plain, is suited for guerilla warfare in the mountains. On all these grounds we believe that the Anglo-Turkish army would not have to fear a guerilla warfare in the Caucasian mountains, and that the possession of the latter could be decided by a contest of the regular armies.

As a rule, war on a large scale avoids high mountains, or at most chooses them as a secondary scene of operations. An Anglo-Turkish army, however, on the Kura and the Rion with head-quarters at Tiflis has no other object of attack than a high range of mountains, and if this army does not wish to relinquish further offensive tactics, it must operate against the Caucasian mountains. These mountains stretch obliquely across the Caucasus from the Black Sea to the Caspian, are very inaccessible, there being but a single practicable road from Tiflis to Vladikavkas, and are about 600 miles in length, and 60 to 150 miles in width. The Caucasian range of mountains is a difficult object of attack; but it must not be forgotten on what suppositions we are discussing such an attack. An Anglo-Turkish army at Tiflis is equivalent to a victorious army, which has already defeated the Russian forces, and that too at a time when Russia, engaged in a decisive combat on her western frontier, cannot send a fresh army into the Caucasus. And an army elated with victory may venture on much against a beaten army; the more so as the Caucasian mountain range is not prepared for defence. This may be accounted for by the fact that the Russians are contemplating the conquest of Turkish Armenia—in which they will probably be successful, and not the defence of the Caucasus. Consequently in the case we are discussing there would not be time to put the Caucasian mountains into a state of defence. Besides, for a shaken army a position at the foot of high mountains, with the latter in its rear, is exceedingly dangerous in view of maintenance and retreat.

On the mountains themselves only inferior forces can at best be deployed and brought into action, so that the defender will merely hold certain points, and watch the *débouchés* on the opposite side so as to attack the assailant as he emerges from the defiles. Nowhere does a bold initiative produce such results as in mountain warfare, and a determined opponent may appear where he is not expected, and upset the defender's admirably laid plans.

Lastly, the Anglo-Turkish fleet would command the Black Sea. Therefore, when its army proceeds to the attack of the Caucasian mountain range strong detachments of troops might be landed on the north side, and support the army debouching from the mountain defiles.

On these grounds we hold that a judiciously and energetically conducted attack on the Caucasian mountains under the conditions stated is capable of realization.

A conquest, however, only secures permanent results when it can be upheld. We must consequently consider whether Great Britain and Turkey would be able to retain possession of the northern slopes of the Caucasian mountains.

ENGLAND'S VALUE TO THE COALITION

The boundary mentioned would be approximately 360 miles long, and might be rendered very secure if it were fortified according to all the rules of science. The necessary funds for this purpose would have to be provided by Great Britain, she rightly judging that the money would be laid out with far greater advantage for India's security than if expended on strengthening the defences of Peshawar or Quetta. Turkey, which in the event of the victory of the coalition would be completely secured, would have to transfer the bulk of her forces to the Northern Caucasus, instead of as of yore to the Danube. Great Britain would have to take part, too, in the defence of this frontier, by occupying in force fortified points on the Black and Caspian Seas, and by maintaining in conjunction with Turkey the command of both those seas. The latter would be desirable in order to secure British influence in Central Asia.

We believe, notwithstanding, that Great Britain and Turkey thrown on their own resources would be as little able to hold, as to conquer, the Caucasus, if Russia could bring her whole strength against them. In the case we have considered, however, Great Britain figures as the ally of the Central European Coalition. The allied Powers would have to conclude a joint treaty of peace, and mutually engage to uphold its conditions. Each State would of course have to secure its own frontier adequately, and to take care of its own army. The assertion of Field Marshal von Moltke, that Germany would have to hold the provinces of Elsass and Lothringen at the sword's point for fifty years more, would probably, *mutatis mutandis*, be applicable here too. In this way only could Great Britain interpose a strong barrier to Russia's encroachments, instead of mere diplomatic notes, and impotent protests, as hitherto.

We have now come to the end of our task. Our readers have learnt that Great Britain is both politically and strategically almost powerless against Russia in Asia, and that Russia times her advance at her own discretion with due regard to the European political situation. With every forward step which Russia makes Great Britain's authority suffers, her position becomes a worse one, and the last hour of her power in India seems no longer to loom in immeasurable distance. If, then, Great Britain does not wish to lose her Indian Imperial crown, and three hundred millions of customers in Asia, she must, in recognition of the fact that she cannot contend with Russia single-handed, take part in the coming contest of Europe with the northern colossus, and secure her most vital interests by a procedure regulated in conformity with the aims it has in view.

INDEX

INDEX

Abd-ul-Khair, 34
Abdur Rahman Khan, x, xi, 109; A. as Amir of Afghanistan, 130
Aberdeen, Earl of, 93
Abkasia, 21
Abramov, General, 47
Adrianople, Treaty of, 21, 76
Afghans, Collision between A. and Russians, 130; A. in Indian Army, 183
Afghan-Turkestan, 85
Afghan Boundary Commission, 52 53, 91; A. boundary on the north, xv, 127; Joint Commission arranged, 128, 131
Afghanistan, 84; war with A., 86; A. and Bokhara, 109, 114, 116; A. as a strong and friendly power, 114, 115; as beyond Russian influence, 117, 124; British war of 1878 against, 126; ceases to be an independent State, 126; Ishak Khan's revolt in A., 1888, 131; opportunity for fresh risings, 131; routes through A. to the Indus, 174; British pledges towards A., 189
Ahmed Khan Abdalli, 112
Akhal Tekkehs, 51
Aktash, xviii
Alabama, The, 18, 163

Alaska occupied by Russia, 17; ceded to the United States, 18
Alexander the Great, 176, 178, 181
Alexander I. (of Russia), 20, 71, 72
Alexander II., 72, 106, 136
Alexander III., 72, 164
Alexander Bay, 32
Alexandrovsk Fort, 40
Algerians, 99
Ali Musjid, 125
Alichur Pamir, xvi
Alsace-Lorraine, 205, 221
Aman-ul-Mulk, xix
Ametkul, leader of the Kipchaks, 43
Amu-daria, *see* Oxus
Amur territory acquired from China, 13, 160
Andkhui, 41, 109, 118, 177
Anglo-Indian army, 182; its mobilisation, 185, 187
Anglo-Russian war of the future inevitable, 78
Aralsk, 45
Araxes, River, 108
Argyll, Duke of, 103, 104
Army, British regular, 140, 144; officers of, 147
Artillery, Field, in England, 149
Asmar, xiii, xiv
Asterabad, 71, 72, 96, 136
Astrakhan, 7, 30, 213

Q

INDEX

Atek, Russian influence in, 133,
Atrek, 123, 124
Attock, 174
Auckland, Lord, 114
Aulie-Ata, 45
Australia, Possibility of A. being attacked by Russia, 163
Austria, Attitude of and policy during Crimean war, 94; conflicting interests of A. and Russia, 4
Avaria, 24

Baber, Sultan, 177, 178, 180
Badakhshan, 53, 118
Bajaur, xiii
Baker, Sir T. D., 189
Baktria, 176, 178
Baku, 19
Balkh, 41, 109, 118, 131, 132, 174, 176, 177
Baltic, The, 159
Baluchis, 183
Baroghil Pass, xvi, 175
Bariatynski, Prince, 27, 72, 136
Bash-Kadiklar, Battle of, 26
Batoum acquired by Russia, 22, 76; 160, 217
Bashkirs, 30. 54, 55, 56, 57, 58, 59, 60, 61
Batyr Shah, 59
Bebutov, General, 26
Bekovitch, Prince, 32, 33, 70
Belgium, Neutrality of, 207, 208, 209
Bereshaven, 165
Berlin, Congress of, 125; 155
Bey Mahomed, 62
Bibikov, General, 2
Bismarck, Prince, 206
Black Sea, 159, 205
Blaramberg, General, 44
Boghdanovitch, General, 44
Bukhárá, Khan of, 32, 42; at war with Kokand, 42, 43; at war with Khiva, 43; Amir of B. defeated at Irjar, 46; Amir of B. beheads Stoddart and Conolly, 84; Amir of B. defeated by Russia, 107; 109, 123, 124
Bolan Pass, 179, 181
Bonaparte, Napoleon, invited by Paul I. to join in campaign against India, 71; proposes fresh campaign to Alexander I., 71; his Egyptian expedition, 79
Bosai-i-Gumbaz, xvi
Brassey, Lord, 150
Britain, Great, *see* England
British officers sent to Persia, 81, 83; B. treaty with Persia, 81; B. interests, 208, 210, 212
Broad Arrow, The, 137, 144, 147, 162
Buda-Pesth, 155
Bukeian horde of Kirghiz, 36
Bukéef, Sultan, 36
Bulgaria, 205
Buller, Sir Redvers, 147
Beeruts, 64
Burzila jai, xvi
Butakov's survey of Sea of Aral, 40

Cabul, xi, xii, 110, 115, 174, 176, 177, 180, 202
Calmucks, The, 34; their Mongolian extraction, 35; their hostilities with the Kirghiz; 36; 64
Camp followers in Indian army, 184
Candahar, 110, 174, 179, 180, 181, 202
Caspian Sea, 213
Catherine II., Empress, 19
Caucasus described as the greatest fortress in the world, 22; war begins, 22; C. conquered, 27; its present population, 29;

INDEX 227

strategical importance of, 91; C. during Crimean war, 91, 96, 136; 159, 205, 212, 213, 214; sketch of a campaign in the C., 216; the C. as a theatre of war, 218

Central Asia, Trade in, 37; Russian literature on, 73; Russian and English policies in, contrasted, 86; the only place where a duel between Russia and England can have result, 165; C. A. merely a stepping-town to India, 168; routes from, to the Indus, 174

Chalt, xiv
Chamberlain, General Sir Neville, 125
Chandawul, xiii
Charjui ceded to Russia, 47
Chechénia, 27
Chelyabinsk, 30, 38
Chemkent, 46, 105
Chikishlar, 47, 48
Chinaz, 46
Chingiz Khan, 34, 68, 178, 179
Chitral, xvi, xix, 175, 176, 179, 194, 195, 202
Choroshkin, Colonel, 8, 10, 12
Chotiali Pass, 179
Chrulov, General, 73
Churchill, Lord R., 189, 201
Chrzanovski, General, 93
Cimbria, The, cruiser, 164
Circassians, removal of C. south of Kuban, 13; their struggle against the Russians, 23; they emigrate from the Caucasus, 28; 97, 98, 108
Cucheval-Clarigny, M., 196
Clarendon, Lord, 92, 117
Constantinople, Russia's advance on, 1; R.'s desire for, 68, 205
Cossacks, First appearance of, 7; they develop into an army,
8; the Border-C. submit to the Muscovite Government, 9; Don - Cossacks dispersed by John the Terrible, 9; encircle Muscovite empire on S. and S.E., 10; independence put down by Peter the Great, 10; hordes and lines organised by Government, 10; their functions, 11, 14; rising and forced transmigrations, 12; their present hordes, 13; numbers and military strength, 14; popularity of "Cossackdom," 16; 33, 38

Cotton, Mr. H. J. S., 199
Crimean war, Causes of, 88; 92, 93
Cronstadt, 158
Cruisers for British Navy, 164

Daghestan, 21, 24, 25
Davidson, Lieut., xvi, xvii
Delhi, Capture of, by Nadir Shah, 112
Dera Ghazi Khan, 179, 181, 194
Dera Ismail Khan, 179, 181
Derbend, 19
Dhuleep Singh, Maharajah, 201
Dilke, Sir Charles, 141, 147, 156, 161, 209
Dir (on Indian N.W. frontier), 176
"Divide et Impera" practised by Russia in Central Asia, 63
Don-Cossacks, *see* Cossacks
Dondoukov-Korsakov, Prince, 130
Dora Pass, 175
Dost Mahomed, Amir of Afghanistan, 86, 109, 115
Dufferin, Earl, 130
Durassier, "Aide Memoire de l'Officier de Marine," 150

Ellis, Mr. Henry, 82
Elsass, *see* Alsace

228   INDEX

England, conflicting interests of
   E. and Russia, 3, 4; her alarm
   at Russian progress in the
   sixties, 51 ; her power to
   arrest Russia's advance, 79 ;
   E. sends military officers to
   Persia, 81, 83; first Afghan
   war, 86 ; massacre of the garrisons, 86; E.'s policy towards
   Central Asia contrasted with
   that of Russia, 86; E.'s inability
   to protect Persia, 89; E.'s
   influence in Central Asia *nil*,
   90 ; policy of excessive modera-
   tion during Crimean war, 93,
   94; E.'s failure to grasp military problems, 99; military
   questions in E., 101 ; public
   opinion in E. on Central Asian
   question, 103 ; E. sends Sir
   Neville Chamberlain on a mission to Cabul, 125; war declared against Amir, 126; relations in 1885 with Russia become strained, 129 ; preparations for war, 129; E.'s land
   forces, 140-149; her naval
   forces, 149; her power to attack
   Russia by sea, 158, 159 ; E.'s
   fleet in Chinese waters, 162; her
   mercantile marine, 163; construction of cruisers for navy,
   165 ; E.'s value for the Central
   European Coalition, 204-222
Erivan, 83

Fadéev, 29
Fadieiev, General, 96
Faizabad, 175, 177
Ferghana, 178
Fergusson, Sir James, 207
France, her attitude in event of
   European war, 205, 206
Fraser, Baillie, 87, 88
Freitag, General, 26

Gagarin, Prince, 31
Gamul Pass, xiv, 179, 180, 181
Gandamak, Treaty of, 126
Gardanne, General, 72, 80
Gazi, Mahomed, 24
Geok-Tepe captured, 49, 51, 126
George XIII., King of Grusia, 20
Germans in Russia, 2, 3, 66 ; G.
   Ocean, 204; the German Em-
   peror, 207 ; Germany and the
   neutrality of Belgium, 209
Ghilzai rising, 85, 131, 169, 190
Gholam Haidar Khan, xiii
Gilgit, xiv, 175, 194
Gladstone, Mr., 103
Goltz, Freiherr v. d., 215
Gorst, Sir J., 190
Gortchakov, Prince, 105, 106, 107,
   117, 118, 127
Gounib, 27
Great Britain, *see* England
Grombtchersky, xv
Grusia, 20 ; incorporated in Russia,
   20
Gulistan, Treaty of, 21, 81
Guriev founded by Cossacks, 31
Gurkhas, 183
Gwáyi Lári Pass, 179, 180

Hamley, General Sir E. B., 192,
   193
Hamzat Beg, 24
Hartmann, Herr, 4, 206
Haymerle, General A. R. von, 118,
   175, 177
Hazaras, ix, x
Hazrat Imam, 174, 177
Heidelberg, 117
Helmand River, 181
Heraclius, King of Grusia, 20
Herat, 72 ; attacked by Persians,
   85, 86; 110, 112 ; its value to
   Russia, 113 ; 132, 170, 174,
   176, 180, 181, 206
Heri Rud, River, viii, 131

INDEX

Hindu Kush Mts., described by Russians as the natural boundary of India, 132, 170; 175, 177, 178, 180
Hong Kong, 163
Hunza-Nagar, xiv, xv

Ilek, River, 38
Ili river, Russians establish themselves on the, 37
Ilovasiki, 68
Imeretia, 19, 20, 21
India, Khiva regarded as stepping-stone towards, 38; conquest of I., desired by Central Asian nations, 69; Peter the Great's designs on, 70; Napoleon Bonaparte's schemes against India, 71; projected invasion of, by Prince Bariatynski, 72; Russian plans of campaigns against, 73; Bonaparte and Paul I.'s designs on, 80; smouldering discontent in I., 87; general-question of invasion of I., 110; anti-British classes in, 110, 111; Russia's advance towards I. likened to siege tactics, 111; Bariatynski's plan of campaign against I., 136; I. and her continental position, 137; probable strength of an invading army, 172; routes into I. from Central Asia, 174; British forces available for defence of N.W. frontier, 181, 188; Indian Native States' armies, 187; N.W. frontier of I., 191; Great Britain's work in I., 196; commerce and industry in I., 197; her loyalty to England, 198; not a homogeneous State, 198; plurality of races, 199; the natives of I. fear the Russians, 200.

Indus, River, 108, 181
Irtish, River, 32
Ishak Khan, 131, 169
Issik-Kul, Lake, 105, 136
Italy and European coalition, 204
Ivan the Terrible, 7, 9, 17, 30

Jamshidis, 44
Jany-Kurhan fort, 45
Japan sea, Russia's fleet in the, 162
Jelalabad, 176
Jermak, The Cossack hetman, 17
Jermolov, General, 22, 25
Jizak, 46
Jones, Sir Harford, 80
Juchakov, 79
Julek fort, 45

Kadi Mulla Mahomed, The, 23
Kafiristan, 176
Kahwak Pass, 176, 178
Kajar Khan, 50
Kaluga, 27
Karamzin, 68
Karkaralinsk, 34
Kars acquired by Russia, 22, 76; 217
Karun, River, 133
Kasan, 7, 30
Kashgar, 41
Kashmir, 110, 175, 176, 201
Kastek, 45
Katkov's saying "The 20th Century belongs to Russia," 3
Kaufmann, General, takes Kokand, 125; his secret treaty with Sher Ali, 132
Kelat, 72
Kerki ceded to Russia, 47
Khanates in Central Asia and their mutability, 41
Khiva, Khan of, defeats Netchai and Shamaj, 31; K., Khan of, defeats Prince Bekovitch, 33; K. the chief obstacle to

development of Central Asian trade, 38; Perovski's expedition against K., 39; K. at war with Bokhara, 43; with Yomut Turcomans, 44; K., campaign of 1873 against, 47; K., Prince Bekovitch's expedition to, 70, 84, 118; K., expedition against and annexation of, 119
Khodayar, Khan of Kokand, 47
Khoja Saleh, 118, 127, 174
Khojend, 106
Khora Bhort Pass, xvii
Khorasan, Russian influence in, 133
Khotan, 41
Khulm, 41, 109, 177
Khyber Pass, 126, 178, 179, 180
Kila Kum, 175
Kilif, 177
Kilik Pass, xv
Kipchaks, 42, 43
Kirghiz, 33, 34, 35, 36, 37; order established in K. desert, 40; K. war against the Bashkirs, 59, 61; K. desert, 97
Kisil-Takir, 48
Kitab taken by Abramov, 47
Knorring, 20
Kokand, Russia brought into contact with, 41, 42; K. incorporated with Russia, 48; 84, 105, 106, 125
Kokcha, River, 53, 118, 119, 175
Komarov, General, 49, 50, 91, 128, 130
Kos-Aral fort, 40, 45
Kos-Kurhan fort, Capture of, 44
Kostomarov, 65
Kotlarevski, General, defeats Abbas Mirza, 21
Kovalevski, 20
Kozin, Lieut., 70
Krasnovodsk, 32, 47, 123, 124, 125
Kuchuk-Kaimardji, Treaty of, 20, 21

Kudriavcev, Governor of Kasan, 56
Kuhn, Baron, 74
Kulja incorporated with Russia, 47; portion of its territory restored to China, 47
Kunduz, 109, 118, 177
Kura, River, 217
Kuropatkin, General, 77
Kurram, 126
Kushk, Collision between Russians and Afghans on the, 52, 129, 198

Langar Kisht, xviii
Lawrence, Lord, his policy of "masterly inactivity," 114
Lessar, M., 128
Lenkoran, 21
Littledale, Mr., xvi
Lockhart, Sir W., xv
Loftus, Lord Augustus, 120
Lough Swilly, 165
Lomakin, General, in Trans-Caspian, 48; defeated by the Tekkehs, 49, 125
Lumley, Mr., British Chargé d'Affaires at St. Petersburg, 106
Lumsden, Sir P., 52, 91, 128

Makhdúm Kúlí Khán, 49
Madras army, 183
Magazine rifle, 148
Mahmud of Ghazni, 179
Mahomed Aga Khan, Shah of Persia, 20
Mahomed Guri, 179, 181
Mahommedan races, 98, 99
Mahrattas, Ahmed Khan Abdalli's campaign against, 112
Maimana, 109, 118, 131, 132
Malcolm, General, 79
Mangishlak Peninsula, 32
Martens, F., viii, 108, 119

INDEX

Maurice, Colonel, 147, 156, 157, 206, 215
McNeill, Sir John, 87, 88
Medemin-Khan of Khiva, 43
Menchikov, Prince, 66
Mertvi Bay, 212, 213
Merv, Capture of, by Khivans, 43; submits to Russian authority, 50; 121, 124, 126, 174
Meshed, Russian Consul at, 133
Metcheraks, 59, 63
Michni Pass, 126
Military operations, Question as to open discussion of, 157; m. experts in England and the Government, 100
Militia, British, 143
Mingrelia, 20, 21
Miurids, The, 23
Miyan, xiv
Mobilisation in Russia, 139; in England, 146
Moltke, Field Marshal von, 221
Moscow, Grand Duchy of, shakes off the Mongolian yoke, 7; 153, 155
Mouraviev, Count, 13
Mula Pass, 181
Mulla Mahomed, founder of Miuridism, 23
Murghab River, 131,
Muzaffar Edin, Amir of Bokhara, 43
Muzzle-loading cannon, 148

Nachitchevan, 83
Nadir Shah, 180, 181
Napoleon Bonaparte's Grand Army, 153; his designs against India, 71 (see also under *Bonaparte*)
Napoleon III., 93
Nasr-Ullah, Khan of Bokhara, 42; beheads Stoddart and Conolly, 84
Native army in India, 182, 185
Native States, Indian armies of, 187

Naval forces, British and Russian, 149
Nepliuiev, Governor-General, 59
Netchai takes Urgenj but defeated by Khivans, 31
Neutral zone suggested by Lord Beaconsfield, 52; Question of, 117, 123, 127
Neva, The, 159
New Hebrides, 206
Nicholas I., 72
Nicolaievsk, 160
Nilt, xiv
Nizam-ul-Mulk, xix
Northcote, Sir Stafford, 107
Novgorod, 167
Novo-Alexandrovsk, 38
Nuksan Pass, 176
Nuski fort, 47

Obrutchev, General, 39
Odessa, 160
Omer Pasha lands force at Sukhum Kale, 28, 96
Omsk, Governor-General of, placed over Kirghiz, 37
Orenburg, O. line of Cossacks, 33; Governor-General of O. placed over Kirghiz; 36, 37, 136
Orlov-Denissov, Prince, 71 (note)
Orsk, 34
Ouseley, Sir Gore, 82
Oxus river, viii, xv, Old channel of, 32, 53; 109; O. proposed as dividing line in Central Asia, 117; accepted by Russia, 118; 175

Pacific, Russia's opportunity in the, 162
Palmerston, Lord, his views on Russian policy, 92, 93, 136
Pamir plateau, viii, xv, 174, 176
Panjdeh, 129, 131, 174
Paszkévitch, General, 21, 25
Paul I. and his plan of campaign against India, 71

Perovski, Count, and his Khivan expedition, 38, 39, 44
Persia cedes some of her northern provinces to Russia, 19; her wars, treaties, and boundary with Russia, 21; and her policy towards Russia, 51; Perso-Russian boundary agreed upon, 51; Russia's policy towards P., 74; P. provinces ceded to Russia, 80; Sir Harford Jones's treaty with, 81; Treaty of Gulistan with Russia, 81; Sir Gore Ouseley's treaty with P., 82; P. concludes Treaty of Turkmantchai with Russia, 83; P. advances on Herat, 85, 86; her fear of Russia, 89, 90; British policy towards P., 114; P. guaranteed by Great Britain, 210
Perovski fort, 45
Peshawar, 110, 174, 176, 178, 202
Peter the Great leads an army against Persia, 19; sends Buchholz into Central Asia, 31; his expeditions to Central Asia, 33; his attempt to reach India, 70
Petro-Alexandrofsk, 47
Peiwar Pass, 180
Pir Mahomed, 179, 181
Pishpek (Kokandi fort) captured, 45
Pishin, 126, 179
Pobiedonostsef's ultra-national theory, 3
Poland, 155
Poles, The, 97, 98
Polish insurrection quelled, 2
Portfolio, The, 88
Potemkin, Prince, 19
Poti, 21
Pul-i-Kisti, 129
Purgatchev, 60
Pyne, Mr., xii

Quetta, 115, 181, 191, 193, 202

Raimsk, Fort, afterwards Fort Aralsk, 40
Rawal Pindi, Durbar at, 130
Rawlinson, General Sir H., 53, 77, 91; on Crimean War, 94, 95; 99, 103; his Central Asian "Memorandum," vii, viii, 107 *et seq.*, 170
Regimental organisation in England, 149
Rion, River, 217
Ripon, Lord, his popularity in India, 199
Roberts, Lord, 78, 103
Robertson, Dr., C.I.E., xx
Rohrberg, General, organises Trans-Caspian territory, 49
Romanofski, General, 46
Rosen, General, 24, 25
Roshan, xv, 53
Roumania, 205
Russell, Lord John, 106
Russian Foreign Office, 103
Russo-Afghan frontier, 51, 52, 53
Russo-Persian frontier, 51, 132
Russia, her expansiveness, 1; her contempt for Western ideas, 2; war between R. and Austria in Europe and R. and England in Asia a mere question of time, 3; R.'s treatment of conquered nations, 4; her interests conflict with those of England and Austria, 4; serfdom in R. abolished, 16; occupies Alaska, 17; cedes it to the United States, 18; her advance towards Southern Asia, 18; acquires Persian provinces, 19; advances against Persia, 19; incorporates Grusia, 20; Persia recommences war against R., 21; comes into direct contact with Turkey in Asia, 21; begins to wage war

INDEX

against the Caucasian tribes, 22; conquers Caucasus, 27; her policy towards the Circassians, 28; further advance in Central Asia, 30; founds towns in Bashkir country, 30; her trade in Central Asia, 37; advance in Kirghiz desert, 37; has "no limits" in the East, 40; at war with Kokand, 44, Ak-Masjed taken, 44; advances further in Central Asia, 46; concludes peace with Kokand, 46; her progress east of Caspian Sea, 50; crushes the Bashkirs, 57, 58; her position in Central Asia, 65; people of Great R. contrasted with Ruthenians and Sclavonic races, 65; idea of universal empire, 67; her policy towards Persia, 74; her greater activity on Balkan Peninsula and in Central Asia, 76; her war against India a mere question of time, 78; Treaty of Gulistan with Persia, 81; policy towards Central Asian countries contrasted with that of England, 86; R. and Caucasus during Crimean war, 96; R.'s forces in the Caucasus, 98; declares her limit of Central Asian progress attained, 106; defeats Amir of Bokhara, 107; her influence in India, 110; her Central Asian advances likened to siege tactics, 111; her progress has justified Sir H. Rawlinson's prediction, 113; proximity to Afghanistan, 116; regards Afghanistan as beyond her influence, 117, 118; her assurances regarding Khiva, 119, 120; issues Memorandum of 1875 on Central Asia, 122; entire freedom of action adopted in the two countries, 124; takes Kokand, 125; sends missson to Cabul, 125; renews her activity in Trans-Caspia and takes Merv, 126; annexes Old Sarakhs, 127; agrees to a joint Afghan boundary commission, 128; relations in 1885 with England become strained, 129; preparations for war, 130; R.'s influence in Khorasan, 133; strategical relations with England, 135; her land forces, 138; naval forces, 149; offensive tactics might be largely adopted against R., 153; scene of the future war, 155; her merchant fleet, 158; powers of defence against naval attack, 158, 159; fleet in the Japan Sea, 162; purchase of cruisers, 164; position in Central Asia, 166; reasons for fighting in the Crimea in 1854, 167; her aspirations in the Balkan peninsula, 209; position in Asia, 211; her position if deprived of the Caucasus, 212, 213

Rustam, ix

Safed Koh Mountains, 179
Salisbury, Lord, and his views on the Central Asian question, 76; on civil government, 99, 101
Samarkand, 46, 137, 169, 213
Sar-i-Pul, 109
Sarakhs, 127, 174, 180
Sarakhs, Old, annexed by Russia, 51, 126
Sarhadd, 175, 202
Schachkov, 68
Schouvalov, Count, 119

"Schwerlinie," 152
Sebastopol, 160, 161
Secrecy in military discussions, Expediency of, questioned, 156
Serfdom abolished in Russia, 16
Sergieev, Governor of Ufa, 56
Seryn, Chief of the Calmucks, 35
"Scythian" warfare, 154
Shah Sujah, 86
Shamaj, 31
Shamil, 24, 95, 99, 136
Shar taken by Abramov, 47
Shefshenko, 4
Sher Ali, 109, his treaty with General Kaufmann, 132
Shibirkhan, 177
Shignan, xv, 53, 132
Shikarpur, 180, 181
Shuturgardan Pass, 180
Siahposhes, 176
Siberia, Cossack conquest of, 17
Sibi, 126
Sikhs, 183
Sir Daria, and Siberian lines connected, 45; 104, 105, 106
Skobelev, General, and his expedition against the Tekkehs, 49, 73, 126, 193
Sobolev, General, 73, 132, 170, 171, 175, 178, 201
Sogdiana, 178
Soldier's Pocket-book for Field Service, 102
Somatash, xviii
Staff Corps, Indian, 183
Stanitza, A, compared to a plant, 17
State of California, The, cruiser, 164
Stavropol colonised, 15, 19
Stchapov, 68
Stewart, Sir Herbert, 147
Stolietov, General, 125
St. Petersburg, 159, 205
Suez Canal, 208, 210

Sukhum Kale, 28, 96
Suliman Mountains, 179, 180, 194
Swat valley, 176

Tal, 179
Tal Pass, 178
Tajmar, 56
Tamerlane, 34, 68
Taras Shefchenko, 4
Tartars in the Crimea, 8; Kasan T., 54
Tartary, Gulf of, 163
Tashkend, 46, 106, 136
Tashkurghan, xviii
Tcherniaiev, General, 45, 46
Tejend oasis, 50
Teheran, Treaty of, 82
Tekkeh Turcomans, 48, 49, 124
Temple, Sir R., 110, 190
Teteclev, the Tartar, 70
Terek River, 7, 19
Thysenhauzen, 73
Tiflis, 217
Timur the Tartar, 176, 178, 179, 180
Tokmak (Kokandi fort) captured, 45
Transbaikal Cossacks, 13
Trans-Caspian military government constituted, 48
Trans-Caspian railway, viii, 109, 173, 212
Turcoman desert, 48, 97
Turcomans, The, 51, 64, 125, 132
Turkestan Khanates, 32; Russian T., 46; its economic value, 77; 109, 118
Turkey, worsted by Russia in 1829 and 1878, 76, 214; her military resources, 215
Turkey in Asia, 208, 210
Turkmantchai, Treaty of, 21, 74, 83

Uguz Khan, 175

INDEX

"Ultima Thule," Von Haymerle's, 175
Umra Khan, xiii
Unkiar Skelessi, Treaty of, 88
Ural Province, head-quarters of, 31
Uratiube, capture of, 42; 46
Urquhart, David, 87, 88
Urussov, Prince, 57
Uruzghan, ix
Uzbeks, 64; U. Governments will soon cease to exist, 109; U. Khanates powerless against Russia, 114, 136

Vambéry, Professor, 92, 132
Varna, 205
Vedeno, 27
Veliaminov, General, 22, 25
Veniukov, Colonel, 61, 63
Vernoe fort, 45
Vienna, 155
Vierovkin, Colonel, 45
Vitkevitch's mission to Cabul, 86
Vladivostock, 156, 160, 161
Vladykin, 15, 16, 29
Volga, Races settled on the, 61
Volunteers, British, 141
Volunteers, Indian, 187
Volynski, Artemius, 70
Vorontzof, Prince, 26, 27
Vrevsky, General, xvi

Wakhan, 53, 118
Walsh, Lovett & Co., xi
Waziristan, xiv
Wellesley, Marquis, 79
Wolseley, Viscount, 100, 101, 102, 147
Woodthorpe, Col., C.B., xv

Yakub Beg, xvi, 42
Yanopp, Col., xvi, xvii, xviii
Yarkand, 31, 41
Yassin, 195, 202
Yate, Lieut., 91, 92, 133, 171, 184
Yeomanry, British, 142

Yomut Turcomans, 43; their country annexed by Russia, 48, 51
Younghusband, Capt., xvi

Zaleski's opinion of Russian influence, 54
Zamoiski, General, 93
Zelenoi, General, 128
Zimmermann, Colonel, 45
Zizianov, Prince, 20; his murder, 21
Zubov, Count, 20
Zulfikar, 131
Zviernigolovskoia Stanitza, 33

**PLEASE DO NOT REMOVE
CARDS OR SLIPS FROM THIS POCKET**

UNIVERSITY OF TORONTO LIBRARY

D
378
P82
1893
c.1
ROBA

www.ingramcontent.com/pod-product-compliance
Lightning Source LLC
Chambersburg PA
CBHW032205230426
43672CB00011B/2518